are filled

s, and it is

who can

t one

another"

THE NEW Comparative WORLD ATLAS

Hammond Incorporated, Maplewood, New Jersey

New Comparative World Atlas

Printed in The United States of America

Library of Congress
Cataloging-in-Publication Data

Hammond Incorporated.
The new comparative world atlas.
p. cm.
Includes index.
ISBN 0-8437-7101-1
ISBN 0-8437-7100-3 (pbk.)
1. Atlases. I. Title.
G1021. H38 1996 <G&M>
912--DC20 96-27383
CIP
MAPS

Contents

Interpreting Maps

Designed to enhance your knowledge and enjoyment of maps, these pages explain map scales and projections, describe how to locate information quickly and show you how to weave together the sections of this atlas to gain a more dynamic world view.

4-5 Using This Atlas
6-7 Map Projections

Quick Reference Guide

The world at your fingertips: a concise, current alphabetical listing of the world's continents, countries, states, provinces and territories, with the size, population and capital of each. Page numbers and reference keys for each entry are visible at a glance.

8-9 Quick Reference Guide

Global Relationships

Beginning with general world physical and political maps, subsequent chapters highlight a variety of the earth's natural features, dealing first with its structure and then with its air, water and land components. Next, maps, charts and graphs unveil the complex relationships between people and their environments. Coverage includes: demographic trends, population distribution and growth, and global energy production; assessing the consequences of pollution: acid rain, deforestation, ozone depletion and global warming; also revealing comparisons of GNP per capita and literacy and life expectancy around the globe.

10-11 World - Physical Map
12-13 World - Political Map
14-15 Structure of the Earth
16-17 Atmosphere and Oceans
18-19 Climate
20-21 Vegetation and Soils
22-23 Environmental Concerns
24-25 Population
26-27 Languages and Religions
28-29 Standards of Living
30-31 Agriculture and Manufacturing
32-33 Energy and Resources
34-35 Transportation and Trade
36 Global Politics

Maps of the World

This new collection of regional maps artfully balances political and physical detail while proprietary map projections present the most distortion-free views of the continents yet seen. Special thematic maps are included in each continental section. Numbers following each entry indicate map scale (M= million).

Europe and Northern Asia

38 Europe - Physical 1:21M
39 Europe - Political 1:21M
40 Europe - Temperature; Rainfall; Climate
41 Europe - Population; Vegetation; Energy Sources; Environmental Concerns
42 Western Europe 1:10.5M
43 Northern Europe 1:10.5M
44 South Central Europe 1:10.5M
45 Central Eurasia 1:10.5M
46-47 Russia and Neighboring Countries 1:21M

Asia

48 Asia - Physical 1:49M
49 Asia - Political 1:49M
50 Asia - Temperature; Rainfall; Climate
51 Asia - Population; Vegetation; Energy Sources; Environmental Concerns
52 Southwestern Asia 1:14M
53 Indian Subcontinent 1:14M
54-55 Eastern Asia 1:14M
56-57 Southeastern Asia 1:14M

Australia and Pacific

58 Australia and New Zealand - Physical 1:19.4M
59 Australia and New Zealand - Political 1:19.4M
60 Australia and New Zealand - Temperature; Rainfall; Climate
61 Australia and New Zealand - Population; Vegetation; Energy Sources; Environmental Concerns
62-63 Pacific Ocean 1:31.5M

Africa, Polar Regions

64 Africa - Physical 1:35M
65 Africa - Political 1:35M
66 Africa - Temperature; Rainfall; Climate
67 Africa - Population; Vegetation; Energy Sources; Environmental Concerns
68-69 Northern Africa 1:17.5M
70 Southern Africa 1:17.5M
71 Arctic Ocean 1:35M
Antarctica 1:49.5M

North America

72 North America - Physical 1:35M
73 North America - Political 1:35M
74 North America - Temperature; Rainfall; Climate
75 North America - Population; Vegetation; Energy Sources; Environmental Concerns
76-77 United States 1:14M
78 Eastern United States, Southestern Canada 1:10.5M
79 Canada 1:21M
80-81 Mexico, Central America and West Indies 1:10.5M

South America

82 South America - Physical 1:28M
83 South America - Political 1:28M
84 South America - Temperature; Rainfall; Climate
85 South America - Population; Vegetation; Energy Sources; Environmental Concerns
86-87 Northern South America 1:15M
88 Southern South America 1:15M

Populations and Index

City population figures are given for all major cities, including capitals. A Master Index lists places and features appearing in this atlas, complete with page numbers, latitude and longitude.

89-90 Population of Major World Cities
91-96 Index of the World

Using This Atlas

How to Locate Information Quickly

For familiar locations such as continents, countries and major political divisions, the Quick Reference Guide helps you quickly pinpoint the map you need. For less familiar places, begin with the Master Index.

Quick Reference Guide

This concise guide lists continents, countries, states, provinces and territories in alphabetical order, complete with the size, population and capital of each. Page numbers and alpha-numeric reference keys are visible at a glance.

A
Aberdeen, Scot. ....
Abidjan, Côte d'Ivoire..............
Abilene, Texas ....
Abu Dhabi,* Un. Arab Emirates
Abuja,* Nigeria ....
Acapulco, Mex. ....
Accra,* Ghana ....
Aconcagua (mt.) ....
Adana, Turkey.............

Master Index

When you're looking for a specific place or physical feature, your quickest route is the Master Index. This 2,000-entry alphabetical index lists both the page number and latitude-longitude coordinates for major places and features found on the Reginal Maps.

This New Comparative World Atlas has been thoughtfully designed to be easy and enjoyable to use, both as a general reference and as a valuable addition to the classroom. A short time spent familiarizing yourself with its organization will help you to benefit fully from its use.

Map Projections

This chapter explores some of the most widely used examples of how map-makers project the curved earth's surface onto a flat plane. Included is Hammond's new Optimal Conformal Projection which keeps scale distortion over selected areas to the minimum degree possible.

Global Relationships

Double spread World Physical and World Political maps are accompanied by Land Elevation/Ocean Depth Profiles and Comparative Land Areas and Population graphics. World thematic maps, charts and diagrams highlight important social, cultural, economic and geographic factors affecting today's world. Here, readers can explore complex relationships among such topics as population growth, environmental problems, climate and agriculture or compare worldwide standards of living, resources and manufacturing.

Continent Comparisons

Eight thematic maps are shown for each continent (except Antarctica) enabling the map reader to visualize a variety of topics for the same region or to compare similar topics for different regions.

Regional Maps

This atlas section is grouped by continent starting with facing-page physical and political maps. Following two pages of thematic topics, in-depth regional maps offer abundant detail

World Thematic Topic

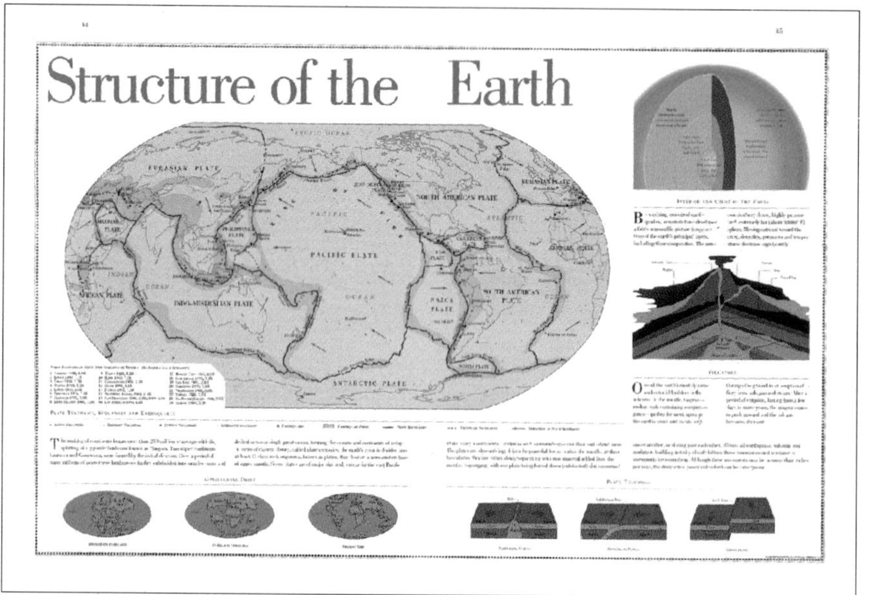

Continent Physical and Political Maps

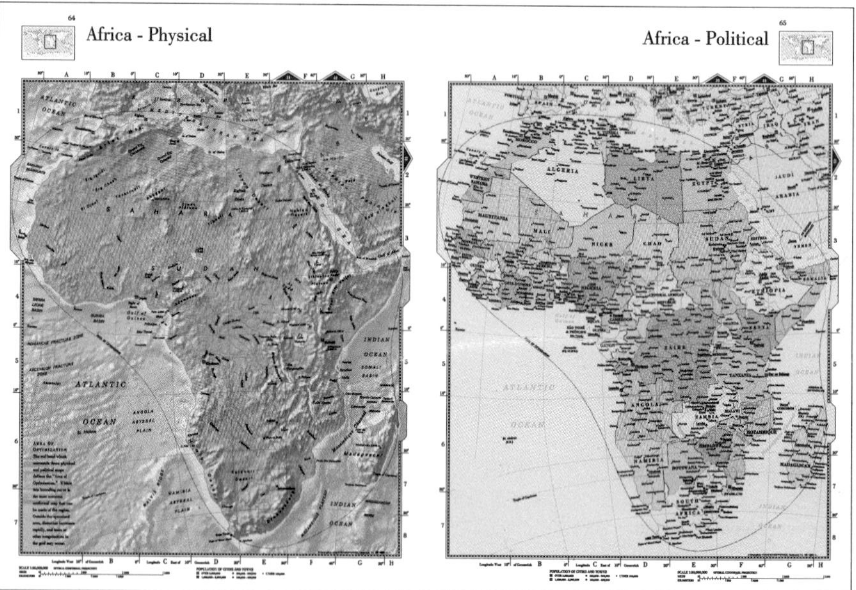

Continent Thematic Maps

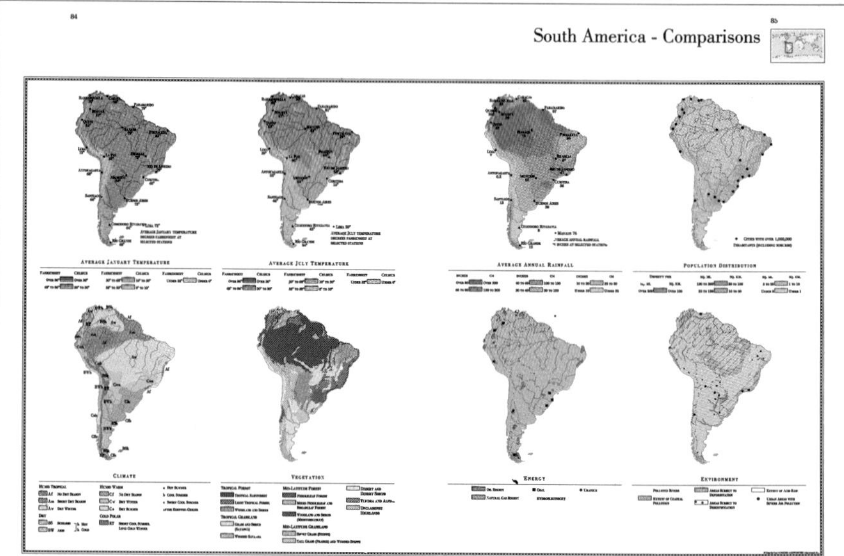

Regional Map

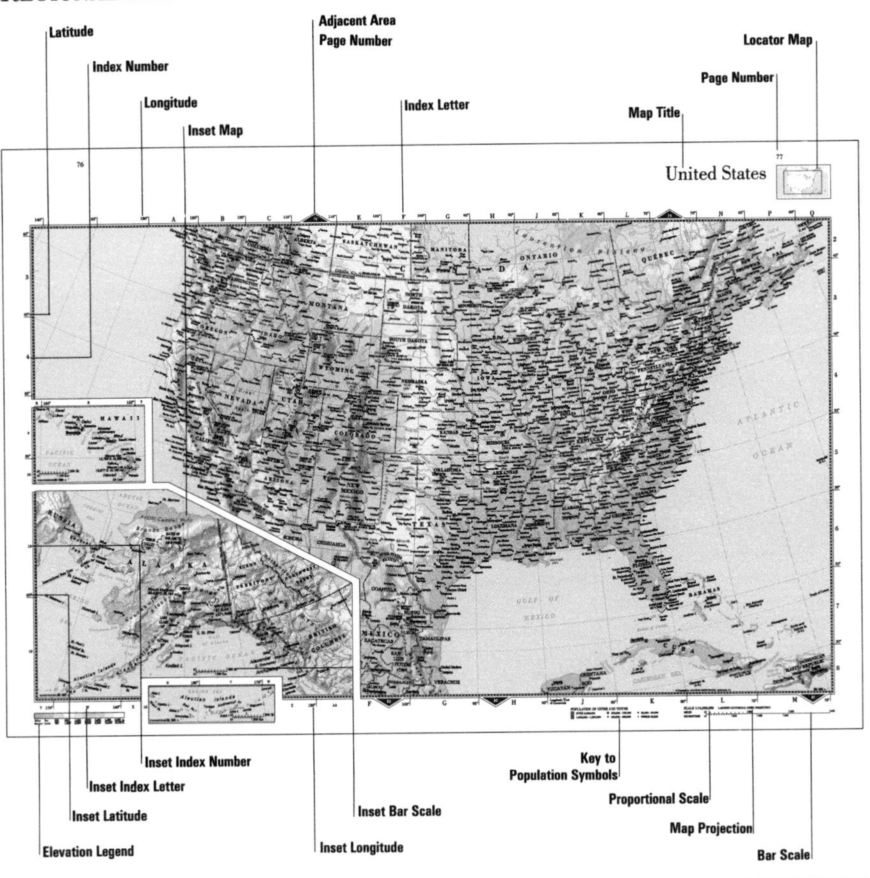

Symbols Used on Regional Maps

First Order (National) Boundary	Intermittent Lake	Pass
First Order Water Boundary	Dry Lake	Ruins
First Order Disputed Boundary	Salt Pan	Falls
Second Order (Internal) Boundary	Desert/Sand Area	Rapids
Third Order (Internal) Boundary	Swamp	Dam
Undefined Boundary	Lava Flow	Point Elevation
International Date Line	Glacier	Park
Shoreline, River	Stockholm First Order (National) Capital	Point of Interest
Intermittent River	Lausanne Second Order (Internal) Capital	Well
Canal/Aqueduct		
Highways/Roads		
Railroads		
Lake, Reservoir		

Below Sea Lev.	Sea Level	200 / 700	500 / 1,600	1,000 / 3,300	1,500 / 5,000	2,000 / 6,500	4,000 / 13,000	6,000 m. / 19,700 ft.

The colors in this bar represent elevation ranges of land areas above or below sea level. Boundaries between colors are labeled both in feet and meters. Selective shading highlights those regions with significant relief variations.

Principal Map Abbreviations

Arch.	Archipelago	Har.	Harbor	Pk.	Peak
Aut.	Autonomous	I., Is.	Island(s)	Plat.	Plateau
B.	Bay	Int'l	International	PN	Park National
C.	Cape	L.	Lake	Prsv.	Preserve
Can.	Canal	Lag.	Lagoon	Pt.	Point
Cap.	Capital	Mt.	Mount	R.	River
Chan.	Channel	Mtn.	Mountain	Ra.	Range
Cr.	Creek	Mts.	Mountains	Rep.	Republic
Des.	Desert	Nat'l	National	Res.	Reservoir, Reservation
Fd.	Fiord, Fjord	No.	Northern		
Fed.	Federal	NP	National Park	Sa.	Sierra
Fk.	Fork	Obl.	Oblast	Sd.	Sound
Ft.	Fort	Occ.	Occupied	So.	Southern
G.	Gulf	Okr.	Okrug	Str.	Strait
Gd.	Grand	Passg.	Passage	Terr.	Territory
Gt.	Great	Pen.	Peninsula	Vol.	Volcano

including boundaries, cities, transportation networks, rivers and major mountain peaks. Map backgrounds are shown in a pleasing combination of elevation coloration and relief shading, with boundary bands defining the extent of each nation's internal and external limits.

City Populations

In addition to population symbols locating cities and towns on the regional maps, an alphabetical listing by country provides at a glance the population of all major cities plus the country's capital.

World Statistics

These tables list the dimensions of the earth's principal mountains, islands, rivers and lakes, along with other useful geographic information.

Master Index

This is an A to Z listing of names found on the world, continent and regional maps. Each entry is accompanied by a page location, as well as latitude and longitude coordinates.

Map Scales

A map's scale is the relationship of any length on that map to an identical length on the earth's surface. A scale of 1:7,000,000 means that one inch on the map represents 7,000,000 inches (110 miles, 178 kilometers) on the earth's surface. Thus, a 1:7,000,000 scale is larger than a 1:14,000,000 scale just as 1/7 is larger than 1/14.

Along with these proportional scales, each map is accompanied by a linear (bar) scale, useful in making accurate measurements between places on the maps.

In this atlas, the most densely populated regions are shown at a scale of 1:10,500,000. Other major regions are presented at 1:14,000,000 and smaller scales, allowing you to accurately compare areas and distances of similar regions.

Boundary Policies

This atlas observes the boundary policies of the U.S. Department of State. Boundary disputes are customarily handled with a special symbol treatment, but de facto boundaries are favored if they seem to have any degree of permanence, in the belief that boundaries should reflect current geographic and political realities. The portrayal of independent nations in the atlas follows their recognition by the United Nations and/or the United States government.

Hammond also uses accepted conventional names for certain major foreign places. Usually, space permits the inclusion of the local form in parentheses. To make the maps more readily understandable to English-speaking readers, many foreign physical features are translated into more recognizable English forms.

A Word About Names

Our source for all foreign names and physical names in the United States is the decision lists of the U.S. Board of Geographic Names, which contain hundreds of thousands of place names. If a place is not listed, the Atlas follows the name form appearing on official foreign maps or in official gazetteers of the country concerned. For rendering domestic city, town and village names, this atlas follows the forms and spelling of the U.S. Postal Service.

Map Projections

There is only one way to represent a sphere with absolute precision: on a globe. All attempts to project our planet's surface onto a plane unevenly stretch or tear the sphere as it flattens, inevitably distorting shapes, areas, distances and/or directions.

Map makers show features on the curved surface of the earth by utilizing an evenly-spaced, imaginary grid pattern on the globe. Points and lines on this pattern are then transferred, or projected, to a corresponding flat surface pattern which has been previously selected and constructed from one of a wide variety of mathematical formulas.

In order to understand some of the most widely used map projections, a brief explanation of the earth's grid pattern is necessary.

The earth rotates around its *axis* once a day. The two end points of this axis are the North and South *poles*; the line circling the earth midway between the poles is the *equator*. The arc from the equator to either pole is divided into 90 degrees. The distance, expressed in degrees, from the equator (0 degrees) north or south to any point is its *latitude*, and circles of equal latitude are called *parallels*. On maps, it is customary to show parallels of evenly-spaced degrees such as every fifth or every tenth degree.

The equator is divided into 360 degrees. Lines circling the globe from pole to pole through the degree points on the equator are called *meridians*. All meridians are equal in length, but by international agreement the meridian passing through the Greenwich Observatory near London has been chosen as the *prime meridian*.

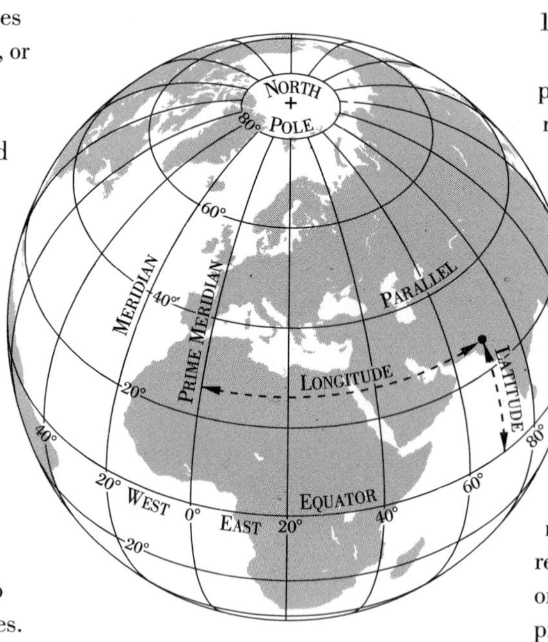

The distance, expressed in degrees, from the prime meridian (0 degrees) east or west to any point is its *longitude*.

While meridians are all equal in length, parallels become shorter as they approach the poles. Whereas one degree of latitude represents approximately 69 miles (112 kilometers) anywhere on the globe, a degree of longitude varies from 69 miles (112 kilometers) at the equator to zero at the poles. Each degree of latitude and longitude is divided into 60 minutes and each minute into 60 seconds. One minute of latitude equals one nautical mile (1.15 land miles or 1.85 kilometers).

On a flat surface, any regular set of parallels and meridians upon which a map can be drawn makes a *map projection*. Since representing a sphere on a flat plane always creates distortion, only the parallels or the meridians or some other set of lines can be *true* (the same length as on a globe at corresponding scale).

The larger the area covered by the map the larger the amount of distortion; thus, distortion is greatest on world maps. Many maps seek to preserve either true area relationships (equal-area projections) or true angles and shapes (conformal projections). Other maps are more concerned with achieving true distance and directional accuracy. Some maps reflect an overall balance by compromise instead of trying to preserve any single true relationship.

World Map Projections

A globe's surface can be transformed to fit within any outline on a flat surface. In fact, such shapes as diamonds, hearts, stars and even stylistic butterflies have enclosed a map of the earth. However, three traditional shapes - rectangles, circles and ovals - are used to portray most maps of the world.

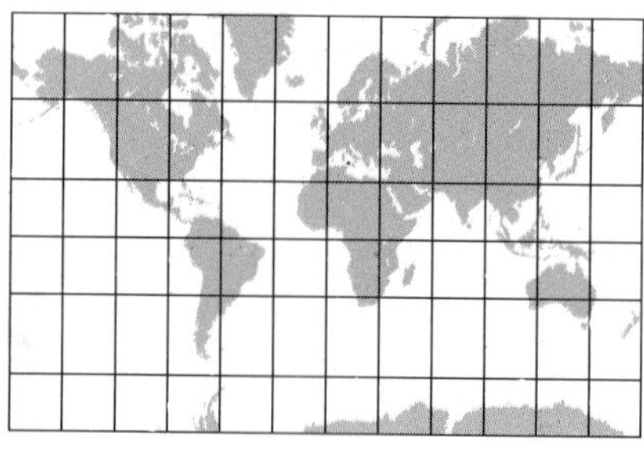

Mercator Projection

A rectangular- shaped map with vertical meridians and horizontal parallels, it is the only map on which a straight line, drawn anywhere on the map, indicates true direction along its entire length. The map has reasonably true shapes and distances within 15 degrees of the equator, but distortion increases dramatically into the higher latitudes.

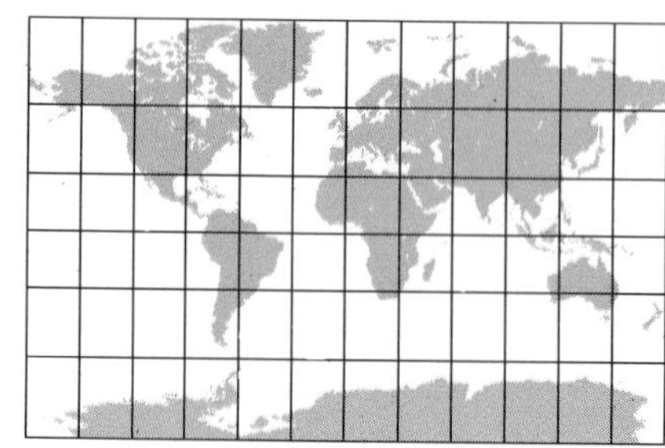

Miller Cylindrical Projection

Similar in appearance to the Mercator Projection, the Miller Cylindrical lessens distortions in the higher latitudes by closing up the spacing between parallels. Although this destroys the unique navigational property or the Mercator, it does present a more realistic view of land areas in the northern parts of Europe, Asia and North America.

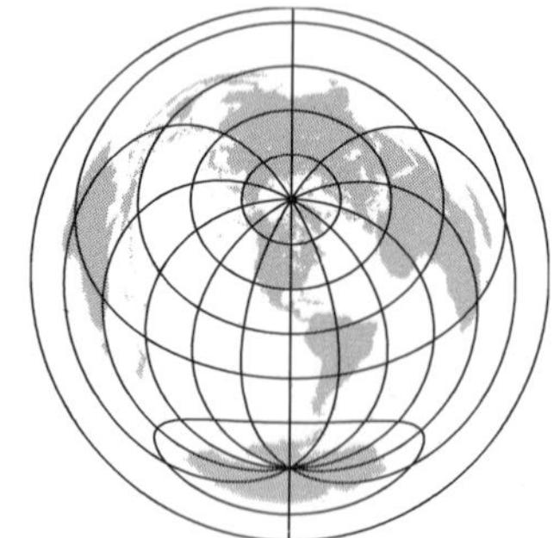

Azimuthal Equidistant Projection

A circular-shaped projection whose oblique view is the only projection in which directions and distances are depicted accurately from the projection's center point to any other place on the globe. Any straight line passing through the center is a great circle route. Distortion of areas and shapes increases away from the center.

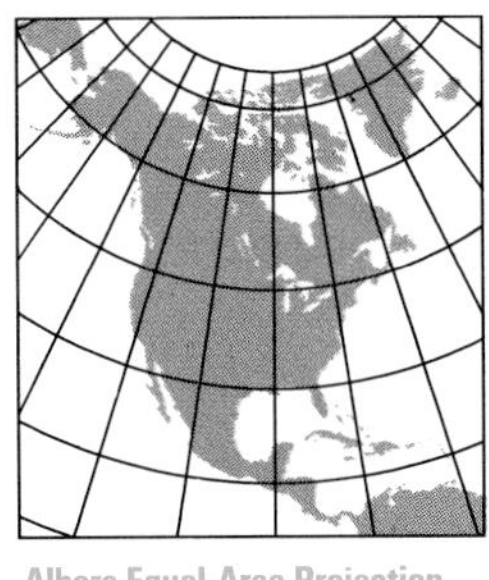
Albers Equal-Area Projection

Other Map Projections

Since continents and smaller regions occupy only a part of the entire earth's surface, other projections can be employed to minimize distortion and, where possible, preserve true shapes, areas, distances or directions. But, although smaller in size, the areas being mapped are still parts of a sphere and the flattening process will still result in distortions in the maps.

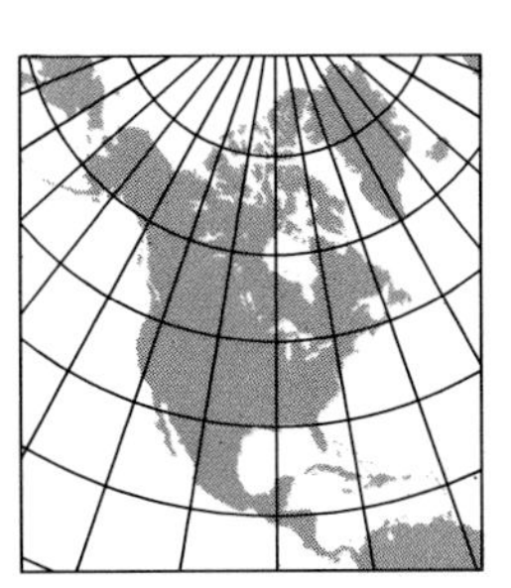
Lambert Conformal Conic Projection

Conic Projections

These maps are created by mathematically projecting points and lines from a globe onto a cone which caps the globe. The cone can be placed either tangent to the globe at a preselected parallel or it can intersect the globe at two preselected parallels. The use of two standard parallels, one near the top of the map, the other near the bottom of the map, reduces the scale error. In one type of conic projection, Albers, the parallels are spaced evenly to make the projection equal-area. In the Lambert Conformal Conic Projection the parallels are spaced so that any small quadrangle of the grid will have the same shape as on the globe.

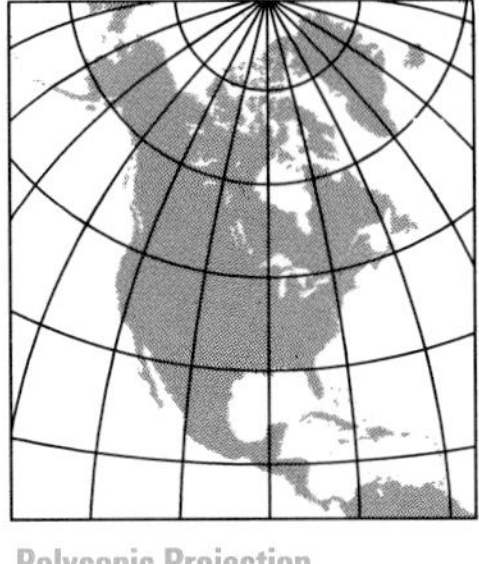
Polyconic Projection

Polyconic Projection

Best suited for maps with a long north-south orientation, this projection is mathematically based upon an infinite number of cones tangent to an infinite number of points (parallels) on the globe. All meridians are curved lines except for the central meridian, which shows true distance and direction.

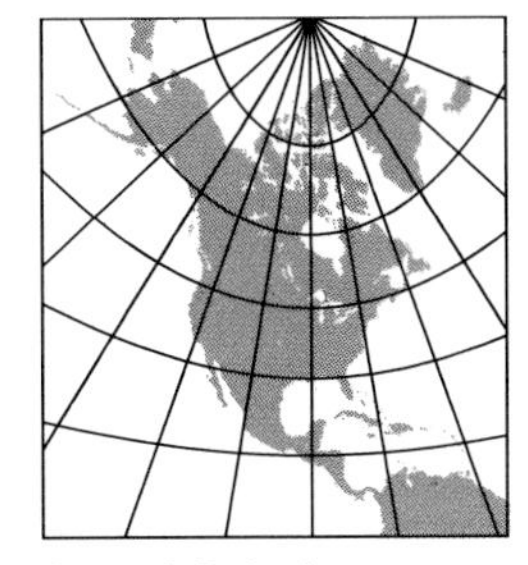
Gnomonic Projection

Gnomonic Projection

Viewing the surface of the globe from its center point creates this projection with very bad distortions away from the map's center. However, this projection has a unique quality - all great circles (shortest lines between points on a sphere) are shown as straight lines. Therefore, the path of the shortest distance between any two points on the map is a straight line.

Lambert Azimuthal Equal-Area Projection

Mathematically projected on a plane surface tangent to any point on a globe, this is the most common projection (also known as Zenithal Equal-Area) used for maps of the Eastern and Western hemispheres. It is also a good projection for continents, as it shows correct areas with little distortion of shape.

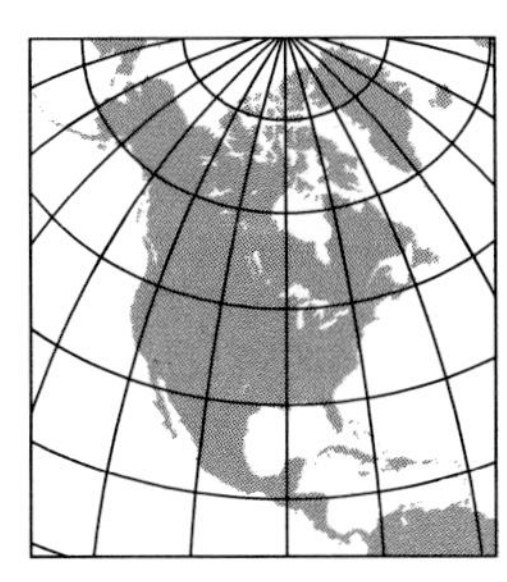
Lambert Azimuthal Equal-Area Projection

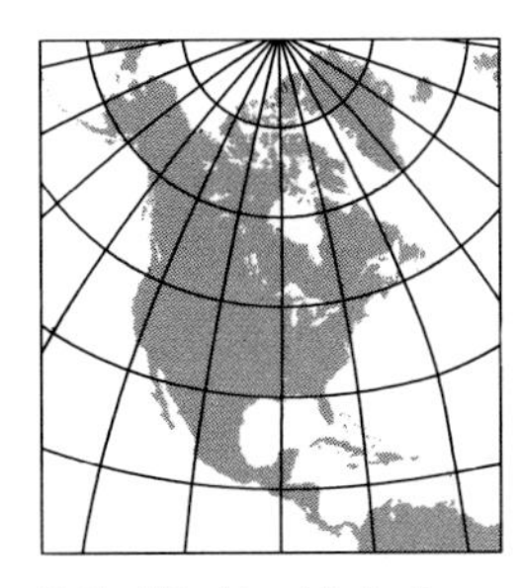
Optimal Conformal Projection

Hammond's Optimal Conformal Projection

As its name implies, this new conformal projection presents the optimal view of an area by reducing shifts in scale over an entire region to the minimum degree possible. While conformal maps generally preserve all small shapes, large shapes can become very distorted because of varying scales, causing considerable inaccuracy in distance measurements. Consequently, unlike other projections, the Optimal Comformal does not use one standard formula to construct a map. Each map is a unique projection - the optimal projection for that particular area. The result is the most distortion-free conformal map possible.

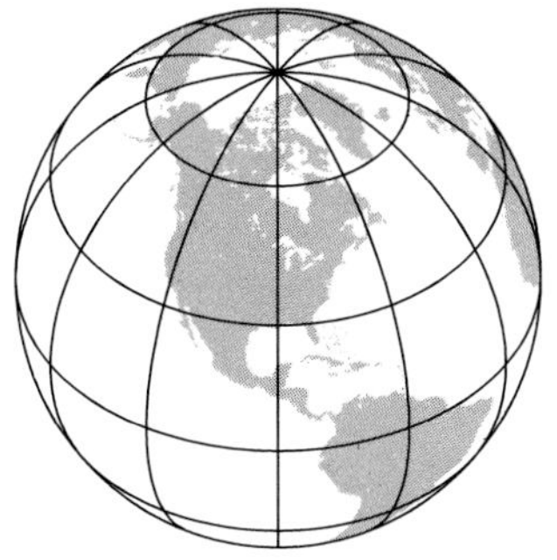

Orthographic Projection

This projection looks like a picture of a globe. It is neither conformal nor equal-area. Although the distortion on the peripheries is extreme, we see it correctly, because the eye perceives it not as a map but as a picture of a three-dimensional globe. Obviously, only a hemisphere (half globe) can be shown.

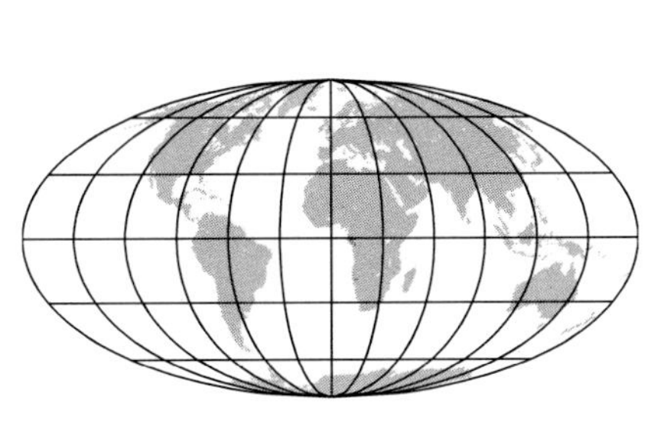

Mollweide Projection

An early example of an oval-shaped (also called pseudocylindrical) projection is this equal-area map of the earth within an ellipse. Shapes are elongated in the lower latitudes. Since its presentation in 1805 it has been an inspiration for similar oval-shaped maps and has even been "interrupted" to minimize distortion of continental or ocean areas.

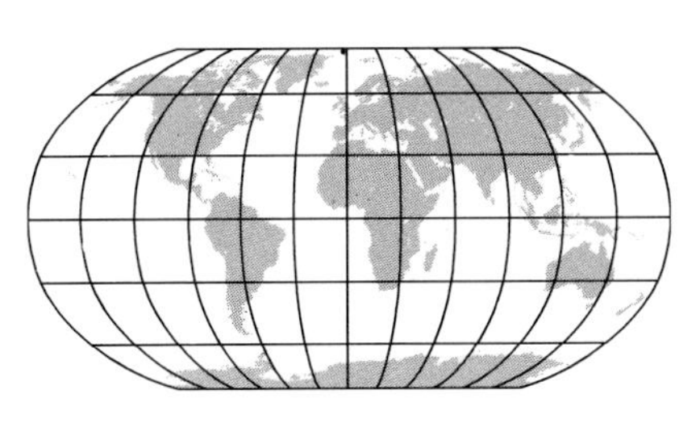

Robinson Projection

This modern, oval-shaped projection uses tabular coordinates rather than mathematical formulas to make the world "look right." Although not true with respect to shapes, sizes, distances or directions, its compromising features show a better balance of size and shape in high latitude lands and very low distortion near the equator.

Quick Reference Guide

This concise alphabetical reference lists continents, countries, states, territories, possessions and other major geographical areas, complete with the size, population and capital or chief town of each. Page numbers and alpha-numeric reference keys (which refer to the grid squares of latitude and longitude on each map) are visible at a glance. The population figures are the latest and most reliable figures obtainable.

	Place	Square Miles	Square Kilometers	Population	Capital or Chief Town	Page/ Index Ref.
A	**Afghanistan**	250,775	649,507	21,251,821	Kabul	49/F 6
	Africa	11,707,000	30,321,130	705,924,000	....	65
	Alabama, U.S.	51,705	133,916	4,040,587	Montgomery	78/C 4
	Alaska, U.S.	591,004	1,530,700	550,043	Juneau	76
	Albania	11,100	28,749	3,413,904	Tiranë	44/C 3
	Alberta, Canada	255,285	661,185	2,545,553	Edmonton	79/F 4
	Algeria	919,591	2,381,740	28,539,321	Algiers	68/F 2
	Andorra	188	487	65,780	Andorra la Vella	42/E 5
	Angola	481,351	1,246,700	10,069,501	Luanda	70/C 3
	Antarctica	5,500,000	14,245,000	....	....	71
	Antigua and Barbuda	171	443	65,176	St. John's	81/J 4
	Argentina	1,072,070	2,776,661	34,292,742	Buenos Aires	88/D 4
	Arizona, U.S.	114,000	295,260	3,665,228	Phoenix	76/D 5
	Arkansas, U.S.	53,187	137,754	2,350,725	Little Rock	77/H 4
	Armenia	11,506	29,800	3,557,284	Yerevan	45/C 4
	Asia	17,128,500	44,362,815	3,407,967,000	....	49
	Australia	2,966,136	7,682,300	18,322,231	Canberra	59
	Austria	32,375	83,851	7,986,664	Vienna	42/G 4
	Azerbaijan	33,436	86,600	7,789,886	Baku	45/D 4
B	**Bahamas**	5,382	13,939	256,616	Nassau	81/F 2
	Bahrain	240	622	575,925	Manama	52/F 3
	Bangladesh	55,126	142,776	128,094,948	Dhaka	53/E 4
	Barbados	166	430	256,395	Bridgetown	81/J 5
	Belarus	80,154	207,600	10,437,418	Minsk	43/G 5
	Belgium	11,781	30,513	10,081,880	Brussels	42/E 3
	Belize	8,867	22,966	214,061	Belmopan	80/D 4
	Benin	43,483	112,620	5,522,677	Porto-Novo	68/F 5
	Bhutan	18,147	47,000	1,780,638	Thimphu	53/E 3
	Bolivia	424,163	1,098,582	7,896,254	La Paz; Sucre	86/F 7
	Bosnia & Herzegovina	19,940	51,129	3,201,823	Sarajevo	44/C 3
	Botswana	224,764	582,139	1,392,414	Gaborone	70/D 5
	Brazil	3,284,426	8,506,663	160,737,489	Brasília	83/D 3
	British Columbia, Canada	366,253	948,596	3,282,061	Victoria	79/E 4
	Brunei	2,226	5,765	292,266	Bandar Seri Begawan	56/E 4
	Bulgaria	42,823	110,912	8,775,198	Sofia	44/D 3
	Burkina	105,869	274,200	10,422,828	Ouagadougou	68/E 5
	Burma (Myanmar)	261,789	678,034	45,103,809	Rangoon	49/J 7
	Burundi	10,747	27,835	6,262,429	Bujumbura	70/E 1
C	**California, U.S.**	158,706	411,049	29,760,021	Sacramento	76/C 4
	Cambodia	69,898	181,036	10,561,373	Phnom Penh	56/C 3
	Cameroon	183,568	475,441	13,521,000	Yaoundé	68/H 7
	Canada	3,851,787	9,976,139	28,434,545	Ottawa	79
	Cape Verde	1,557	4,033	435,983	Praia	12/H 5
	Central African Republic	242,000	626,780	3,209,759	Bangui	69/J 6
	Chad	495,752	1,283,998	5,586,505	N'Djamena	69/J 4
	Chile	292,257	756,946	14,161,216	Santiago	88/B 3
	China, People's Rep. of	3,691,000	9,559,690	1,203,097,268	Beijing	54/G 4
	China, Republic of (Taiwan)	13,971	36,185	21,500,583	Taipei	55/M 7
	Colombia	439,513	1,138,339	36,200,251	Bogotá	86/D 3
	Colorado, U.S.	104,091	269,596	3,294,394	Denver	76/E 4
	Comoros	719	1,862	549,338	Moroni	65/G 6
	Congo	132,046	342,000	2,504,996	Brazzaville	65/D 4
	Connecticut, U.S.	5,018	12,997	3,287,116	Hartford	78/F 2
	Costa Rica	19,575	50,700	3,419,114	San José	80/E 5
	Côte d'Ivoire	124,504	322,465	14,791,257	Yamoussoukro	68/D 5
	Croatia	22,050	56,538	4,665,821	Zagreb	44/C 2
	Cuba	44,206	114,494	10,937,635	Havana	81/F 3
	Cyprus	3,473	8,995	736,636	Nicosia	52/B 1
	Czech Republic	30,449	78,863	10,432,774	Prague	44/B 2
D	**Delaware, U.S.**	2,044	5,294	666,168	Dover	78/E 3
	Denmark	16,629	43,069	5,199,437	Copenhagen	43/C 4
	District of Columbia, U.S.	69	179	606,900	Washington	78/E 3
	Djibouti	8,880	23,000	421,320	Djibouti	69/P 5
	Dominica	290	751	82,608	Roseau	81/J 4
	Dominican Republic	18,704	48,443	7,511,263	Santo Domingo	81/H 4
E	**Ecuador**	109,483	283,561	10,890,950	Quito	86/C 4
	Egypt	386,659	1,001,447	62,359,623	Cairo	69/L 2
	El Salvador	8,260	21,393	5,870,481	San Salvador	80/C 5
	England, U.K.	50,516	130,836	48,068,400	London	42/D 3
	Equatorial Guinea	10,831	28,052	420,293	Malabo	68/G 7
	Eritrea	36,170	93,679	3,578,709	Āsmara	69/N 5
	Estonia	17,413	45,100	1,625,399	Tallinn	43/G 4
	Ethiopia	435,606	1,128,220	55,979,018	Addis Ababa	69/N 5
	Europe	4,057,000	10,507,630	732,653,000	....	39
F	**Fiji**	7,055	18,272	772,891	Suva	62/G 6
	Finland	130,128	337,032	5,085,206	Helsinki	43/G 3
	Florida, U.S.	58,664	151,940	12,937,926	Tallahassee	78/D 5
	France	210,038	543,998	58,109,160	Paris	42/E 4
	French Guiana	35,135	91,000	145,270	Cayenne	87/H 3
	French Polynesia	1,544	4,000	219,999	Papeete	63/L 6
G	**Gabon**	103,346	267,666	1,155,749	Libreville	68/H 7
	Gambia	4,127	10,689	989,273	Banjul	68/B 5
	Gaza Strip	139	360	813,322	Gaza	52/B 2
	Georgia	26,911	69,700	5,725,972	Tbilisi	45/C 4
	Georgia, U.S.	58,910	152,577	6,478,216	Atlanta	78/D 4
	Germany	137,753	356,780	81,337,541	Berlin	42/F 3
	Ghana	92,099	238,536	17,763,138	Accra	68/E 6
	Greece	50,944	131,945	10,647,511	Athens	44/D 4
	Greenland, Denmark	840,000	2,175,600	57,611	Nuuk (Godthåb)	72/N 2
	Grenada	133	344	94,486	St. George's	81/J 5
	Guatemala	42,042	108,889	10,998,602	Guatemala	80/C 4
	Guinea	94,925	245,856	6,549,336	Conakry	68/C 5
	Guinea-Bissau	13,948	36,125	1,124,537	Bissau	68/B 5
	Guyana	83,000	214,970	723,774	Georgetown	86/G 3
H	**Haiti**	10,694	27,697	6,539,983	Port-au-Prince	81/G 4
	Hawaii, U.S.	6,471	16,760	1,108,229	Honolulu	76
	Honduras	43,277	112,087	5,459,743	Tegucigalpa	80/D 4
	Hong Kong, U.K.	403	1,044	5,542,869	Victoria	55/K 7
	Hungary	35,919	93,030	10,318,838	Budapest	44/C 2
I	**Iceland**	39,768	103,000	265,998	Reykjavík	39/B 2
	Idaho, U.S.	83,564	216,431	1,006,749	Boise	76/C 3
	Illinois, U.S.	56,345	145,934	11,430,602	Springfield	78/B 2
	India	1,269,339	3,287,588	936,545,814	New Delhi	53/C 4
	Indiana, U.S.	36,185	93,719	5,544,159	Indianapolis	78/C 2
	Indonesia	788,430	2,042,034	203,583,886	Jakarta	56/E 6
	Iowa, U.S.	56,275	145,752	2,776,755	Des Moines	77/H 3
	Iran	636,293	1,648,000	64,625,455	Tehran	52/F 2
	Iraq	172,476	446,713	20,643,769	Baghdad	52/D 2
	Ireland	27,136	70,282	3,550,448	Dublin	42/C 3
	Ireland, Northern, U.K.	5,452	14,121	1,610,000	Belfast	42/C 3
	Israel	7,847	20,324	5,433,134	Jerusalem	52/B 2
	Italy	116,303	301,225	58,261,971	Rome	39/F 4
J	**Jamaica**	4,411	11,424	2,574,291	Kingston	81/F 4
	Japan	145,730	377,441	125,506,492	Tokyo	55/Q 4
	Jordan	35,000	90,650	4,100,709	Amman	52/C 2
K	**Kansas, U.S.**	82,277	213,097	2,477,574	Topeka	77/G 4
	Kazakstan	1,048,300	2,715,100	17,376,615	Aqmola	46/G 5
	Kentucky, U.S.	40,409	104,659	3,685,296	Frankfort	77/J 4
	Kenya	224,960	582,646	28,817,227	Nairobi	65/F 4
	Kiribati	291	754	79,386	Bairiki	62/H 5
	Korea, North	46,540	120,539	23,486,550	P'yŏngyang	55/N 3
	Korea, South	38,175	98,873	45,553,882	Seoul	55/N 4
	Kuwait	6,532	16,918	1,817,397	Al Kuwait	52/E 3
	Kyrgyzstan	76,641	198,500	4,769,877	Bishkek	46/H 5
L	**Laos**	91,428	236,800	4,837,237	Vientiane	49/K 8
	Latvia	24,595	63,700	2,762,899	Riga	43/G 4
	Lebanon	4,015	10,399	3,695,921	Beirut	52/B 2
	Lesotho	11,720	30,355	1,992,960	Maseru	70/E 6
	Liberia	43,000	111,370	3,073,245	Monrovia	68/D 6
	Libya	679,358	1,759,537	5,248,401	Tripoli	69/J 2
	Liechtenstein	61	158	30,654	Vaduz	42/F 4
	Lithuania	25,174	65,200	3,876,396	Vilnius	43/F 4
	Louisiana, U.S.	47,752	123,678	4,219,973	Baton Rouge	77/H 5
	Luxembourg	999	2,587	404,660	Luxembourg	42/F 4
M	**Macedonia**	9,889	25,713	2,159,503	Skopje	44/D 3
	Madagascar	226,657	587,041	13,862,325	Antananarivo	70/K10

Place	Square Miles	Square Kilometers	Population	Capital or Chief Town	Page/ Index Ref.
Maine, U.S.	33,265	86,156	1,227,928	Augusta	78/G 1
Malawi	45,747	118,485	9,808,384	Lilongwe	70/F 3
Malaysia	128,308	332,318	19,723,587	Kuala Lumpur	56/D 4
Maldives	115	298	261,310	Male	49/G 9
Mali	464,873	1,204,021	9,375,132	Bamako	68/E 4
Malta	122	316	369,609	Valletta	44/B 4
Manitoba, Canada	250,999	650,087	1,091,942	Winnipeg	79/H 4
Marshall Islands	70	181	56,157	Majuro	62/G 3
Maryland, U.S.	10,460	27,091	4,781,468	Annapolis	78/E 3
Massachusetts, U.S.	8,284	21,456	6,016,425	Boston	78/F 2
Mauritania	419,229	1,085,803	2,263,202	Nouakchott	68/C 4
Mauritius	790	2,046	1,127,068	Port Louis	13/M 7
Mexico	761,601	1,972,546	93,985,848	Mexico City	80/A 3
Michigan, U.S.	58,527	151,585	9,295,297	Lansing	78/C 1
Micronesia, Federated States of	....	....	122,950	Kolonia	62/D 4
Minnesota, U.S.	84,402	218,601	4,375,099	St. Paul	77/G 2
Mississippi, U.S.	47,689	123,515	2,573,216	Jackson	78/B 4
Missouri, U.S.	69,697	180,515	5,117,073	Jefferson City	77/H 4
Moldova	13,012	33,700	4,489,657	Chişinău	44/E 2
Monaco	368 acres	149 hectares	31,515	....	42/F 5
Mongolia	606,163	1,569,962	2,493,615	Ulaanbaatar	54/G 2
Montana, U.S.	147,046	380,849	799,065	Helena	76/D 2
Morocco	172,414	446,550	29,168,848	Rabat	68/C 1
Mozambique	303,769	786,762	18,115,250	Maputo	70/G 4
N					
Namibia	317,827	823,172	1,651,545	Windhoek	70/C 5
Nauru	7.7	20	10,149	Yaren (district)	62/F 5
Nebraska, U.S.	77,355	200,349	1,578,385	Lincoln	76/F 3
Nepal	54,663	141,577	21,560,869	Kathmandu	53/D 3
Netherlands	15,892	41,160	15,452,903	The Hague; Amsterdam	42/F 3
Nevada, U.S.	110,561	286,353	1,201,833	Carson City	76/C 4
New Brunswick, Canada	28,354	73,437	723,900	Fredericton	79/L 5
Newfoundland, Canada	156,184	404,517	568,474	St. John's	79/L 4
New Hampshire, U.S.	9,279	24,033	1,109,252	Concord	78/F 2
New Jersey, U.S.	7,787	20,168	7,730,188	Trenton	78/F 2
New Mexico, U.S.	121,593	314,926	1,515,069	Santa Fe	76/E 5
New York, U.S.	49,108	127,190	17,990,455	Albany	78/E 2
New Zealand	103,736	268,676	3,407,277	Wellington	59/H 6
Nicaragua	45,698	118,358	4,206,353	Managua	80/D 5
Niger	489,189	1,267,000	9,280,208	Niamey	68/G 4
Nigeria	357,000	924,630	101,232,251	Abuja	68/G 6
North America	9,363,000	24,250,170	443,438,000	....	73
North Carolina, U.S.	52,669	136,413	6,628,637	Raleigh	78/D 3
North Dakota, U.S.	70,702	183,118	638,800	Bismarck	76/F 2
Northern Ireland, U.K.	5,452	14,121	1,610,000	Belfast	42/C 3
North Korea	46,540	120,539	23,486,550	P'yŏngyang	55/N 3
Northwest Territories, Canada	1,304,896	3,379,683	57,649	Yellowknife	79/F 3
Norway	125,053	323,887	4,330,951	Oslo	43/C 3
Nova Scotia, Canada	21,425	55,491	899,942	Halifax	79/L 5
O					
Ohio, U.S.	41,330	107,045	10,847,115	Columbus	78/D 2
Oklahoma, U.S.	69,956	181,186	3,145,585	Oklahoma City	77/G 4
Oman	120,000	310,800	2,125,089	Muscat	52/G 4
Ontario, Canada	412,580	1,068,582	10,084,885	Toronto	79/H 4
Oregon, U.S.	97,073	251,419	2,842,321	Salem	76/B 3
P					
Pakistan	310,403	803,944	131,541,920	Islamabad	49/F 7
Palau	188	487	16,661	Koror	62/C 4
Panama	29,761	77,082	2,680,903	Panamá	80/E 6
Papua New Guinea	183,540	475,369	4,294,750	Port Moresby	62/D 5
Paraguay	157,047	406,752	5,358,198	Asunción	83/C 5
Pennsylvania, U.S.	45,308	117,348	11,881,643	Harrisburg	78/E 2
Peru	496,222	1,285,215	24,087,372	Lima	86/C 5
Philippines	115,707	299,681	73,265,584	Manila	57/H 3
Poland	120,725	312,678	38,792,442	Warsaw	39/F 3
Portugal	35,549	92,072	10,562,388	Lisbon	42/C 6
Prince Edward Island, Canada	2,184	5,657	129,765	Charlottetown	79/L 5
Puerto Rico, U.S.	3,515	9,104	3,812,569	San Juan	81/H 4
Q					
Qatar	4,247	11,000	533,916	Doha	52/F 3
Québec, Canada	594,857	1,540,680	6,895,963	Québec	79/K 4
R					
Réunion, France	969	2,510	666,067	St-Denis	13/M 7
Rhode Island, U.S.	1,212	3,139	1,003,464	Providence	78/F 2
Romania	91,699	237,500	23,198,330	Bucharest	44/D 2
Russia	6,592,812	17,075,400	149,909,089	Moscow	46/H 3
Rwanda	10,169	26,337	8,605,307	Kigali	70/E 1
S					
Saint Kitts and Nevis	104	269	40,992	Basseterre	81/J 4
Saint Lucia	238	616	156,050	Castries	81/J 5
Saint Vincent & the Grenadines	150	388	117,344	Kingstown	81/J 5
San Marino	23.4	60.6	24,313	San Marino	42/G 5
São Tomé and Príncipe	372	963	140,423	São Tomé	68/F 7
Saskatchewan, Canada	251,699	651,900	988,928	Regina	79/G 4
Saudi Arabia	829,995	2,149,687	18,729,576	Riyadh	52/D 4
Scotland, U.K.	30,414	78,772	5,111,200	Edinburgh	42/C 2
Senegal	75,954	196,720	9,007,080	Dakar	68/B 5
Seychelles	145	375	72,709	Victoria	13/M 6
Sierra Leone	27,925	72,325	4,753,120	Freetown	68/C 6
Singapore	226	585	2,890,468	Singapore	56/C 5
Slovakia	18,924	49,014	5,432,383	Bratislava	44/C 2
Slovenia	7,898	20,251	2,051,522	Ljubljana	44/B 2
Solomon Islands	11,500	29,785	399,206	Honiara	62/E 6
Somalia	246,200	637,658	7,347,554	Mogadishu	69/Q 6
South Africa	455,318	1,179,274	45,095,459	Cape Town; Pretoria	70/D 6
South America	6,875,000	17,806,250	314,335,000	....	83
South Carolina, U.S.	31,113	80,583	3,486,703	Columbia	78/D 4
South Dakota, U.S.	77,116	199,730	696,004	Pierre	76/F 3
South Korea	38,175	98,873	45,553,882	Seoul	55/N 4
Spain	194,881	504,742	39,404,348	Madrid	42/D 5
Sri Lanka	25,332	65,610	18,342,660	Colombo	53/D 7
Sudan	967,494	2,505,809	30,120,420	Khartoum	69/L 5
Suriname	55,144	142,823	429,544	Paramaribo	87/G 3
Swaziland	6,705	17,366	966,977	Mbabane	70/F 6
Sweden	173,665	449,792	8,821,759	Stockholm	43/D 3
Switzerland	15,943	41,292	7,084,984	Bern	42/F 4
Syria	71,498	185,180	15,451,917	Damascus	52/C 1
T					
Taiwan	13,971	36,185	21,500,583	Taipei	55/M 7
Tajikistan	55,251	143,100	6,155,474	Dushanbe	46/H 6
Tanzania	363,708	942,003	28,701,077	Dar es Salaam	70/F 2
Tennessee, U.S.	42,144	109,153	4,877,185	Nashville	78/C 3
Texas, U.S.	266,807	691,030	16,986,510	Austin	76/F 5
Thailand	198,455	513,998	60,271,300	Bangkok	56/C 2
Togo	21,622	56,000	4,410,370	Lomé	68/F 6
Tonga	270	699	105,600	Nuku'alofa	63/H 7
Trinidad and Tobago	1,980	5,128	1,271,159	Port-of-Spain	81/J 5
Tunisia	63,378	164,149	8,879,845	Tunis	68/G 1
Turkey	300,946	779,450	63,405,526	Ankara	44/F 4
Turkmenistan	188,455	488,100	4,075,316	Ashkhabad	46/F 6
Tuvalu	9.78	25.33	9,991	Funafuti	62/G 5
U					
Uganda	91,076	235,887	19,573,262	Kampala	69/M 7
Ukraine	233,089	603,700	51,867,828	Kiev	44/E 2
United Arab Emirates	32,278	83,600	2,924,594	Abu Dhabi	52/F 4
United Kingdom	94,399	244,493	58,295,119	London	42/D 2
United States	3,536,338	9,159,116	263,814,032	Washington	76
Uruguay	72,172	186,925	3,222,716	Montevideo	88/E 3
Utah, U.S.	84,899	219,888	1,722,850	Salt Lake City	76/D 4
Uzbekistan	173,591	449,600	23,089,261	Tashkent	46/G 5
V					
Vanuatu	5,700	14,763	173,648	Vila	62/F 6
Vatican City	108.7 acres	44 hectares	830	....	42/G 5
Venezuela	352,143	912,050	21,004,773	Caracas	82/E 2
Vermont, U.S.	9,614	24,900	562,758	Montpelier	78/F 2
Vietnam	128,405	332,569	74,393,324	Hanoi	49/K 8
Virginia, U.S.	40,767	105,587	6,187,358	Richmond	78/E 3
Virgin Islands, British	59	153	12,000	Road Town	81/J 4
Virgin Islands, U.S.	132	342	97,229	Charlotte Amalie	81/H 4
W					
Wales, U.K.	8,017	20,764	2,886,400	Cardiff	42/D 3
Washington, U.S.	68,139	176,480	4,866,692	Olympia	76/B 2
West Bank	2,100	5,439	1,319,991	....	52/C 2
Western Sahara	102,703	266,000	217,211	....	68/B 3
Western Samoa	1,133	2,934	209,360	Apia	63/H 6
West Virginia, U.S.	24,231	62,758	1,793,477	Charleston	78/D 3
Wisconsin, U.S.	56,153	145,436	4,891,769	Madison	78/B 1
World	(land) 57,970,000	150,142,300	5,733,687,096	....	12
Wyoming, U.S.	97,809	253,325	453,588	Cheyenne	76/E 3
Y					
Yemen	188,321	487,752	14,728,474	Sanaa	52/E 6
Yugoslavia	38,989	100,982	11,101,833	Belgrade	44/D 3
Yukon Territory, Canada	207,075	536,324	27,797	Whitehorse	79/D 3
Z					
Zaire	905,063	2,344,113	44,060,636	Kinshasa	65/E 5
Zambia	290,586	752,618	9,445,723	Lusaka	70/E 3
Zimbabwe	150,803	390,580	11,139,961	Harare	70/E 4

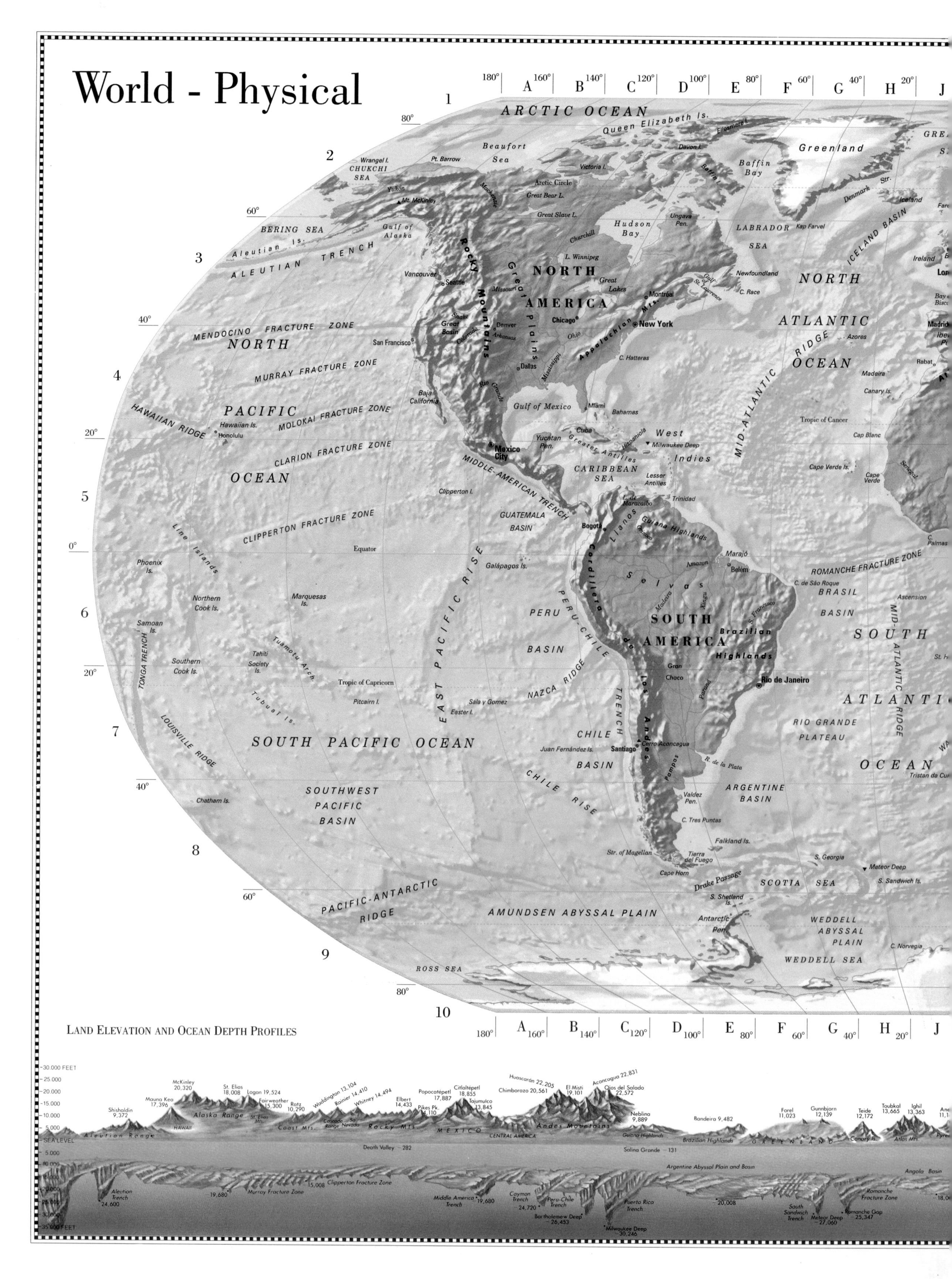
World - Physical
ARCTIC OCEAN
Queen Elizabeth Is.
Ellesmere I.
Greenland
Beaufort Sea
Devon I.
Baffin Bay
Wrangel I.
CHUKCHI SEA
Pt. Barrow
Victoria I.
Yukon
Mt. McKinley
Arctic Circle
Great Bear L.
Iceland
Denmark Str.
Great Slave L.
Ungava Pen.
Hudson Bay
BERING SEA
Gulf of Alaska
LABRADOR SEA
Kap Farvel
ICELAND BASIN
Aleutian Is.
ALEUTIAN TRENCH
Churchill
L. Winnipeg
Ireland
Vancouver
Seattle
Rocky Mountains
Great Plains
NORTH AMERICA
Great Lakes
Gulf of St. Lawrence
Newfoundland
C. Race
NORTH ATLANTIC OCEAN
Missouri
Montréal
Snake
Great Basin
Denver
Colorado
Arkansas
Chicago
Ohio
Appalachian Mts.
New York
MENDOCINO FRACTURE ZONE
NORTH PACIFIC OCEAN
San Francisco
Mississippi
Dallas
C. Hatteras
MID-ATLANTIC RIDGE
Azores
Madrid
Rabat
Madeira
Canary Is.
MURRAY FRACTURE ZONE
Rio Grande
Baja California
Gulf of Mexico
Miami
Bahamas
Tropic of Cancer
HAWAIIAN RIDGE
Hawaiian Is.
Honolulu
MOLOKAI FRACTURE ZONE
Yucatan Pen.
Cuba
Greater Antilles
Hispaniola
West Indies
Milwaukee Deep
Cap Blanc
Mexico City
CLARION FRACTURE ZONE
MIDDLE-AMERICAN TRENCH
CARIBBEAN SEA
Lesser Antilles
Cape Verde Is.
Cape Verde
Clipperton I.
Trinidad
L. de Maracaibo
GUATEMALA BASIN
Bogotá
Llanos
Guiana Highlands
Orinoco
CLIPPERTON FRACTURE ZONE
Line Islands
Equator
Marajó
Belém
Amazon
Phoenix Is.
Galápagos Is.
Cordillera
Selvas
ROMANCHE FRACTURE ZONE
C. de São Roque
BRASIL BASIN
Ascension
Northern Cook Is.
Marquesas Is.
EAST PACIFIC RISE
PERU BASIN
PERU-CHILE TRENCH
Madeira
Xingu
São Francisco
SOUTH AMERICA
Brazilian Highlands
SOUTH ATLANTIC OCEAN
Samoan Is.
TONGA TRENCH
Tuamotu Arch.
Tahiti
Society Is.
Southern Cook Is.
Gran Chaco
Paraná
Rio de Janeiro
Tropic of Capricorn
Pitcairn I.
Sala y Gomez
Easter I.
NAZCA RIDGE
Tubuai Is.
Los Andes
LOUISVILLE RIDGE
SOUTH PACIFIC OCEAN
CHILE BASIN
Juan Fernández Is.
Santiago
Cerro Aconcagua
RIO GRANDE PLATEAU
R. de la Plata
Pampas
Tristan da Cunha
CHILE RISE
ARGENTINE BASIN
SOUTHWEST PACIFIC BASIN
Chatham Is.
Valdez Pen.
C. Tres Puntas
Falkland Is.
Str. of Magellan
Tierra del Fuego
S. Georgia
Meteor Deep
Cape Horn
Drake Passage
SCOTIA SEA
S. Sandwich Is.
PACIFIC-ANTARCTIC RIDGE
AMUNDSEN ABYSSAL PLAIN
S. Shetland Is.
Antarctic Pen.
WEDDELL ABYSSAL PLAIN
WEDDELL SEA
C. Norvegia
ROSS SEA
LAND ELEVATION AND OCEAN DEPTH PROFILES
30,000 FEET
25,000
20,000
15,000
10,000
5,000
SEA LEVEL
5,000
35,000 FEET
Shishaldin 9,372
Mauna Kea 17,396
McKinley 20,320
St. Elias 18,008
Logan 19,524
Fairweather 15,300
Ratz 10,290
Waddington 13,104
Rainier 14,410
Whitney 14,494
Elbert 14,433
Pikes Pk. 14,110
Popocatépetl 17,887
Citlaltépetl 18,855
Tajumulco 13,845
Chimborazo 20,561
Huascarán 22,205
El Misti 19,101
Aconcagua 22,831
Ojos del Salado 22,572
Neblina 9,889
Bandeira 9,482
Forel 11,023
Gunnbjorn 12,139
Teide 12,172
Toubkal 13,665
Ighil 13,363
Aleutian Range
HAWAII
Alaska Range
St. Elias Mts.
Coast Mts.
Cascade Range
Sa. Nevada
Rocky Mts.
MEXICO
CENTRAL AMERICA
Andes Mountains
Guiana Highlands
Brazilian Highlands
GREENLAND
Canary Is.
Atlas Mts.
Death Valley -282
Salina Grande -131
Argentine Abyssal Plain and Basin
Angola Basin
Aleutian Trench 24,600
19,680
Murray Fracture Zone
15,008
Clipperton Fracture Zone
Middle America Trench
19,680
Cayman Trench 24,720
Peru-Chile Trench
Bartholomew Deep 26,453
Puerto Rico Trench
Milwaukee Deep 30,246
20,008
South Sandwich Trench
Meteor Deep 27,060
Romanche Gap 25,347
Romanche Fracture Zone

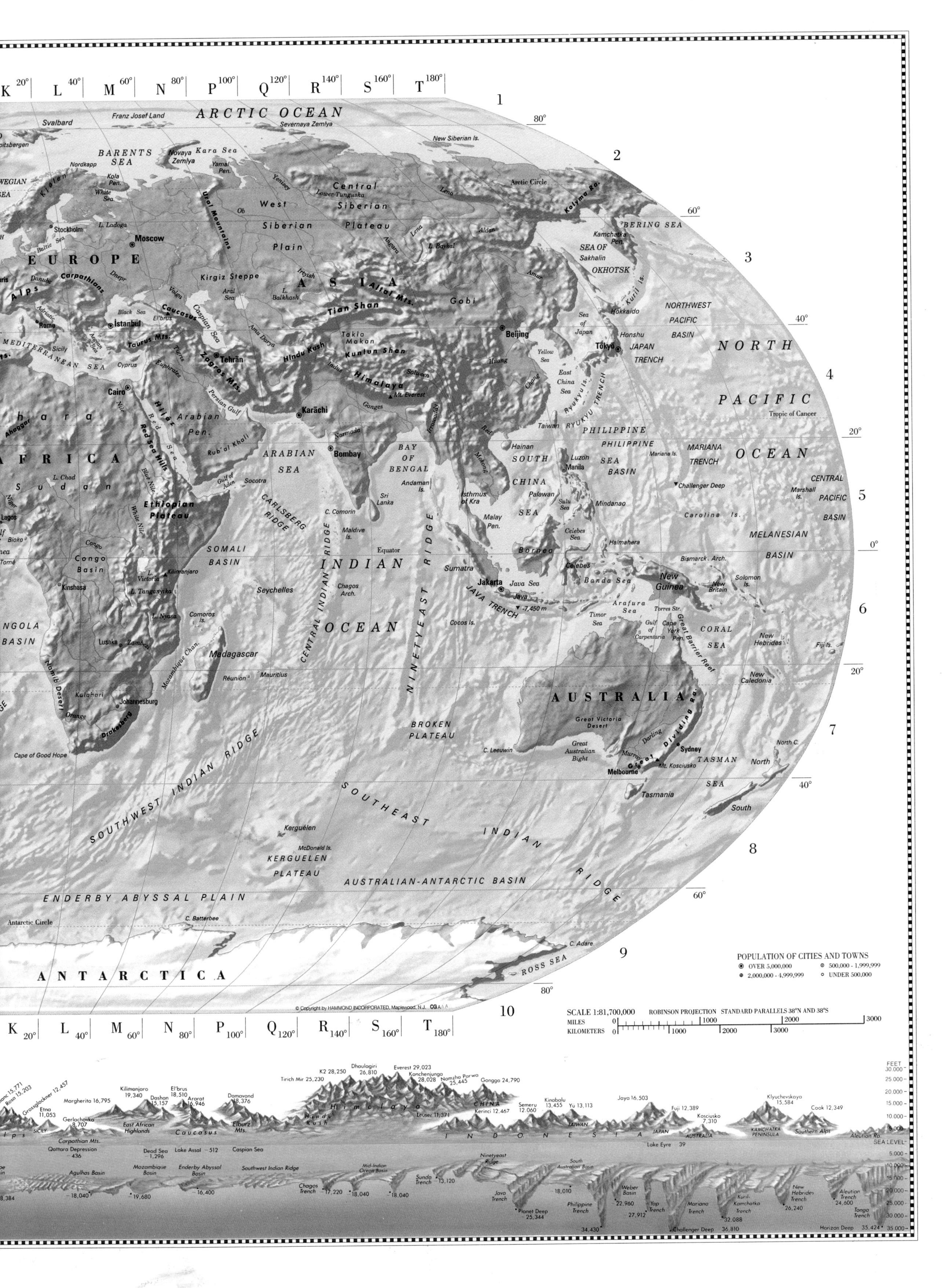

K 20°
L 40°
M 60°
N 80°
P 100°
Q 120°
R 140°
S 160°
T 180°
ARCTIC OCEAN
Svalbard
Franz Josef Land
Severnaya Zemlya
New Siberian Is.
BARENTS SEA
Novaya Zemlya
Kara Sea
Yamal Pen.
Nordkapp
Kola Pen.
White Sea
Central Siberian Plateau
Lower Tunguska
Yenisey
Lena
Arctic Circle
Kolyma Ra.
West Siberian Plain
Ural Mountains
Ob
Stockholm
L. Ladoga
Moscow
Baltic Sea
EUROPE
Danube
Carpathians
Alps
Dnepr
Volga
Kirgiz Steppe
Aral Sea
L. Balkhash
Irtysh
ASIA
Altai Mts.
Tian Shan
Gobi
Angara
L. Baykal
Aldan
Amur
BERING SEA
Kamchatka Pen.
SEA OF OKHOTSK
Sakhalin
Kuril Is.
Hokkaido
Black Sea
Caucasus
El'brus
Caspian Sea
İstanbul
Rome
Adriatic
Sicily
Aegean Sea
MEDITERRANEAN SEA
Cyprus
Taurus Mts.
Tigris
Euphrates
Amu Darya
Tehrān
Zagros Mts.
Hindu Kush
Takla Makan
Kunlun Shan
Beijing
Sea of Japan
Honshu
Tōkyō
JAPAN TRENCH
NORTHWEST PACIFIC BASIN
NORTH PACIFIC OCEAN
Yellow Sea
Huang
East China Sea
Chang
Ryukyu Is.
RYUKYU TRENCH
Taiwan
Tropic of Cancer
Cairo
Nile
Persian Gulf
Arabian Pen.
Hijāz
Red Sea
Red Sea Hills
Rub' al Khali
Karāchi
Indus
Himalaya
Mt. Everest
Ganges
Salween
Irrawaddy
Red
Narmada
Bombay
ARABIAN SEA
BAY OF BENGAL
Hainan
SOUTH CHINA SEA
Luzon
Manila
PHILIPPINE SEA
PHILIPPINE BASIN
PHILIPPINE TRENCH
Mariana Is.
MARIANA TRENCH
Challenger Deep
Ahaggar
Sahara
AFRICA
L. Chad
Sudan
Gulf of Aden
Socotra
Blue Nile
White Nile
Ethiopian Plateau
Niger
Lagos
Bioko
Congo
Congo Basin
CARLSBERG RIDGE
C. Comorin
Sri Lanka
Andaman Is.
Isthmus of Kra
Mekong
Malay Pen.
Palawan
Sulu Sea
Mindanao
Caroline Is.
Marshall Is.
CENTRAL PACIFIC BASIN
MELANESIAN BASIN
Maldive Is.
Equator
SOMALI BASIN
CENTRAL INDIAN RIDGE
INDIAN OCEAN
NINETYEAST RIDGE
Sumatra
Borneo
Celebes Sea
Celebes
Halmahera
Bismarck Arch.
L. Victoria
Kilimanjaro
Kinshasa
L. Tanganyika
Seychelles
Chagos Arch.
Jakarta
Java Sea
Java
JAVA TRENCH
-7,450 m
Banda Sea
New Guinea
New Britain
Solomon Is.
ANGOLA BASIN
L. Nyasa
Comoros Is.
Lusaka
Zambezi
Mozambique Chan.
Madagascar
Cocos Is.
Timor Sea
Arafura Sea
Torres Str.
Gulf of Carpentaria
Cape York Pen.
Great Barrier Reef
CORAL SEA
New Hebrides
Fiji Is.
Namib Desert
Kalahari
Johannesburg
Orange
Drakensberg
Réunion
Mauritius
New Caledonia
AUSTRALIA
Great Victoria Desert
Great Dividing Ra.
Darling
Murray
Sydney
Mt. Kosciusko
Melbourne
Great Australian Bight
C. Leeuwin
BROKEN PLATEAU
TASMAN SEA
Tasmania
North
South
Cape of Good Hope
SOUTHWEST INDIAN RIDGE
SOUTHEAST INDIAN RIDGE
Kerguélen
McDonald Is.
KERGUELEN PLATEAU
AUSTRALIAN-ANTARCTIC BASIN
ENDERBY ABYSSAL PLAIN
Antarctic Circle
C. Batterbee
C. Adare
ROSS SEA
ANTARCTICA
80°
60°
40°
20°
0°
1
2
3
4
5
6
7
8
9
10
POPULATION OF CITIES AND TOWNS
OVER 5,000,000
2,000,000 - 4,999,999
500,000 - 1,999,999
UNDER 500,000
SCALE 1:81,700,000
ROBINSON PROJECTION STANDARD PARALLELS 38°N AND 38°S
MILES 0 1000 2000 3000
KILOMETERS 0 1000 2000 3000
© Copyright by HAMMOND INCORPORATED, Maplewood, N.J.
Grossglockner 12,457
Margherita 16,795
Etna 11,053
Gerlachovka 8,707
Kilimanjaro 19,340
Dashan 15,157
El'brus 18,510
Ararat 16,946
East African Highlands
Caucasus
Damavand 18,376
Elburz Mts.
Tirich Mir 25,230
K2 28,250
Dhaulagiri 26,810
Everest 29,023
Kanchenjunga 28,028
Namzha Parwa 25,445
Gongga 24,790
Himalaya
Hindu Kush
CHINA
Leuser 11,371
Kerinci 12,467
Semeru 12,060
Kinabalu 13,455
Yu 13,113
TAIWAN
Jaya 16,503
Fuji 12,389
Kosciusko 7,310
JAPAN
AUSTRALIA
INDONESIA
Klyuchevskaya 15,584
KAMCHATKA PENINSULA
Cook 12,349
Southern Alps
Aleutian Ra.
Carpathian Mts.
Qattara Depression -436
Dead Sea -1,296
Lake Assal -512
Caspian Sea
Lake Eyre -39
Agulhas Basin
Mozambique Basin
Enderby Abyssal Basin
Southwest Indian Ridge
Mid-Indian Ocean Basin
Ninetyeast Ridge
South Australian Basin
Chagos Trench
Sunda Trench
Java Trench
Philippine Trench
Weber Basin
Yap Trench
Mariana Trench
Kuril-Kamchatka Trench
New Hebrides Trench
Aleutian Trench
Tonga Trench
18,040
19,680
16,400
17,220
18,040
18,040
13,120
18,010
22,960
27,912
32,088
26,240
24,600
Planet Deep 25,344
34,430
Challenger Deep 36,810
Horizon Deep 35,424
FEET
30,000
25,000
20,000
15,000
10,000
5,000
SEA LEVEL
5,000
10,000
15,000
20,000
25,000
30,000
35,000

World - Political

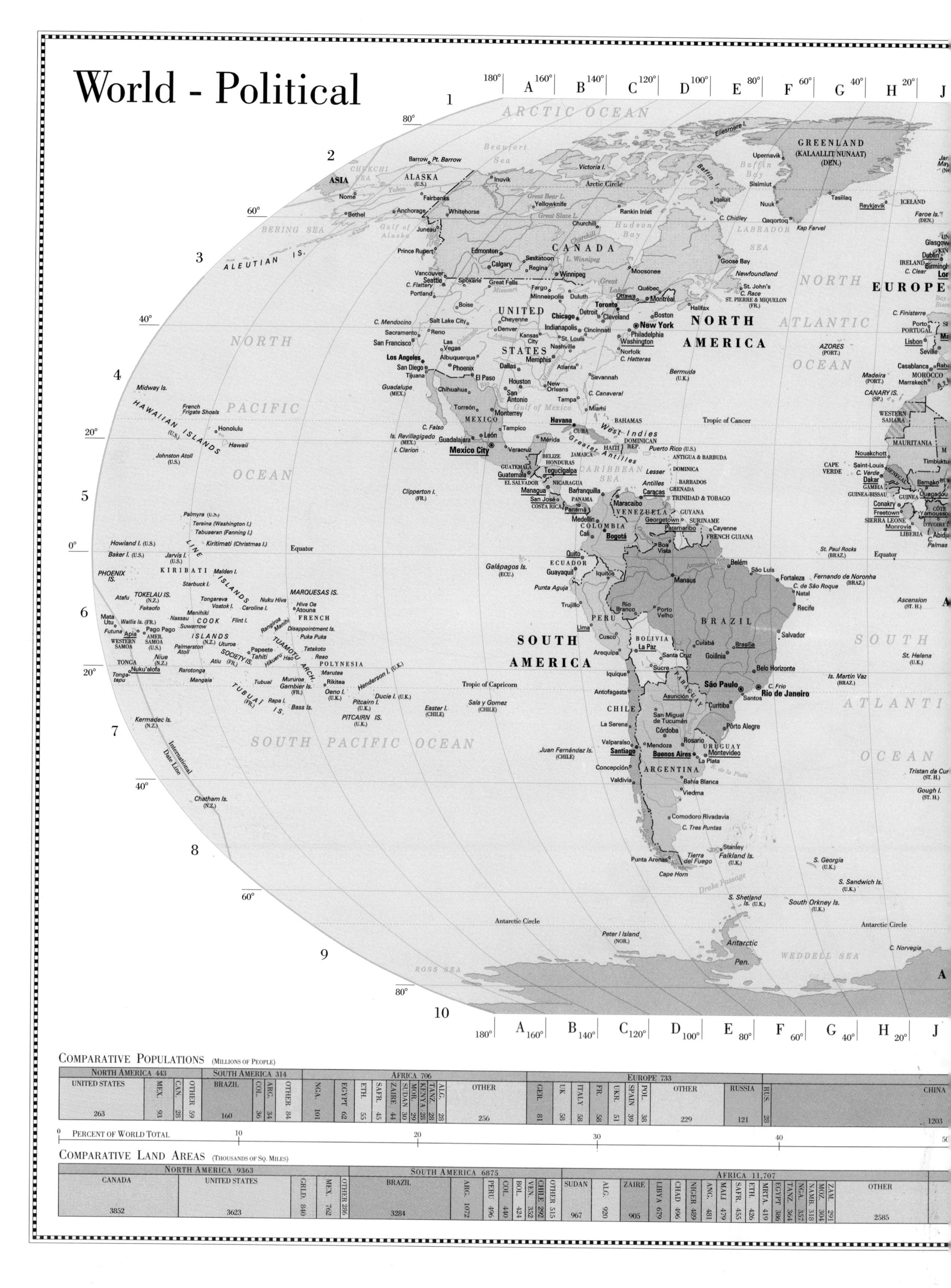

Comparative Populations (Millions of People)

North America 443				South America 314			
UNITED STATES	MEX.	CAN.	OTHER	BRAZIL	COL.	ARG.	OTHER
263	93	28	59	160	36	34	84

Africa 706										
NGA.	EGYPT	ETH.	SAFR.	ZAIRE	SUDAN	MOR.	KENYA	TANZ.	ALG.	OTHER
101	62	55	45	44	30	29	28	28	28	256

Europe 733										
GER.	UK	ITALY	FR.	UKR.	SPAIN	POL.	OTHER	RUSSIA	RUS.	CHINA
81	58	58	58	51	39	38	229	121	28	1203

Percent of World Total: 0, 10, 20, 30, 40, 50

Comparative Land Areas (Thousands of Sq. Miles)

North America 9363				
CANADA	UNITED STATES	GRLD.	MEX.	OTHER
3852	3623	840	762	286

South America 6875							
BRAZIL	ARG.	PERU	COL.	BOL.	VEN.	CHILE	OTHER
3284	1072	496	440	424	352	292	515

Africa 11,707																			
SUDAN	ALG.	ZAIRE	LIBYA	CHAD	NIGER	ANG.	MALI	SAFR.	ETH.	MRTA.	EGYPT	TANZ.	NGA.	NAMB.	MOZ.	ZAM.	OTHER
967	920	905	679	496	489	481	479	455	426	419	386	364	357	318	304	291	2585

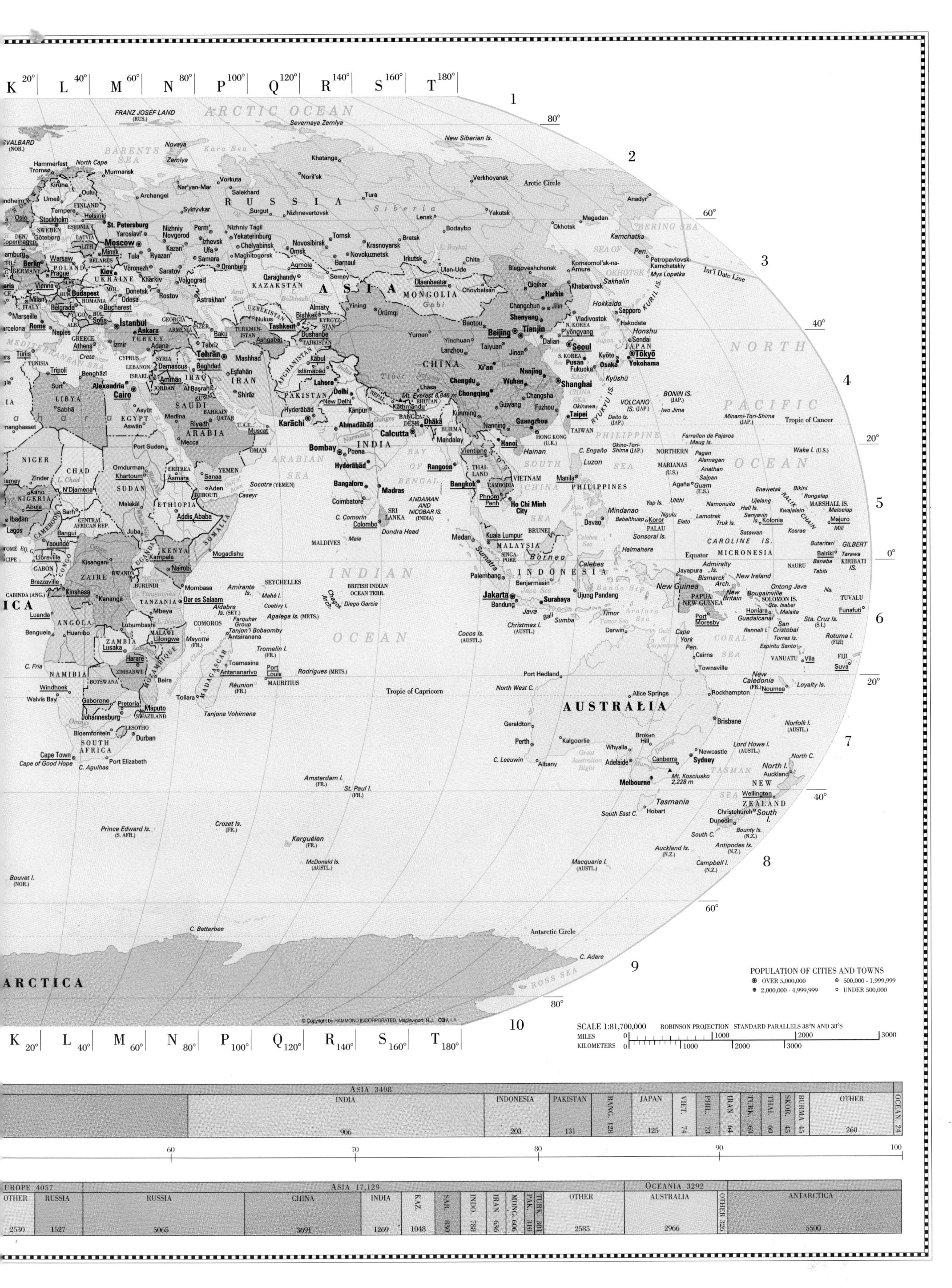
K 20° L 40° M 60° N 80° P 100° Q 120° R 140° S 160° T 180°
ARCTIC OCEAN
FRANZ JOSEF LAND (RUS.)
Severnaya Zemlya
New Siberian Is.
BARENTS SEA
Kara Sea
Novaya Zemlya
R U S S I A
S i b e r i a
Arctic Circle
BERING SEA
SEA OF OKHOTSK
Kamchatka
Int'l Date Line
A S I A
MONGOLIA
KAZAKSTAN
CHINA
Tibet
Gobi
JAPAN
Tōkyō
Beijing
Shanghai
Seoul
N. KOREA
S. KOREA
TAIWAN
PHILIPPINES
Manila
VIETNAM
Hanoi
Ho Chi Minh City
THAILAND
Bangkok
BURMA
Rangoon
CAMBODIA
Phnom Penh
LAOS
Vientiane
INDIA
New Delhi
Bombay
Calcutta
Madras
Bangalore
Hyderābād
PAKISTAN
Karāchi
Islāmābād
NEPAL
Kāthmandu
Mt. Everest 8,846 m
BHUTAN
BANGLADESH
Dhākā
SRI LANKA
Colombo
MALDIVES
AFGHANISTAN
Kābul
IRAN
Tehrān
IRAQ
Baghdad
SAUDI ARABIA
Riyadh
Mecca
YEMEN
OMAN
TURKEY
Ankara
İstanbul
SYRIA
Damascus
ISRAEL
JORDAN
LEBANON
UZBEKISTAN
Tashkent
TURKMENISTAN
Ashgabat
KYRGYZSTAN
Bishkek
TAJIKISTAN
Dushanbe
GEORGIA
ARMENIA
AZER.
Baku
UKRAINE
Kiev
BELARUS
Minsk
Moscow
St. Petersburg
FINLAND
Helsinki
SWEDEN
Stockholm
NORWAY
Oslo
POLAND
Warsaw
GERMANY
Berlin
ITALY
Rome
GREECE
Athens
ROMANIA
Bucharest
BULGARIA
Sofia
MEDITERRANEAN SEA
Black Sea
ARABIAN SEA
BAY OF BENGAL
SOUTH CHINA SEA
PHILIPPINE SEA
EAST CHINA SEA
NORTH PACIFIC OCEAN
INDIAN OCEAN
Tropic of Cancer
Tropic of Capricorn
LIBYA
Tripoli
EGYPT
Cairo
SUDAN
Khartoum
CHAD
NIGER
NIGERIA
Abuja
ETHIOPIA
Addis Ababa
SOMALIA
Mogadishu
KENYA
Nairobi
UGANDA
Kampala
TANZANIA
Dar es Salaam
ZAIRE
Kinshasa
ANGOLA
Luanda
ZAMBIA
Lusaka
ZIMBABWE
Harare
MOZAMBIQUE
Maputo
MADAGASCAR
Antananarivo
NAMIBIA
Windhoek
BOTSWANA
Gaborone
SOUTH AFRICA
Pretoria
Cape Town
Cape of Good Hope
INDONESIA
Jakarta
Borneo
Sumatra
Java
Celebes
MALAYSIA
Kuala Lumpur
SINGAPORE
BRUNEI
New Guinea
PAPUA NEW GUINEA
Port Moresby
AUSTRALIA
Canberra
Sydney
Melbourne
Perth
Brisbane
Tasmania
NEW ZEALAND
Wellington
TASMAN SEA
CORAL SEA
MICRONESIA
CAROLINE IS.
MARSHALL IS.
SOLOMON IS.
Honiara
FIJI
Suva
TUVALU
KIRIBATI
NAURU
New Caledonia (FR.)
Equator
ANTARCTICA
ROSS SEA
Antarctic Circle
© Copyright by HAMMOND INCORPORATED, Maplewood, N.J.
POPULATION OF CITIES AND TOWNS
OVER 5,000,000
2,000,000 - 4,999,999
500,000 - 1,999,999
UNDER 500,000
SCALE 1:81,700,000
ROBINSON PROJECTION STANDARD PARALLELS 38°N AND 38°S
MILES 0 1000 2000 3000
KILOMETERS 0 1000 2000 3000
ASIA 3408
INDIA 906
INDONESIA 203
PAKISTAN 131
BANG. 128
JAPAN 125
VIET. 74
PHIL. 73
IRAN 64
TURK. 63
THAI. 60
SKOR. 45
BURMA 45
OTHER 260
OCEAN. 24
60 70 80 90 100
EUROPE 4057
OTHER 2530
RUSSIA 1527
ASIA 17,129
RUSSIA 5065
CHINA 3691
INDIA 1269
KAZ. 1048
SAR. 850
INDO. 788
IRAN 636
MONG. 606
PAK. 310
TURK. 301
OTHER 2585
OCEANIA 3292
AUSTRALIA 2966
OTHER 326
ANTARCTICA 5500

Structure of the

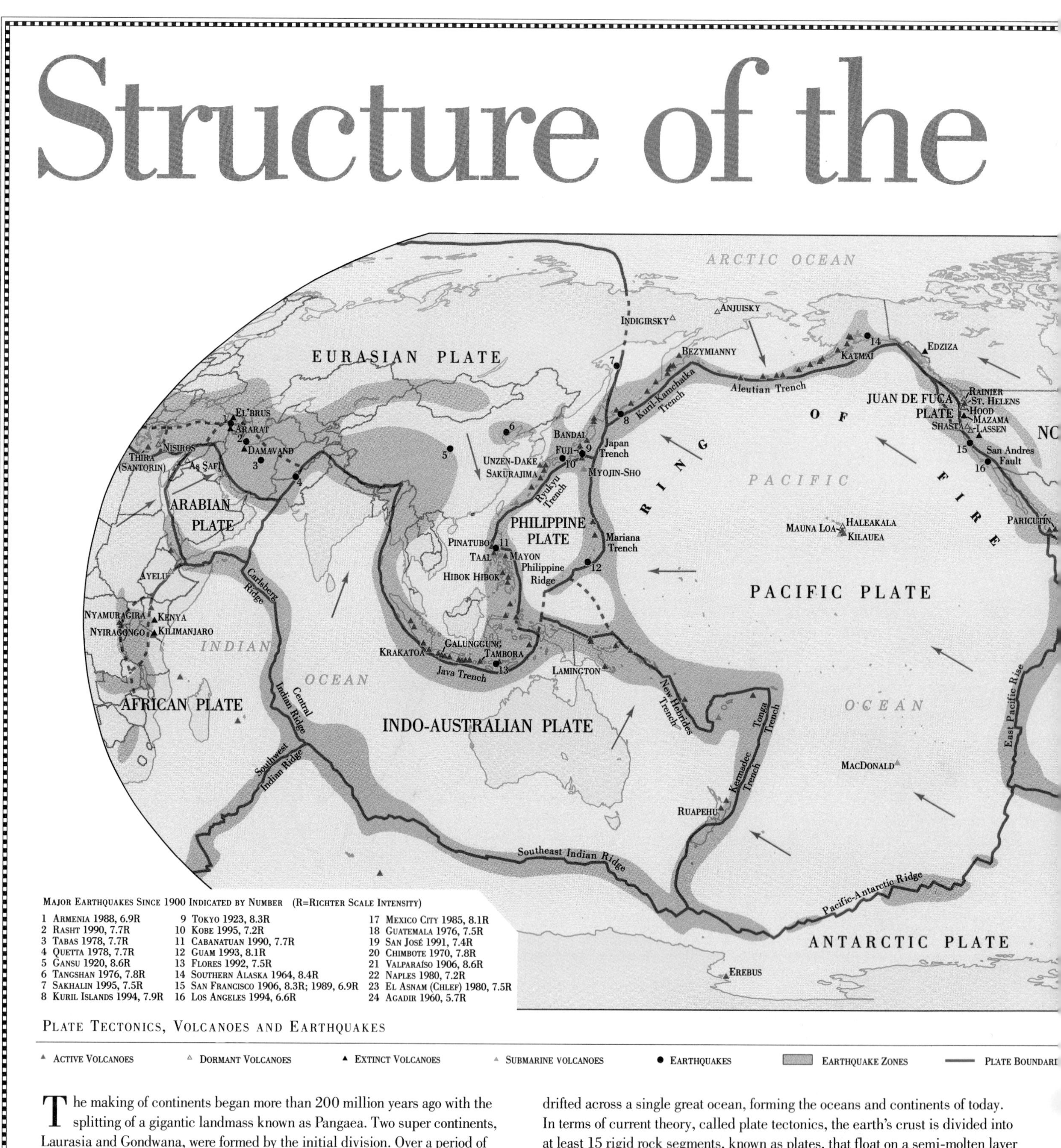

PLATE TECTONICS, VOLCANOES AND EARTHQUAKES

ACTIVE VOLCANOES · DORMANT VOLCANOES · EXTINCT VOLCANOES · SUBMARINE VOLCANOES · EARTHQUAKES · EARTHQUAKE ZONES · PLATE BOUNDARI

The making of continents began more than 200 million years ago with the splitting of a gigantic landmass known as Pangaea. Two super continents, Laurasia and Gondwana, were formed by the initial division. Over a period of many millions of years these landmasses further subdivided into smaller parts and drifted across a single great ocean, forming the oceans and continents of today. In terms of current theory, called plate tectonics, the earth's crust is divided into at least 15 rigid rock segments, known as plates, that float on a semi-molten layer of upper mantle. Seven plates are of major size and, except for the vast Pacific

CONTINENTAL DRIFT

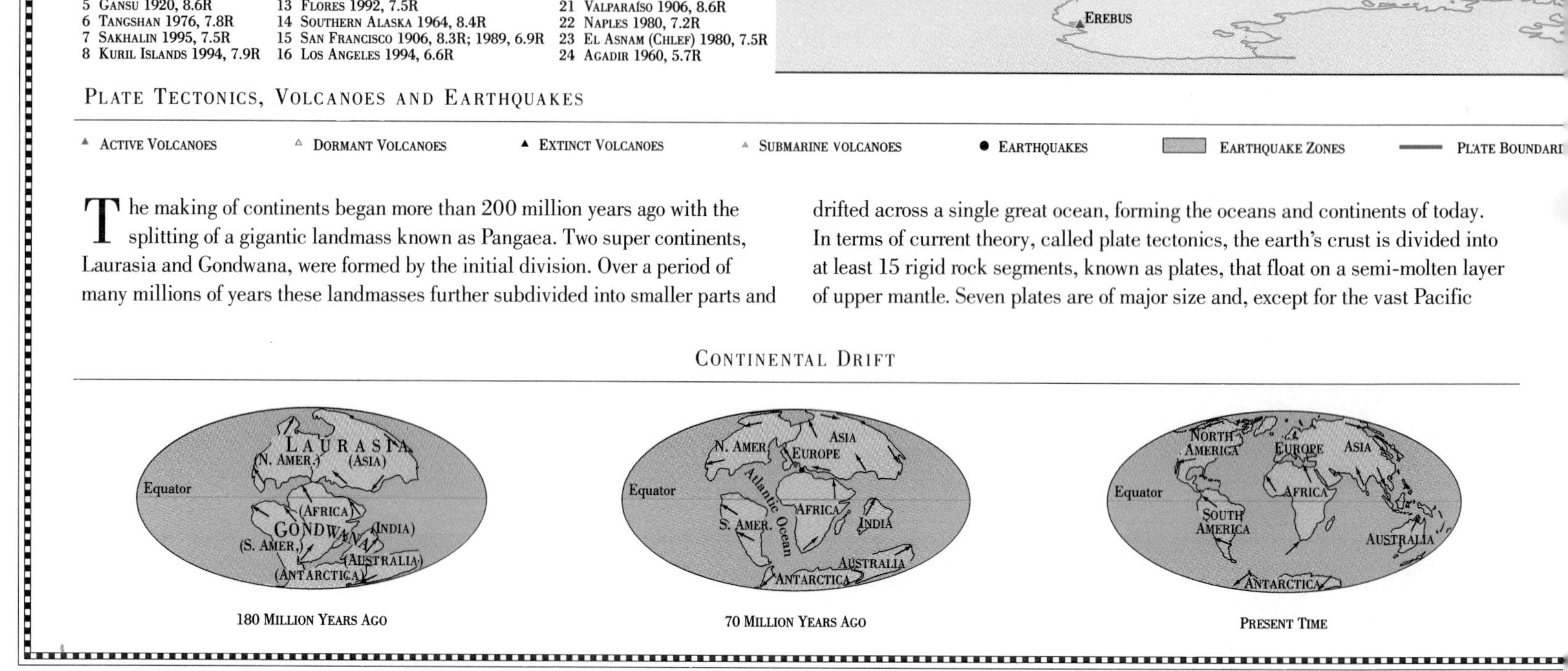

180 MILLION YEARS AGO · 70 MILLION YEARS AGO · PRESENT TIME

Earth

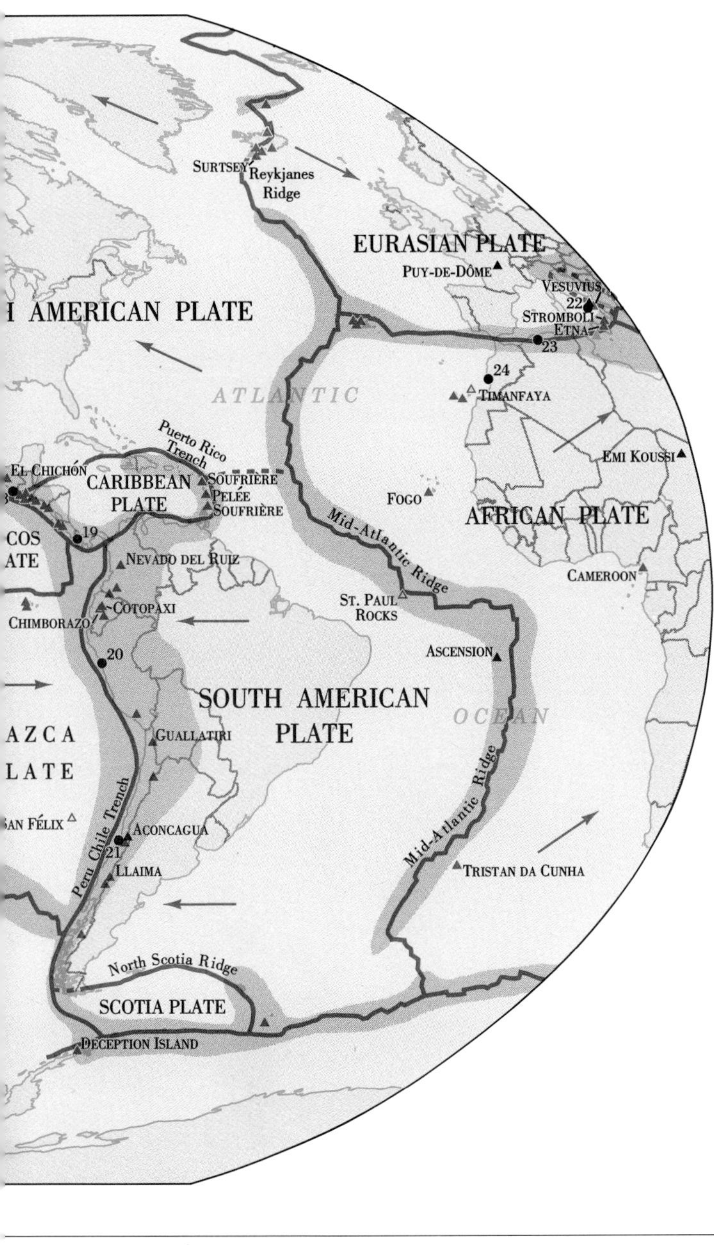

Mantle
1800 miles thick
solid, mostly iron and
magnesium silicates

Continental Crust
25 miles thick
solid, mostly coarse
crystalline rock

Outer Core
1350 miles thick
liquid, iron
and nickel

Oceanic Crust
4 miles thick
solid, mostly fine
crystalline rock

Inner Core
800 mile radius
solid, iron
and nickel

Interior and Crust of the Earth

By studying records of earthquakes, scientists have developed a fairly reasonable picture (cross section) of the earth's principal layers, including their composition. The inner core is a very dense, highly-pressurized, extremely hot (about 9,000° F.) sphere. Moving outward toward the crust, densities, pressures and temperatures decrease significantly.

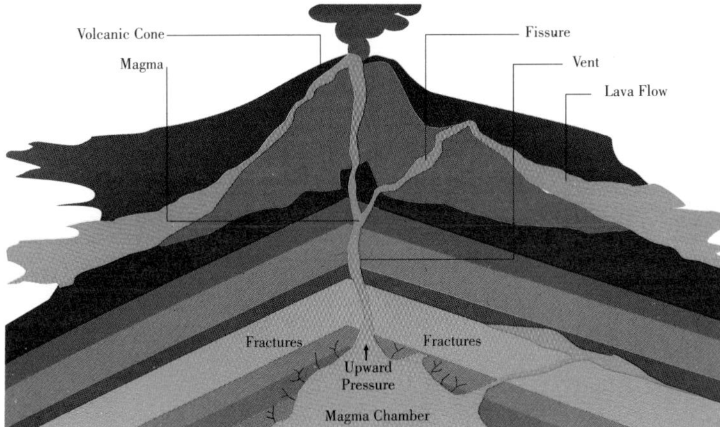

Volcanoes

One of the earth's most dynamic and colorful builders is the volcano. In the mantle, magma—molten rock containing compressed gases—probes for weak spots in the earth's crust and bursts forth through the ground in an eruption of fiery lava, ash, gas and steam. After a period of eruption, lasting from a few days to many years, the magma ceases to push upward and the volcano becomes dormant.

Plate, carry a continental landmass with surrounding ocean floor and island areas. The plates are slow-moving, driven by powerful forces within the mantle. At their boundaries they are either slowly separating with new material added from the mantle, converging, with one plate being forced down (subducted) and consumed under another, or sliding past each other. Almost all earthquake, volcanic and mountain-building activity closely follows these boundaries and is related to movements between them. Although these movements may be no more than inches per year, the destructive power unleashed can be cataclysmic.

Plate Tectonics

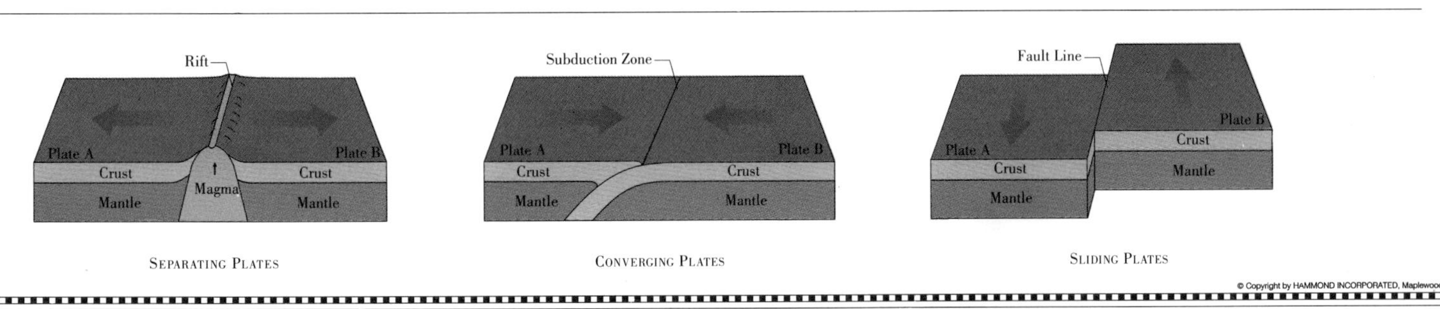

Separating Plates

Converging Plates

Sliding Plates

Atmosphere &

OCEAN CURRENTS

WARM CURRENTS   COLD CURRENTS   DIRECTION OF FLOW

Hurricane

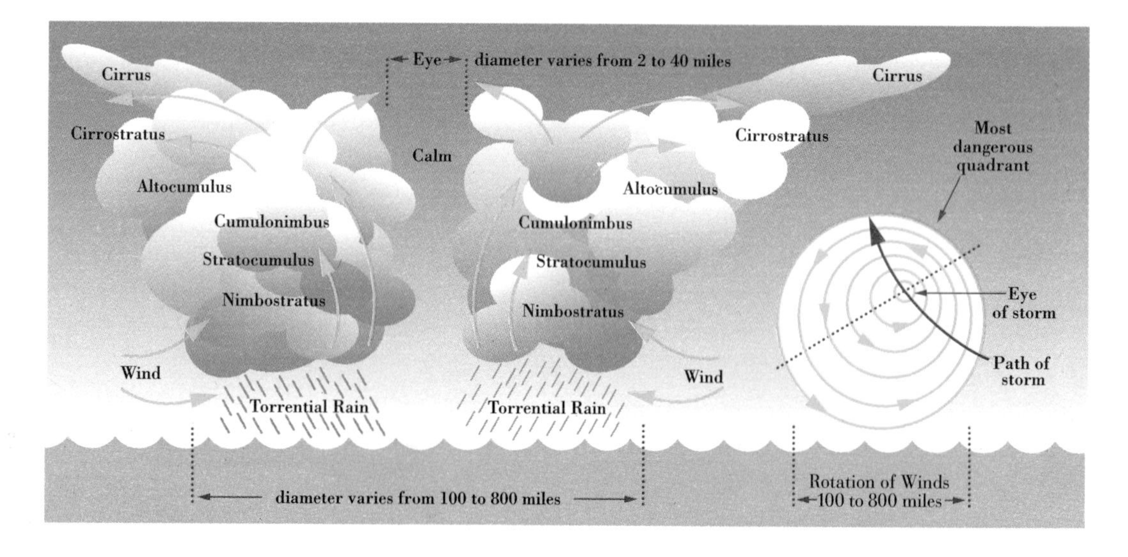

Hurricanes are great whirling storms accompanied by violent destructive winds, torrential rains and high waves and tides. They originate over the oceans, and usually move from lower to higher latitudes with increasing speed, size and intensity. Movement over land quickly reduces their force. Hurricane winds cause severe property damage, but drowning is the greatest cause of hurricane deaths. Floods can be the hurricane's most serious threat.

Oceans

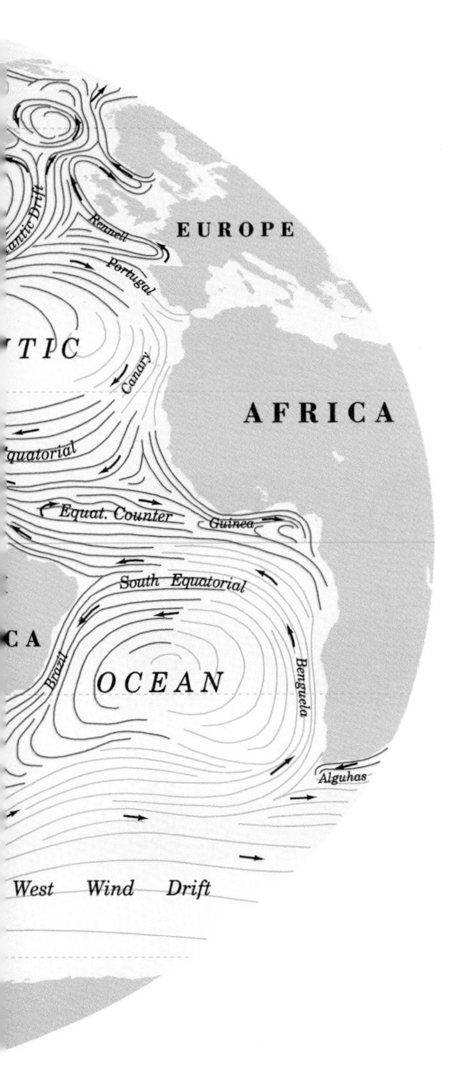

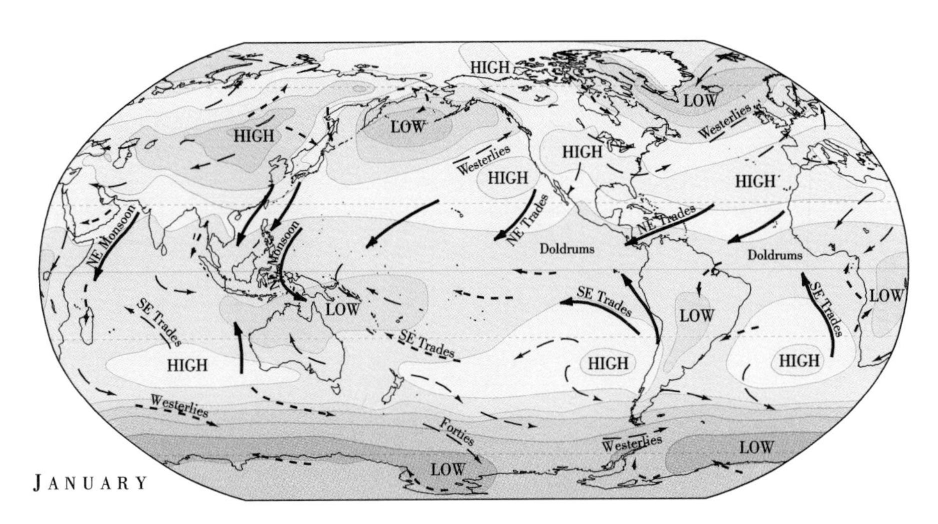

JANUARY

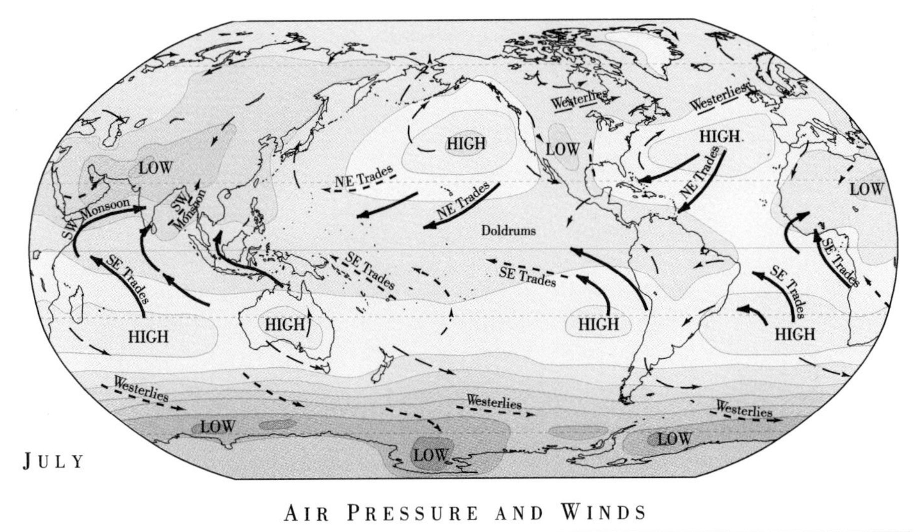

JULY

Air Pressure and Winds

Pressure in Millibars

- Over 1038
- 1032 to 1038
- 1026 to 1032
- 1020 to 1026
- 1014 to 1020
- 1008 to 1014
- 1002 to 1008
- 996 to 1002
- 990 to 996
- 984 to 990
- Under 984

Winds

- Less Often
- More Often
- Constant

Warm Front

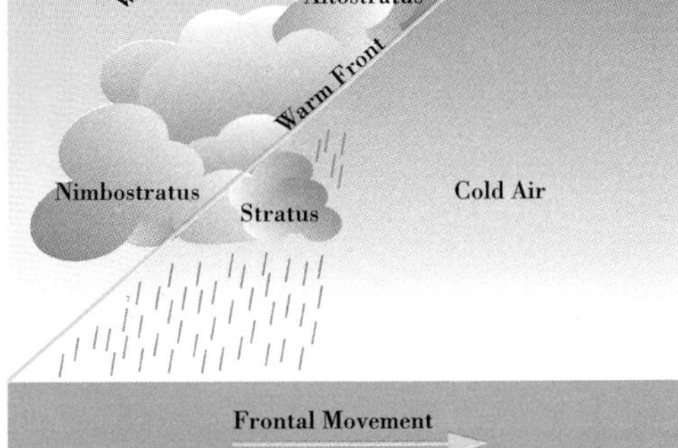

Cold Front

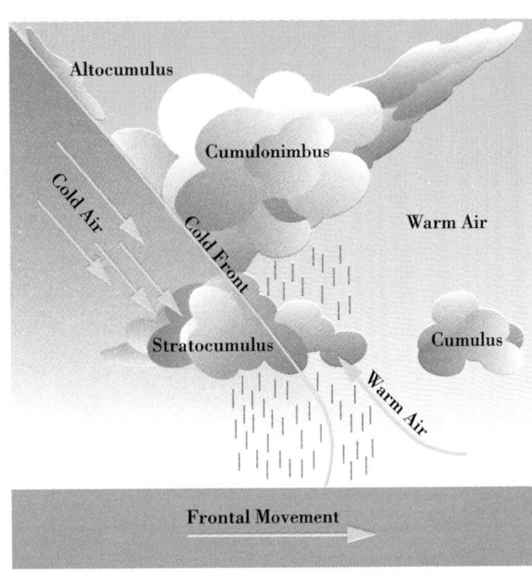

A front is the boundary surface between two air masses which have different characteristics, primarily different temperatures. Depending upon the amount of moisture in the warm air, warm fronts usually produce steady, moderate precipitation over a broad area ahead of the front on the ground. Cold fronts tend to move faster than warm fronts. They are generally confined to a narrower frontal zone but may contain dense thunderheads and severe storms.

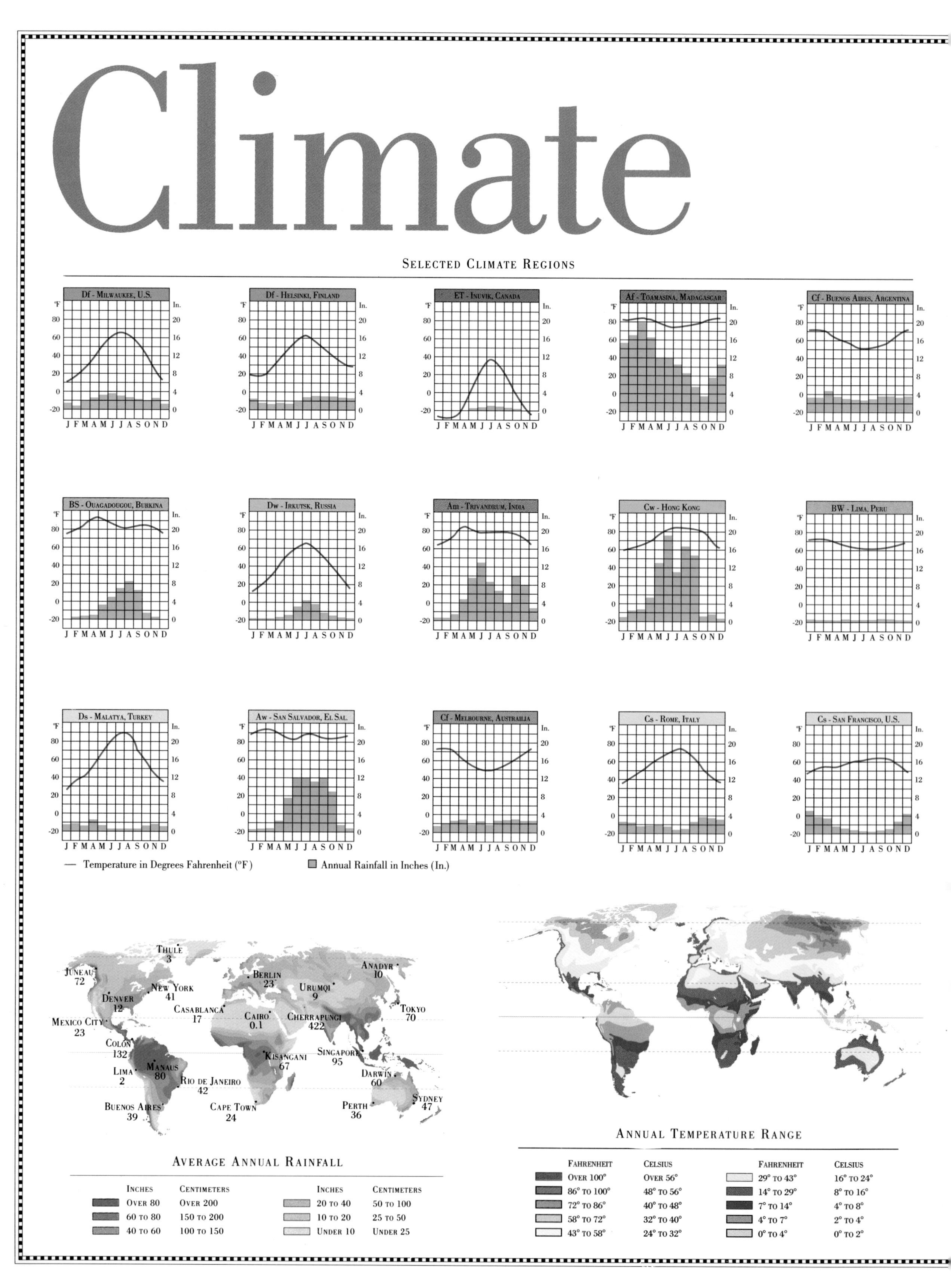

Climate
Selected Climate Regions
Df - Milwaukee, U.S.
Df - Helsinki, Finland
ET - Inuvik, Canada
Af - Toamasina, Madagascar
Cf - Buenos Aires, Argentina
BS - Ouagadougou, Burkina
Dw - Irkutsk, Russia
Am - Trivandrum, India
Cw - Hong Kong
BW - Lima, Peru
Ds - Malatya, Turkey
Aw - San Salvador, El Sal.
Cf - Melbourne, Austrailia
Cs - Rome, Italy
Cs - San Francisco, U.S.
°F
In.
J F M A M J J A S O N D
— Temperature in Degrees Fahrenheit (°F)
Annual Rainfall in Inches (In.)
Thule 3
Juneau 72
Denver 12
New York 41
Mexico City 23
Colon 132
Lima 2
Manaus 80
Rio de Janeiro 42
Buenos Aires 39
Casablanca 17
Berlin 23
Cairo 0.1
Kisangani 67
Cape Town 24
Urumqi 9
Anadyr 10
Cherrapunji 422
Tokyo 70
Singapore 95
Darwin 60
Perth 36
Sydney 47
Average Annual Rainfall
Inches | Centimeters
Over 80 | Over 200
60 to 80 | 150 to 200
40 to 60 | 100 to 150
20 to 40 | 50 to 100
10 to 20 | 25 to 50
Under 10 | Under 25
Annual Temperature Range
Fahrenheit | Celsius
Over 100° | Over 56°
86° to 100° | 48° to 56°
72° to 86° | 40° to 48°
58° to 72° | 32° to 40°
43° to 58° | 24° to 32°
29° to 43° | 16° to 24°
14° to 29° | 8° to 16°
7° to 14° | 4° to 8°
4° to 7° | 2° to 4°
0° to 4° | 0° to 2°

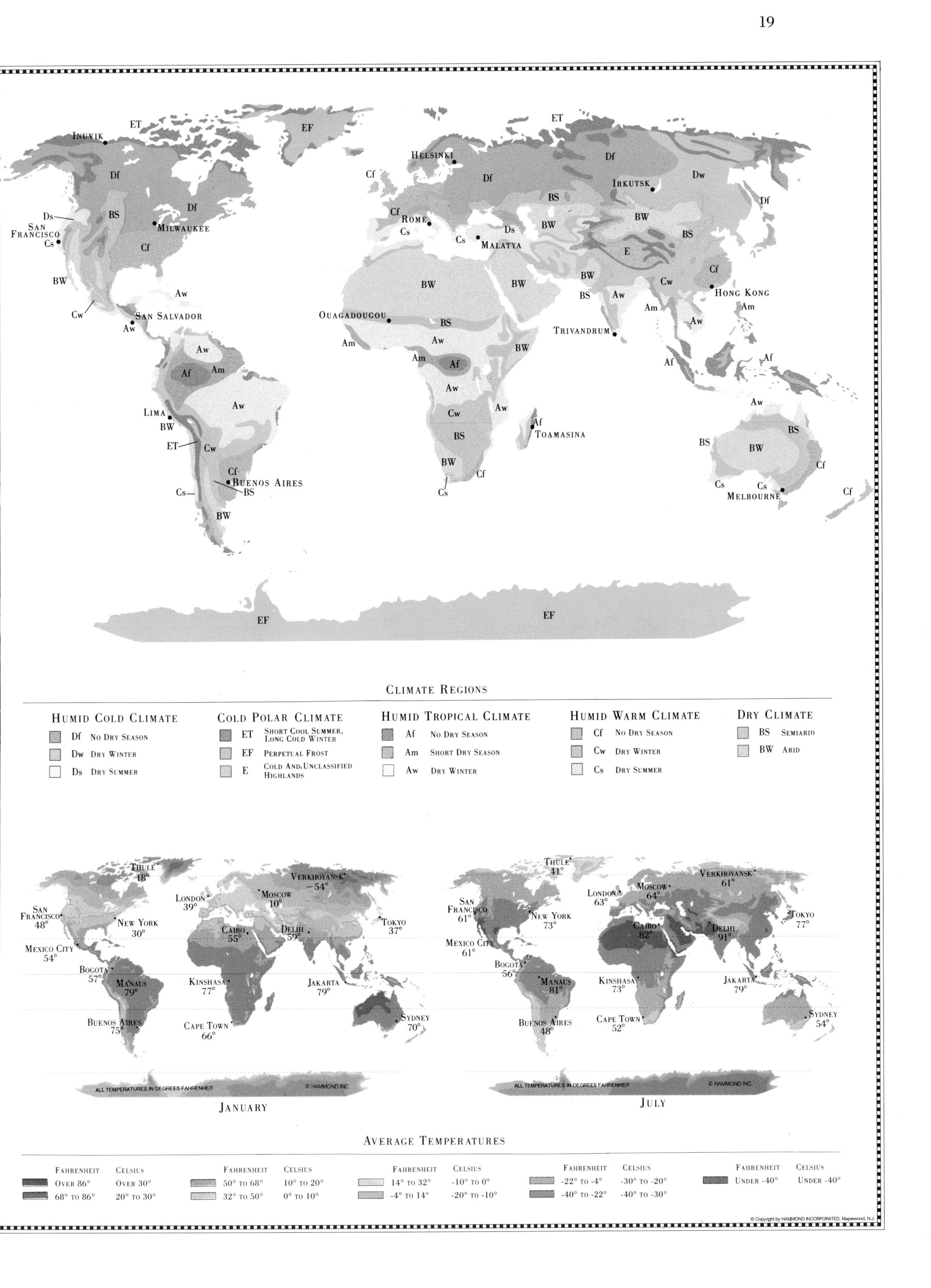

Inuvik
ET
EF
Df
BS
Ds
San Francisco
Cs
Milwaukee
Cf
BW
Cw
Aw
San Salvador
Af
Am
Lima
ET
Buenos Aires
Helsinki
Rome
Malatya
Ouagadougou
Toamasina
Dw
Irkutsk
E
Hong Kong
Trivandrum
Melbourne
Climate Regions
Humid Cold Climate
Df No Dry Season
Dw Dry Winter
Ds Dry Summer
Cold Polar Climate
ET Short Cool Summer, Long Cold Winter
EF Perpetual Frost
E Cold And Unclassified Highlands
Humid Tropical Climate
Af No Dry Season
Am Short Dry Season
Aw Dry Winter
Humid Warm Climate
Cf No Dry Season
Cw Dry Winter
Cs Dry Summer
Dry Climate
BS Semiarid
BW Arid
Thule 18°
Verkhoyansk −54°
London 39°
Moscow 10°
San Francisco 48°
New York 30°
Tokyo 37°
Cairo 55°
Delhi 59°
Mexico City 54°
Bogota 57°
Manaus 79°
Kinshasa 77°
Jakarta 79°
Buenos Aires 75°
Cape Town 66°
Sydney 70°
All temperatures in degrees Fahrenheit
© Hammond Inc.
January
Thule 41°
Verkhoyansk 61°
London 63°
Moscow 64°
San Francisco 61°
New York 73°
Tokyo 77°
Cairo 82°
Delhi 91°
Mexico City 61°
Bogota 56°
Manaus 81°
Kinshasa 73°
Jakarta 79°
Buenos Aires 48°
Cape Town 52°
Sydney 54°
All temperatures in degrees Fahrenheit
© Hammond Inc.
July
Average Temperatures
Fahrenheit Celsius
Over 86° Over 30°
68° to 86° 20° to 30°
50° to 68° 10° to 20°
32° to 50° 0° to 10°
14° to 32° -10° to 0°
-4° to 14° -20° to -10°
-22° to -4° -30° to -20°
-40° to -22° -40° to -30°
Under -40° Under -40°
© Copyright by HAMMOND INCORPORATED, Maplewood, N.J.

Vegetation & Soils

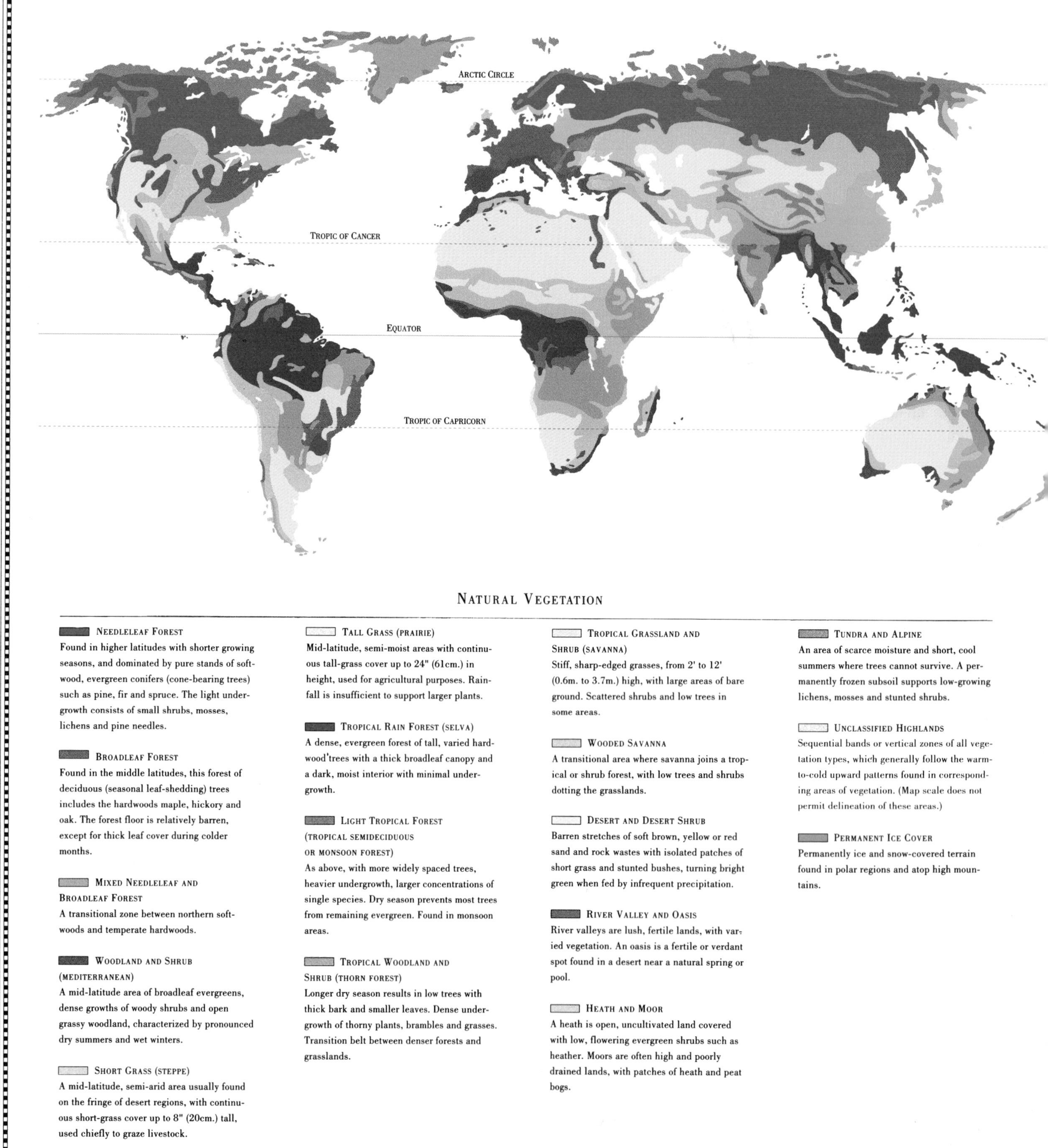

Natural Vegetation

Needleleaf Forest
Found in higher latitudes with shorter growing seasons, and dominated by pure stands of softwood, evergreen conifers (cone-bearing trees) such as pine, fir and spruce. The light undergrowth consists of small shrubs, mosses, lichens and pine needles.

Broadleaf Forest
Found in the middle latitudes, this forest of deciduous (seasonal leaf-shedding) trees includes the hardwoods maple, hickory and oak. The forest floor is relatively barren, except for thick leaf cover during colder months.

Mixed Needleleaf and Broadleaf Forest
A transitional zone between northern softwoods and temperate hardwoods.

Woodland and Shrub (Mediterranean)
A mid-latitude area of broadleaf evergreens, dense growths of woody shrubs and open grassy woodland, characterized by pronounced dry summers and wet winters.

Short Grass (Steppe)
A mid-latitude, semi-arid area usually found on the fringe of desert regions, with continuous short-grass cover up to 8" (20cm.) tall, used chiefly to graze livestock.

Tall Grass (Prairie)
Mid-latitude, semi-moist areas with continuous tall-grass cover up to 24" (61cm.) in height, used for agricultural purposes. Rainfall is insufficient to support larger plants.

Tropical Rain Forest (Selva)
A dense, evergreen forest of tall, varied hardwood'trees with a thick broadleaf canopy and a dark, moist interior with minimal undergrowth.

Light Tropical Forest (Tropical Semideciduous or Monsoon Forest)
As above, with more widely spaced trees, heavier undergrowth, larger concentrations of single species. Dry season prevents most trees from remaining evergreen. Found in monsoon areas.

Tropical Woodland and Shrub (Thorn Forest)
Longer dry season results in low trees with thick bark and smaller leaves. Dense undergrowth of thorny plants, brambles and grasses. Transition belt between denser forests and grasslands.

Tropical Grassland and Shrub (Savanna)
Stiff, sharp-edged grasses, from 2' to 12' (0.6m. to 3.7m.) high, with large areas of bare ground. Scattered shrubs and low trees in some areas.

Wooded Savanna
A transitional area where savanna joins a tropical or shrub forest, with low trees and shrubs dotting the grasslands.

Desert and Desert Shrub
Barren stretches of soft brown, yellow or red sand and rock wastes with isolated patches of short grass and stunted bushes, turning bright green when fed by infrequent precipitation.

River Valley and Oasis
River valleys are lush, fertile lands, with varied vegetation. An oasis is a fertile or verdant spot found in a desert near a natural spring or pool.

Heath and Moor
A heath is open, uncultivated land covered with low, flowering evergreen shrubs such as heather. Moors are often high and poorly drained lands, with patches of heath and peat bogs.

Tundra and Alpine
An area of scarce moisture and short, cool summers where trees cannot survive. A permanently frozen subsoil supports low-growing lichens, mosses and stunted shrubs.

Unclassified Highlands
Sequential bands or vertical zones of all vegetation types, which generally follow the warm-to-cold upward patterns found in corresponding areas of vegetation. (Map scale does not permit delineation of these areas.)

Permanent Ice Cover
Permanently ice and snow-covered terrain found in polar regions and atop high mountains.

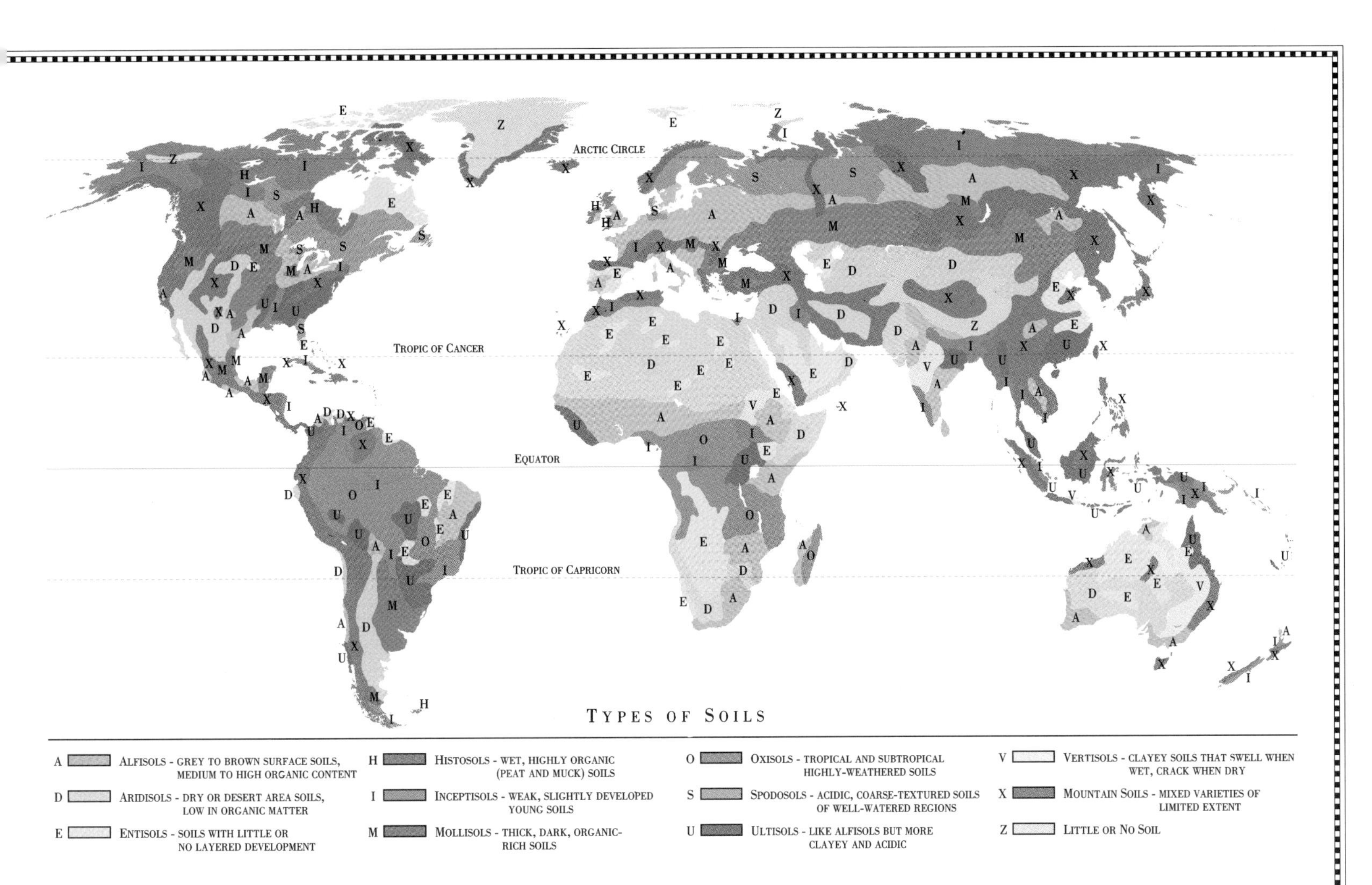

Types of Vegetation

Needleleaf Forest
These typically coniferous softwood forests of Europe, Asia and North America cover about 9 percent of the earth's land.

Broadleaf Forest
Located in the most pleasant habitable climatic regions, temperate broadleaf forests have suffered the greatest destruction by people.

Mixed Forest
These hardwood and softwood forests, when added to the broadleaf forest area, are home to over half the world's population.

Prairie
Unique to the Americas, tall grass prairie lands have been successfully cultivated to become great grain fields of the world

Steppe
Slightly more moist than desert, steppe areas are sometimes cultivated but more often used for livestock ranching and herding.

Tropical Rain Forest
Teak, mahogany, balsawood, quinine, cocoa and rubber are some of the major products found in the world's tropical rain forest regions.

Savanna
A place of winter droughts and summer rainfall, these tropical grass and shrub areas are home to a wide variety of big-game animals.

Mediterranean
In addition to southern Europe and northern Africa, this vegetation also can be found in California, Chile, South Africa and Western Australia.

Desert Shrub
One-fifth of the world's land is desert and desert shrub, too dry for farming and ranching and populated largely by nomads and oases-dwellers.

Tundra
Found along the Arctic fringe of North America and Eurasia, tundra is of little economic significance except for mineral exploitation.

Environmental Concerns

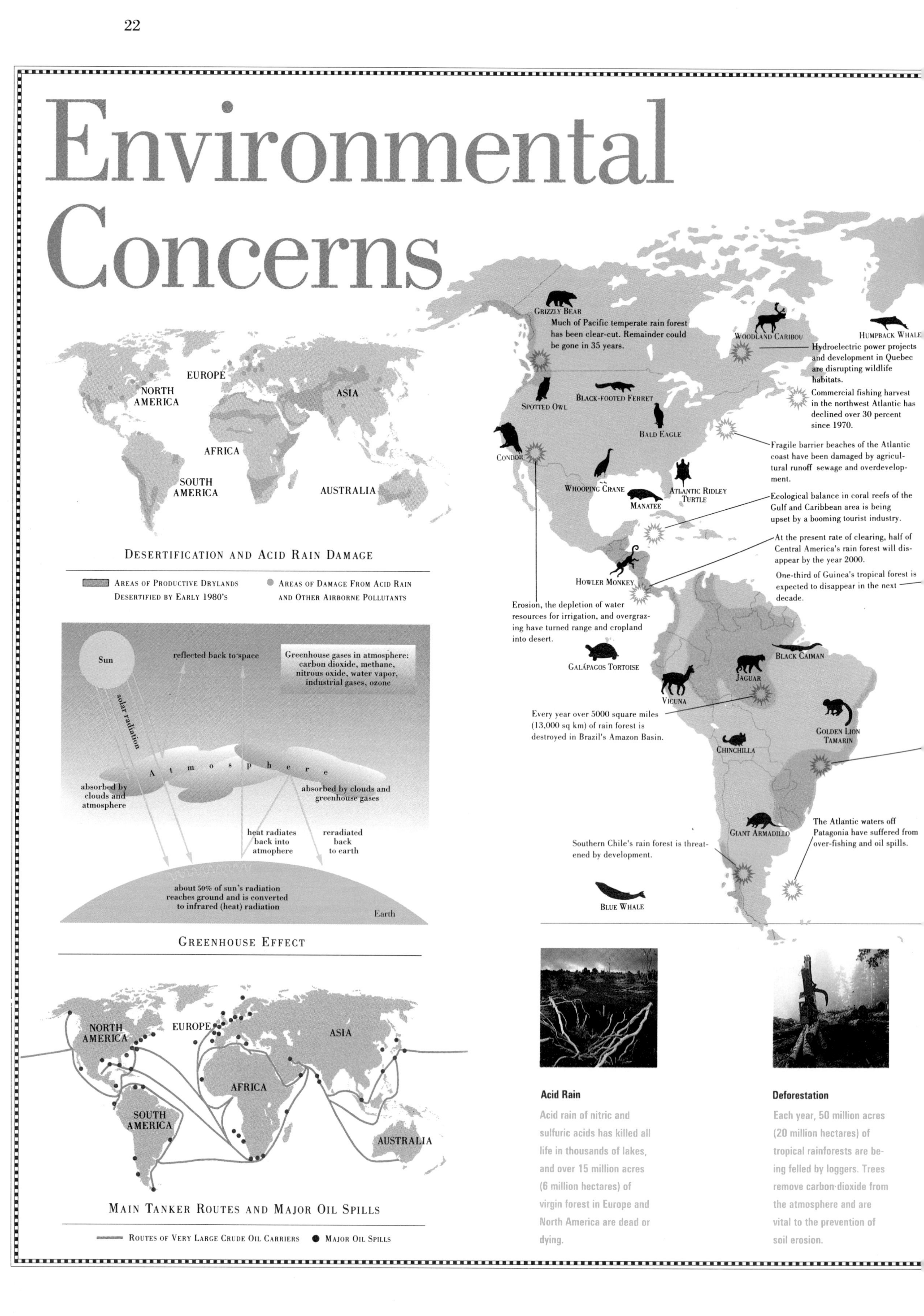

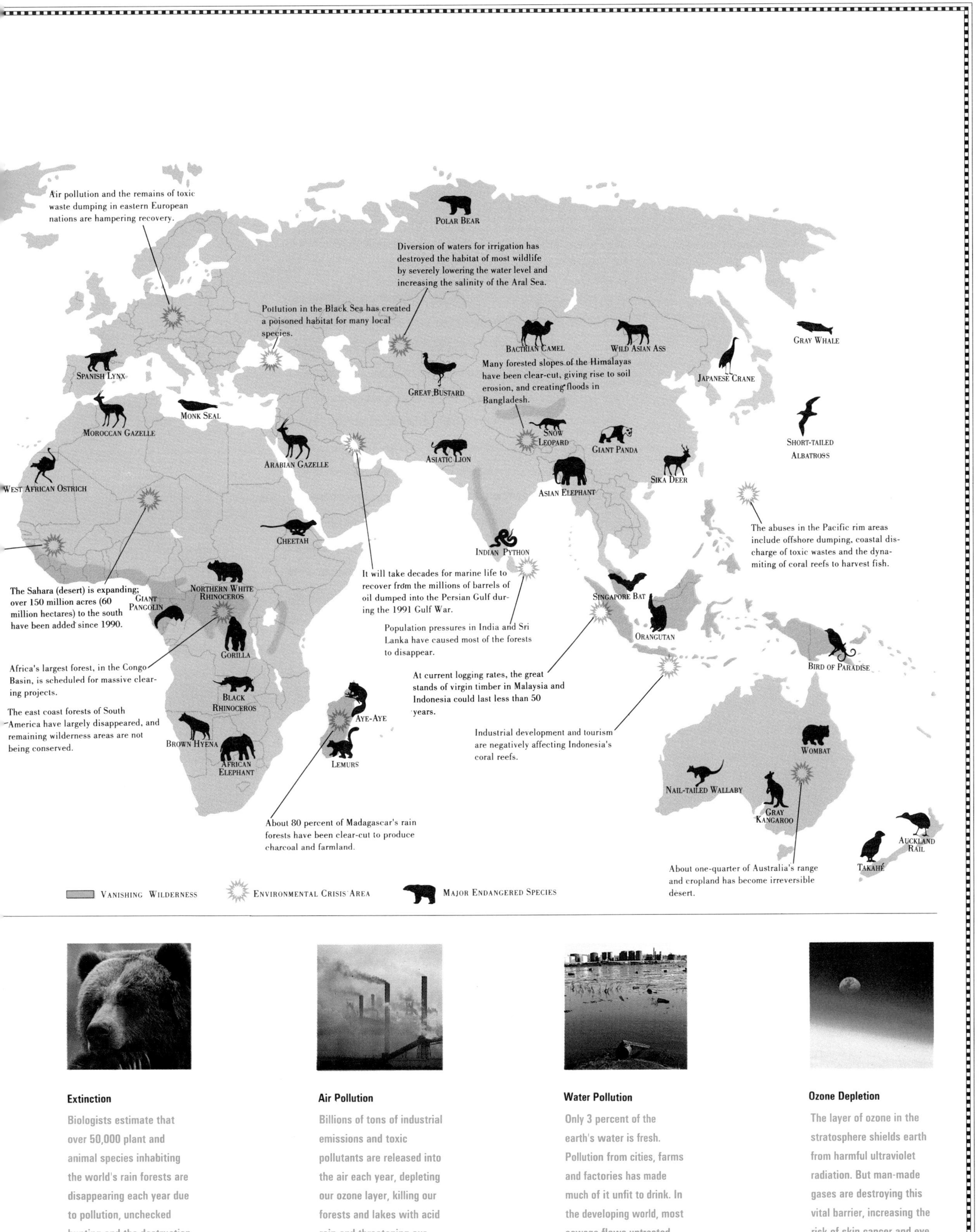

Extinction

Biologists estimate that over 50,000 plant and animal species inhabiting the world's rain forests are disappearing each year due to pollution, unchecked hunting and the destruction of natural habitats.

Air Pollution

Billions of tons of industrial emissions and toxic pollutants are released into the air each year, depleting our ozone layer, killing our forests and lakes with acid rain and threatening our health.

Water Pollution

Only 3 percent of the earth's water is fresh. Pollution from cities, farms and factories has made much of it unfit to drink. In the developing world, most sewage flows untreated into lakes and rivers.

Ozone Depletion

The layer of ozone in the stratosphere shields earth from harmful ultraviolet radiation. But man-made gases are destroying this vital barrier, increasing the risk of skin cancer and eye disease.

Population

Great Cities

World's Largest Urban Areas: Millions of Inhabitants

Tokyo, Japan	26.5
New York, U.S.	18.0
São Paulo, Brazil	16.9
Osaka, Japan	16.9
Seoul, Korea	15.8
Mexico City, Mexico	15.5
Shanghai, China	14.7
Bombay, India	14.5
Los Angeles, U.S.	14.5
Moscow, Russia	13.1
Beijing, China	12.0
Calcutta, India	11.4
London, U.K.	11.1
Rio de Janeiro, Brazil	11.0
Jakarta, Indonesia	11.0

Town & Country

Urban & Rural Population Components of Selected Countries

Urban / Rural

Country	Urban / Rural
Uruguay	87% / 13%
Australia	85% / 15%
Japan	77% / 23%
United States	74% / 26%
Russia	73% / 27%
Hungary	62% / 38%
Iran	54% / 46%
Egypt	44% / 56%
Philippines	37% / 63%
Portugal	30% / 70%
China	26% / 74%
Maldives	20% / 80%
Bangladesh	15% / 85%
Nepal	6% / 94%

Age Distribution

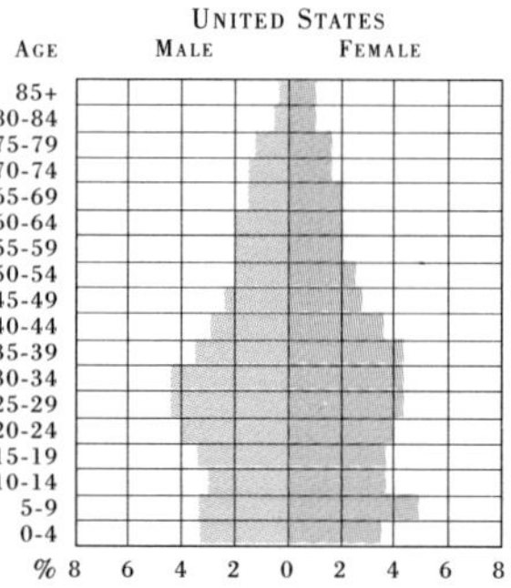

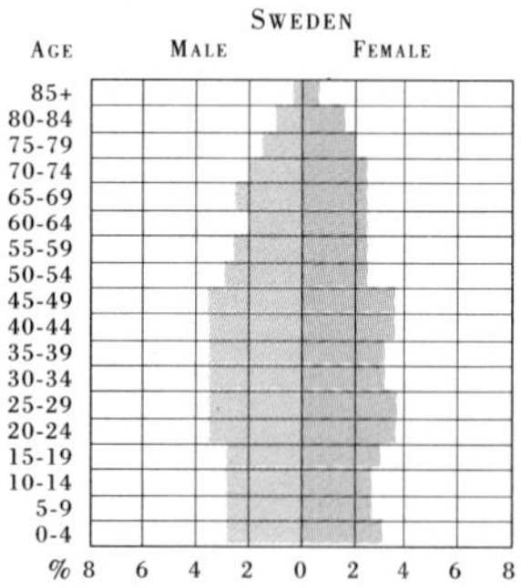

United States

Age: 85+, 80-84, 75-79, 70-74, 65-69, 60-64, 55-59, 50-54, 45-49, 40-44, 35-39, 30-34, 25-29, 20-24, 15-19, 10-14, 5-9, 0-4

Male / Female

% 8 6 4 2 0 2 4 6 8

(Percent of Total Population Male or Female)

Sweden

Age: 85+, 80-84, 75-79, 70-74, 65-69, 60-64, 55-59, 50-54, 45-49, 40-44, 35-39, 30-34, 25-29, 20-24, 15-19, 10-14, 5-9, 0-4

Male / Female

% 8 6 4 2 0 2 4 6 8

(Percent of Total Population Male or Female)

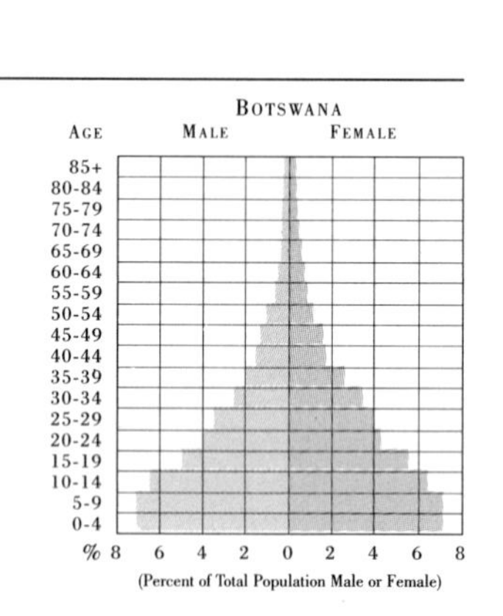

Largest Countries: Estimated Populations in 2020

Millions of Inhabitants: 1995 / 2020 (Estimate)

Country	1995 / 2020
China	1203 / 1541
India	936 / 1317
United States	263 / 294
Indonesia	203 / 287
Brazil	160 / 231
Russia	149 / 153
Pakistan	131 / 251
Bangladesh	128 / 209
Japan	125 / 127
Nigeria	101 /273
Mexico	93 / 147
Vietnam	74 / 102
Iran	64 / 143
Ethiopia	55 / 123

Alaska

Mexic

3.5 percent or more

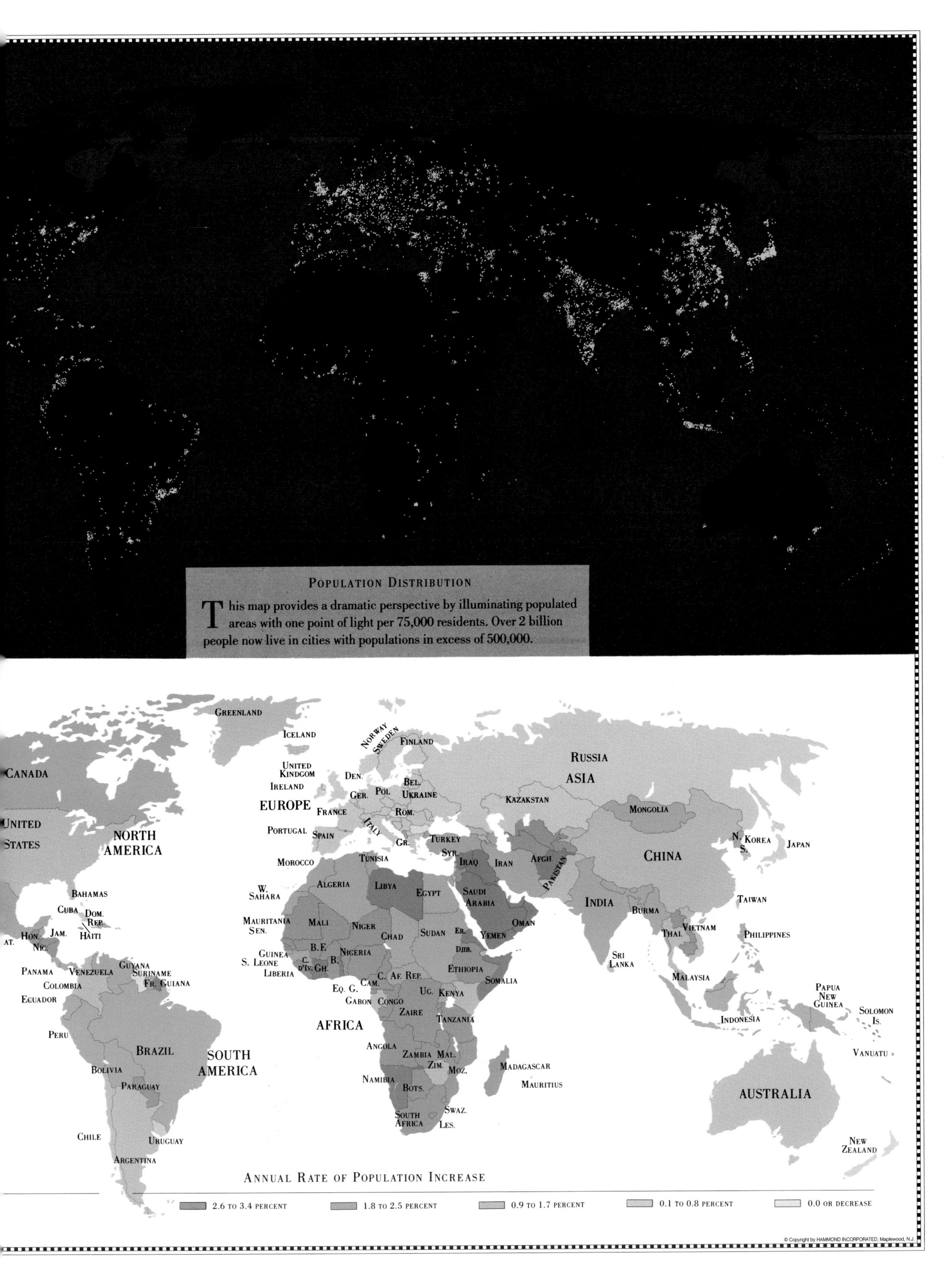
POPULATION DISTRIBUTION
This map provides a dramatic perspective by illuminating populated areas with one point of light per 75,000 residents. Over 2 billion people now live in cities with populations in excess of 500,000.
GREENLAND
ICELAND
NORWAY
SWEDEN
FINLAND
RUSSIA
ASIA
CANADA
UNITED KINGDOM
IRELAND
DEN.
BEL.
GER.
POL.
UKRAINE
KAZAKSTAN
EUROPE
FRANCE
ROM.
MONGOLIA
UNITED STATES
NORTH AMERICA
PORTUGAL
SPAIN
ITALY
GR.
TURKEY
SYR.
IRAQ
IRAN
AFGH.
PAKISTAN
N. KOREA
S.
JAPAN
CHINA
MOROCCO
TUNISIA
W. SAHARA
ALGERIA
LIBYA
EGYPT
SAUDI ARABIA
INDIA
BURMA
TAIWAN
BAHAMAS
CUBA
DOM. REP.
HAITI
MAURITANIA
SEN.
MALI
NIGER
CHAD
SUDAN
ER.
YEMEN
OMAN
THAI.
VIETNAM
PHILIPPINES
HON.
JAM.
NIC.
GUINEA
S. LEONE
LIBERIA
B.F.
C. D'IV.
GH.
B.
NIGERIA
DJIB.
ETHIOPIA
SOMALIA
SRI LANKA
MALAYSIA
PANAMA
VENEZUELA
GUYANA
SURINAME
FR. GUIANA
COLOMBIA
ECUADOR
CAM.
C. AF. REP.
EQ. G.
GABON
CONGO
UG.
KENYA
ZAIRE
TANZANIA
AFRICA
PAPUA NEW GUINEA
SOLOMON IS.
INDONESIA
PERU
BRAZIL
SOUTH AMERICA
BOLIVIA
PARAGUAY
ANGOLA
ZAMBIA
MAL.
ZIM.
MOZ.
NAMIBIA
BOTS.
MADAGASCAR
MAURITIUS
VANUATU
SOUTH AFRICA
SWAZ.
LES.
AUSTRALIA
CHILE
URUGUAY
ARGENTINA
NEW ZEALAND
ANNUAL RATE OF POPULATION INCREASE
2.6 TO 3.4 PERCENT
1.8 TO 2.5 PERCENT
0.9 TO 1.7 PERCENT
0.1 TO 0.8 PERCENT
0.0 OR DECREASE
© Copyright by HAMMOND INCORPORATED, Maplewood, N.J.

Languages & Religions

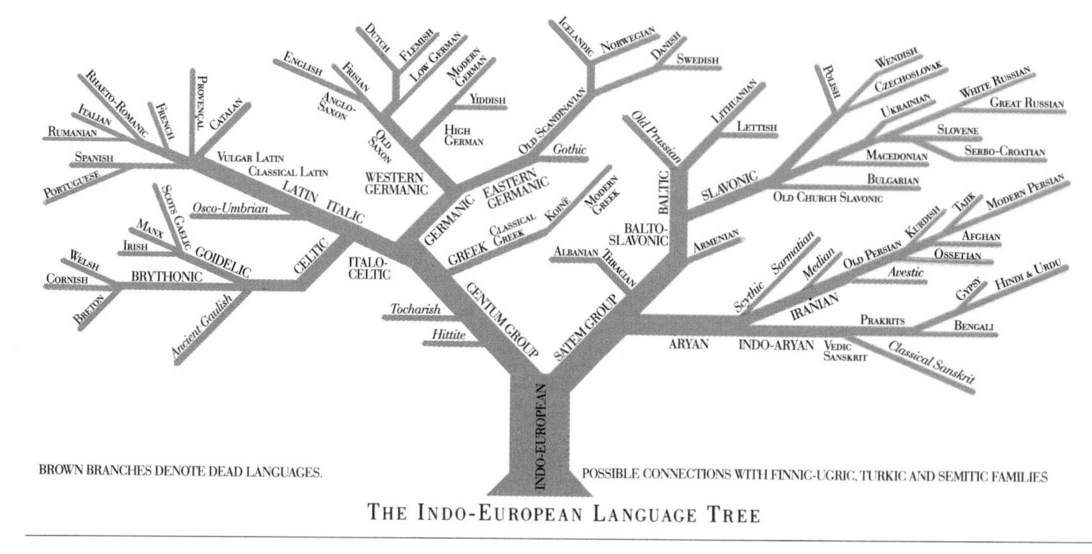

THE INDO-EUROPEAN LANGUAGE TREE

The most well-established family tree is Indo-European. Spoken by more than 2.5 billion people, it contains dozens of languages. Some linguists theorize that all people - and all languages - are descended from a tiny population that lived in Africa some 200,000 years ago.

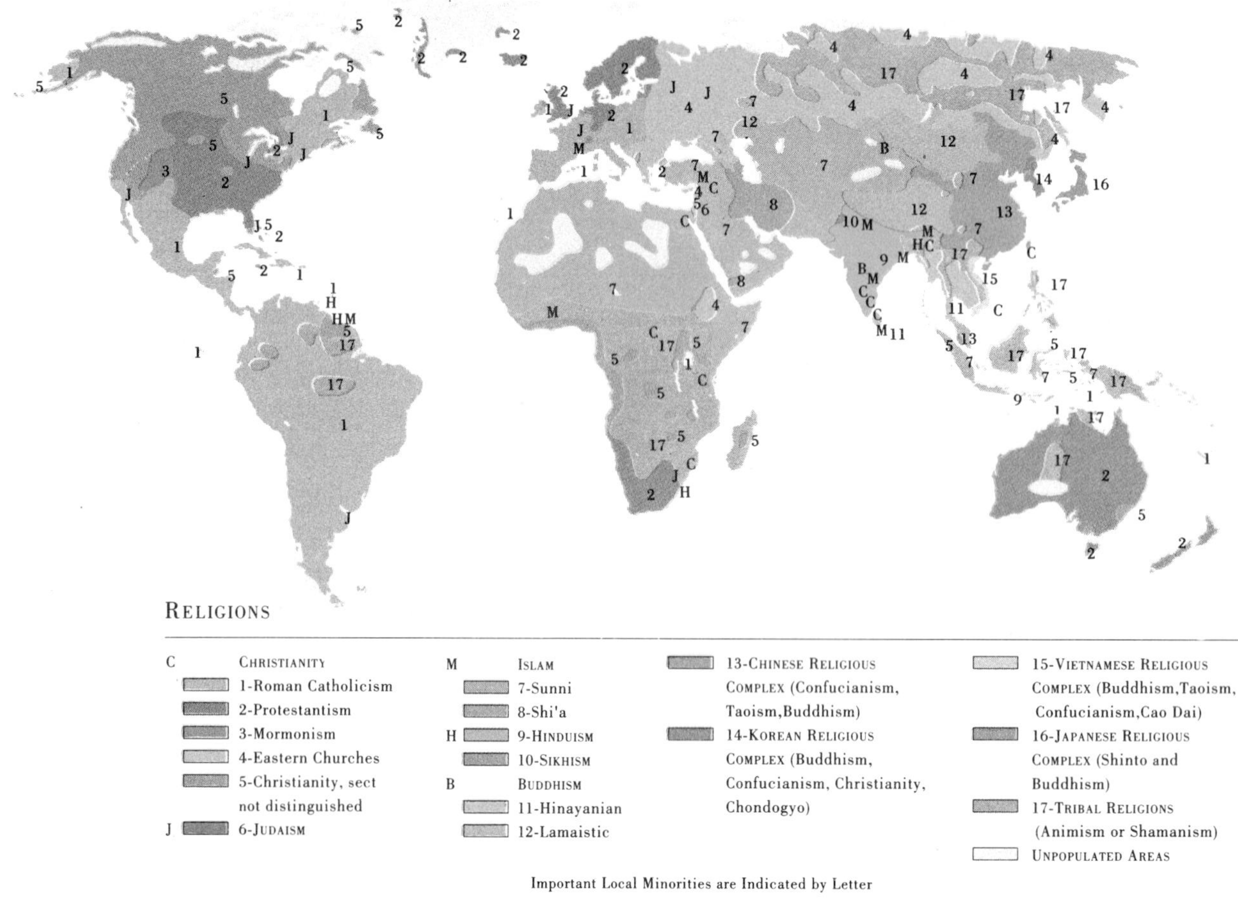

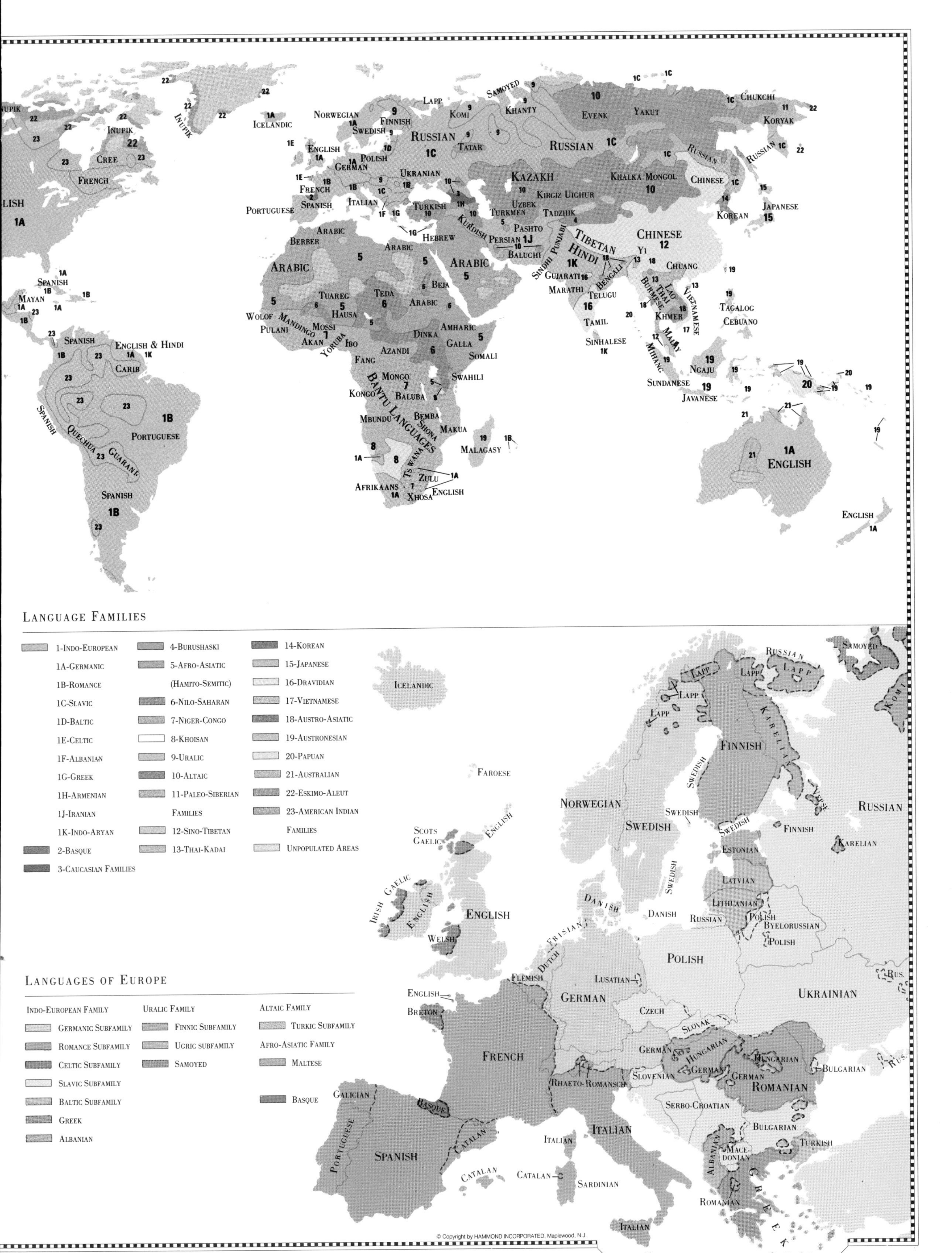
LANGUAGE FAMILIES
1-INDO-EUROPEAN
1A-GERMANIC
1B-ROMANCE
1C-SLAVIC
1D-BALTIC
1E-CELTIC
1F-ALBANIAN
1G-GREEK
1H-ARMENIAN
1J-IRANIAN
1K-INDO-ARYAN
2-BASQUE
3-CAUCASIAN FAMILIES
4-BURUSHASKI
5-AFRO-ASIATIC (HAMITO-SEMITIC)
6-NILO-SAHARAN
7-NIGER-CONGO
8-KHOISAN
9-URALIC
10-ALTAIC
11-PALEO-SIBERIAN FAMILIES
12-SINO-TIBETAN
13-THAI-KADAI
14-KOREAN
15-JAPANESE
16-DRAVIDIAN
17-VIETNAMESE
18-AUSTRO-ASIATIC
19-AUSTRONESIAN
20-PAPUAN
21-AUSTRALIAN
22-ESKIMO-ALEUT
23-AMERICAN INDIAN FAMILIES
UNPOPULATED AREAS
LANGUAGES OF EUROPE
INDO-EUROPEAN FAMILY
GERMANIC SUBFAMILY
ROMANCE SUBFAMILY
CELTIC SUBFAMILY
SLAVIC SUBFAMILY
BALTIC SUBFAMILY
GREEK
ALBANIAN
URALIC FAMILY
FINNIC SUBFAMILY
UGRIC SUBFAMILY
SAMOYED
ALTAIC FAMILY
TURKIC SUBFAMILY
AFRO-ASIATIC FAMILY
MALTESE
BASQUE
INUPIK
CREE
FRENCH
ENGLISH
SPANISH
MAYAN
ENGLISH & HINDI
CARIB
PORTUGUESE
QUECHUA
GUARANI
ICELANDIC
NORWEGIAN
SWEDISH
FINNISH
LAPP
KOMI
SAMOYED
KHANTY
EVENK
YAKUT
CHUKCHI
KORYAK
RUSSIAN
TATAR
POLISH
GERMAN
UKRANIAN
ITALIAN
TURKISH
KURDISH
KAZAKH
KIRGIZ
UIGHUR
UZBEK
TURKMEN
TADZHIK
PASHTO
PERSIAN
BALUCHI
KHALKA MONGOL
CHINESE
KOREAN
JAPANESE
TIBETAN
HINDI
SINDHI
PUNJABI
GUJARATI
MARATHI
BENGALI
TELUGU
TAMIL
SINHALESE
YI
CHUANG
BURMESE
THAI
LAO
VIETNAMESE
KHMER
MALAY
MIHANG
TAGALOG
CEBUANO
NGAJU
SUNDANESE
JAVANESE
HEBREW
ARABIC
BERBER
TUAREG
TEDA
HAUSA
BEJA
AMHARIC
GALLA
SOMALI
DINKA
WOLOF
MANDINGO
PULANI
MOSSI
AKAN
YORUBA
IBO
FANG
AZANDI
MONGO
KONGO
BALUBA
SWAHILI
MBUNDU
BANTU LANGUAGES
BEMBA
SHONA
MAKUA
TSWANA
ZULU
XHOSA
AFRIKAANS
MALAGASY
FAROESE
SCOTS GAELIC
IRISH GAELIC
WELSH
BRETON
FLEMISH
DUTCH
FRISIAN
DANISH
ESTONIAN
LATVIAN
LITHUANIAN
BYELORUSSIAN
KARELIAN
KARELIA
VEPSE
LUSATIAN
CZECH
SLOVAK
HUNGARIAN
SLOVENIAN
RHAETO-ROMANSCH
SERBO-CROATIAN
ROMANIAN
BULGARIAN
MACE-DONIAN
GREEK
ROMANIAN
GALICIAN
CATALAN
SARDINIAN
MALTESE
© Copyright by HAMMOND INCORPORATED, Maplewood, N.J.

Standards of Living

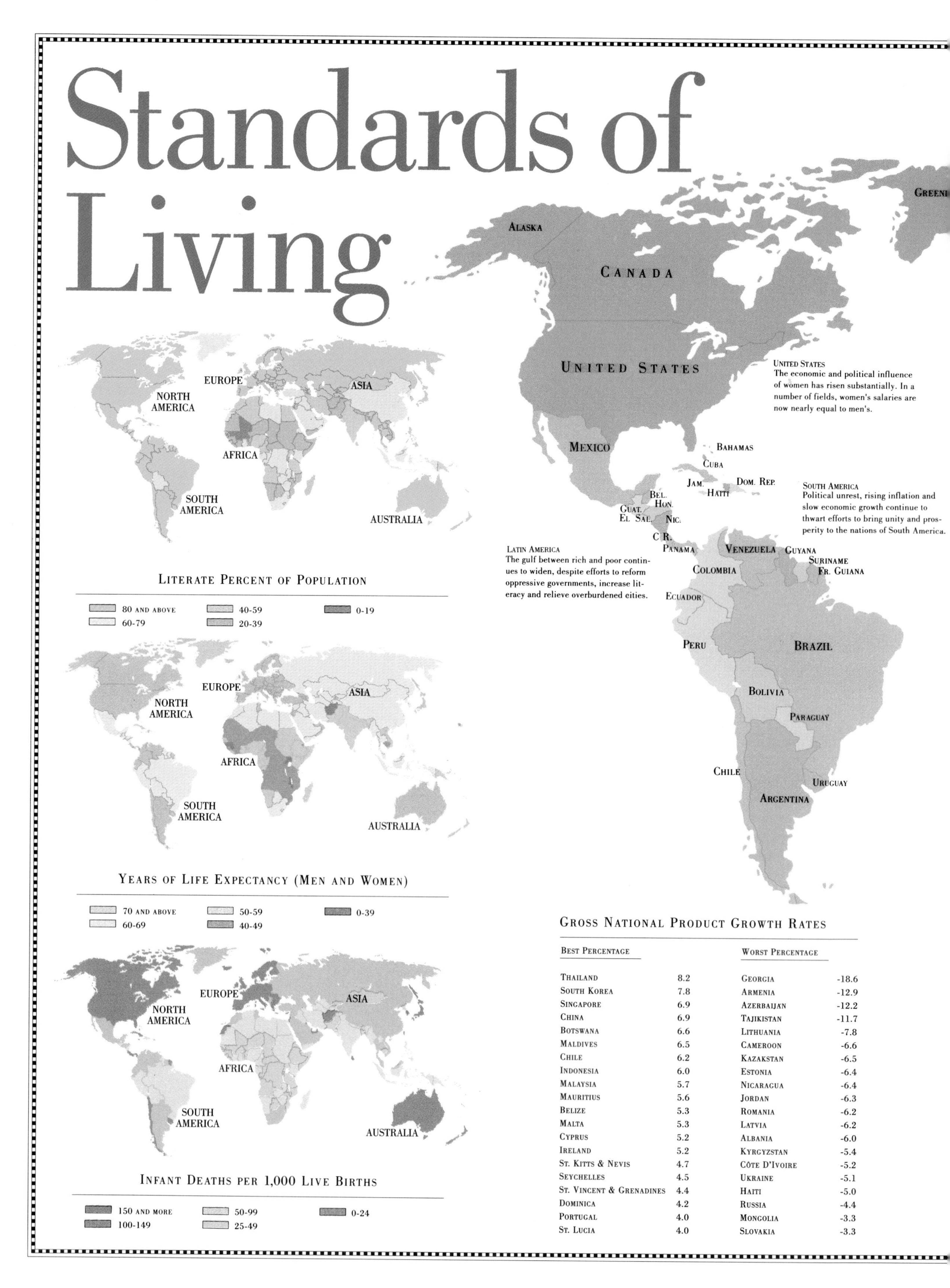

Gross National Product Growth Rates

Best Percentage		Worst Percentage	
Thailand	8.2	Georgia	-18.6
South Korea	7.8	Armenia	-12.9
Singapore	6.9	Azerbaijan	-12.2
China	6.9	Tajikistan	-11.7
Botswana	6.6	Lithuania	-7.8
Maldives	6.5	Cameroon	-6.6
Chile	6.2	Kazakstan	-6.5
Indonesia	6.0	Estonia	-6.4
Malaysia	5.7	Nicaragua	-6.4
Mauritius	5.6	Jordan	-6.3
Belize	5.3	Romania	-6.2
Malta	5.3	Latvia	-6.2
Cyprus	5.2	Albania	-6.0
Ireland	5.2	Kyrgyzstan	-5.4
St. Kitts & Nevis	4.7	Côte D'Ivoire	-5.2
Seychelles	4.5	Ukraine	-5.1
St. Vincent & Grenadines	4.4	Haiti	-5.0
Dominica	4.2	Russia	-4.4
Portugal	4.0	Mongolia	-3.3
St. Lucia	4.0	Slovakia	-3.3

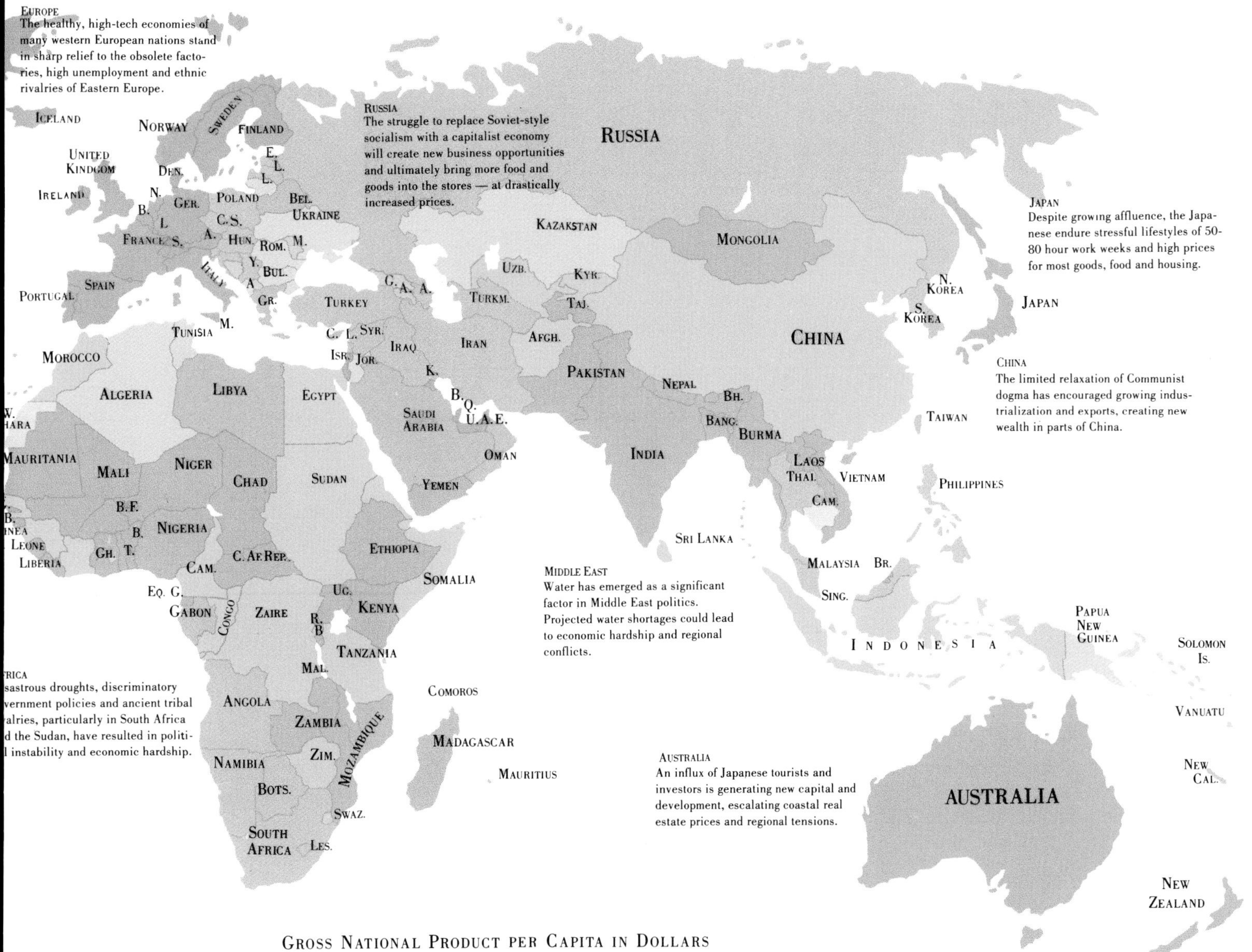

EUROPE
The healthy, high-tech economies of many western European nations stand in sharp relief to the obsolete factories, high unemployment and ethnic rivalries of Eastern Europe.

RUSSIA
The struggle to replace Soviet-style socialism with a capitalist economy will create new business opportunities and ultimately bring more food and goods into the stores — at drastically increased prices.

JAPAN
Despite growing affluence, the Japanese endure stressful lifestyles of 50-80 hour work weeks and high prices for most goods, food and housing.

CHINA
The limited relaxation of Communist dogma has encouraged growing industrialization and exports, creating new wealth in parts of China.

MIDDLE EAST
Water has emerged as a significant factor in Middle East politics. Projected water shortages could lead to economic hardship and regional conflicts.

RICA
sastrous droughts, discriminatory
vernment policies and ancient tribal
alries, particularly in South Africa
d the Sudan, have resulted in politi-
l instability and economic hardship.

AUSTRALIA
An influx of Japanese tourists and investors is generating new capital and development, escalating coastal real estate prices and regional tensions.

GROSS NATIONAL PRODUCT PER CAPITA IN DOLLARS

OVER 8000 PER YEAR · 5000-8000 PER YEAR · 2000-5000 PER YEAR · 1000-2000 PER YEAR · 500-1000 PER YEAR · UNDER 500 PER YEAR · DATA NOT AVAILABLE

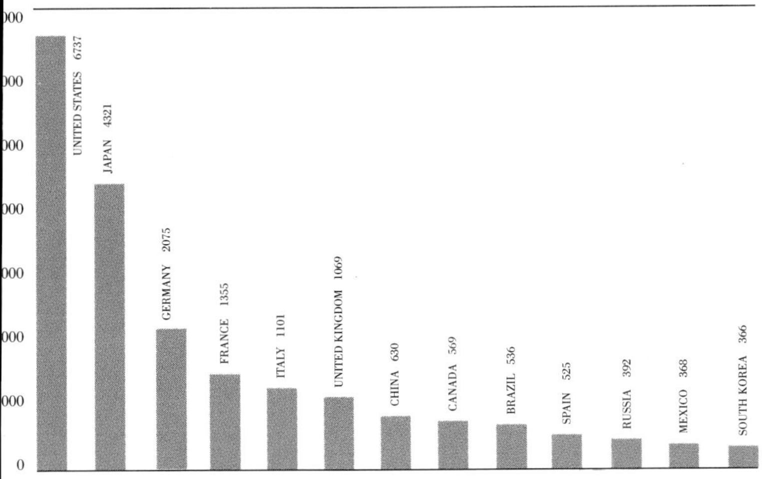

TOTAL GROSS NATIONAL PRODUCT

BILLIONS OF DOLLARS

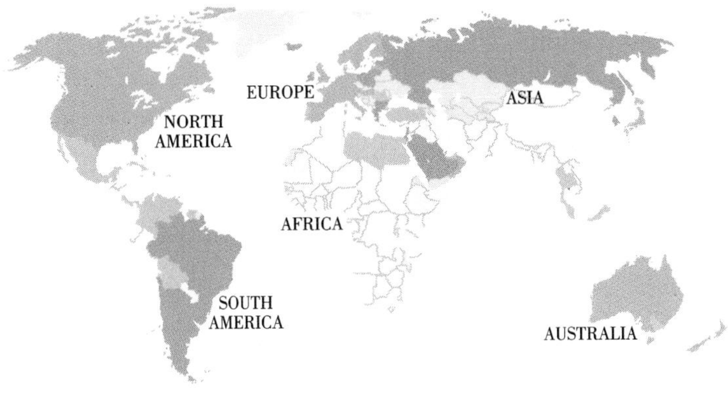

Country	Billions of Dollars
UNITED STATES	6737
JAPAN	4321
GERMANY	2075
FRANCE	1355
ITALY	1101
UNITED KINGDOM	1069
CHINA	630
CANADA	569
BRAZIL	536
SPAIN	525
RUSSIA	392
MEXICO	368
SOUTH KOREA	366

TELEVISION SETS PER 1,000 PEOPLE

400 AND MORE · 200 - 399 · 100 - 199 · 30 - 99 · LESS THAN 30 · DATA NOT AVAILABLE

Agriculture & Manufacturing

Top Five World Producers of Selected Agricultural Commodities

	1	2	3	4	5
Wheat	China	United States	India	Russia	France
Rice	China	India	Indonesia	Bangladesh	Burma
Oats	Russia	Canada	United States	Germany	Ukraine
Corn (Maize)	United States	China	Brazil	Mexico	France
Soybeans	United States	Brazil	China	Argentina	India
Potatoes	China	Russia	Poland	United States	Ukraine
Coffee	Brazil	Colombia	Indonesia	Mexico	Ethiopia
Tea	India	China	Sri Lanka	Kenya	Turkey
Tobacco	China	United States	Brazil	India	Turkey
Cotton	China	United States	India	Pakistan	Uzbekistan
Cattle (Stock)	Brazil	United States	China	Argentina	Russia
Sheep (Stock)	Australia	China	New Zealand	Russia	India
Hogs (Stock)	China	United States	Brazil	Russia	Germany
Cow's Milk	United States	Russia	India	Germany	France
Hen's Eggs	China	United States	Japan	Russia	India
Wool	Australia	New Zealand	China	Russia	Kazakstan
Roundwood	United States	Russia	China	India	Brazil
Natural Rubber	Thailand	Indonesia	Malaysia	India	China
Fish Catches	China	Japan	Peru	Chile	Russia

Names in Black Indicate More Than 10% of Total World Production

Percent of Total Employment in Agriculture, Manufacturing and Other Industries

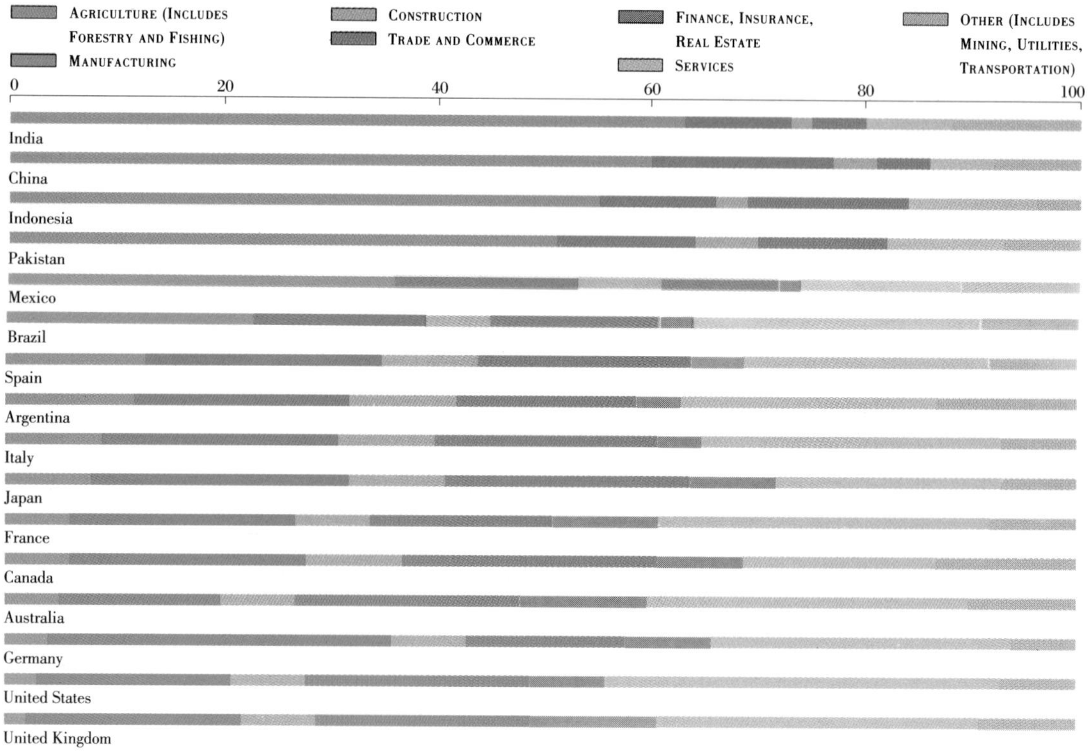

Agriculture (Includes Forestry and Fishing)
Manufacturing
Construction
Trade and Commerce
Finance, Insurance, Real Estate
Services
Other (Includes Mining, Utilities, Transportation)

0 20 40 60 80 100

India
China
Indonesia
Pakistan
Mexico
Brazil
Spain
Argentina
Italy
Japan
France
Canada
Australia
Germany
United States
United Kingdom

Finance, Insurance, Real Estate Data Included With "Other" for India, China, Indonesia and Pakistan

Herding
Livestock Ranching

Seattle - Tacoma
San Francisco - San Jose
Southern California
Mexico City - Puebla

Aircraft
Motor Vehicles
Shipbuilding

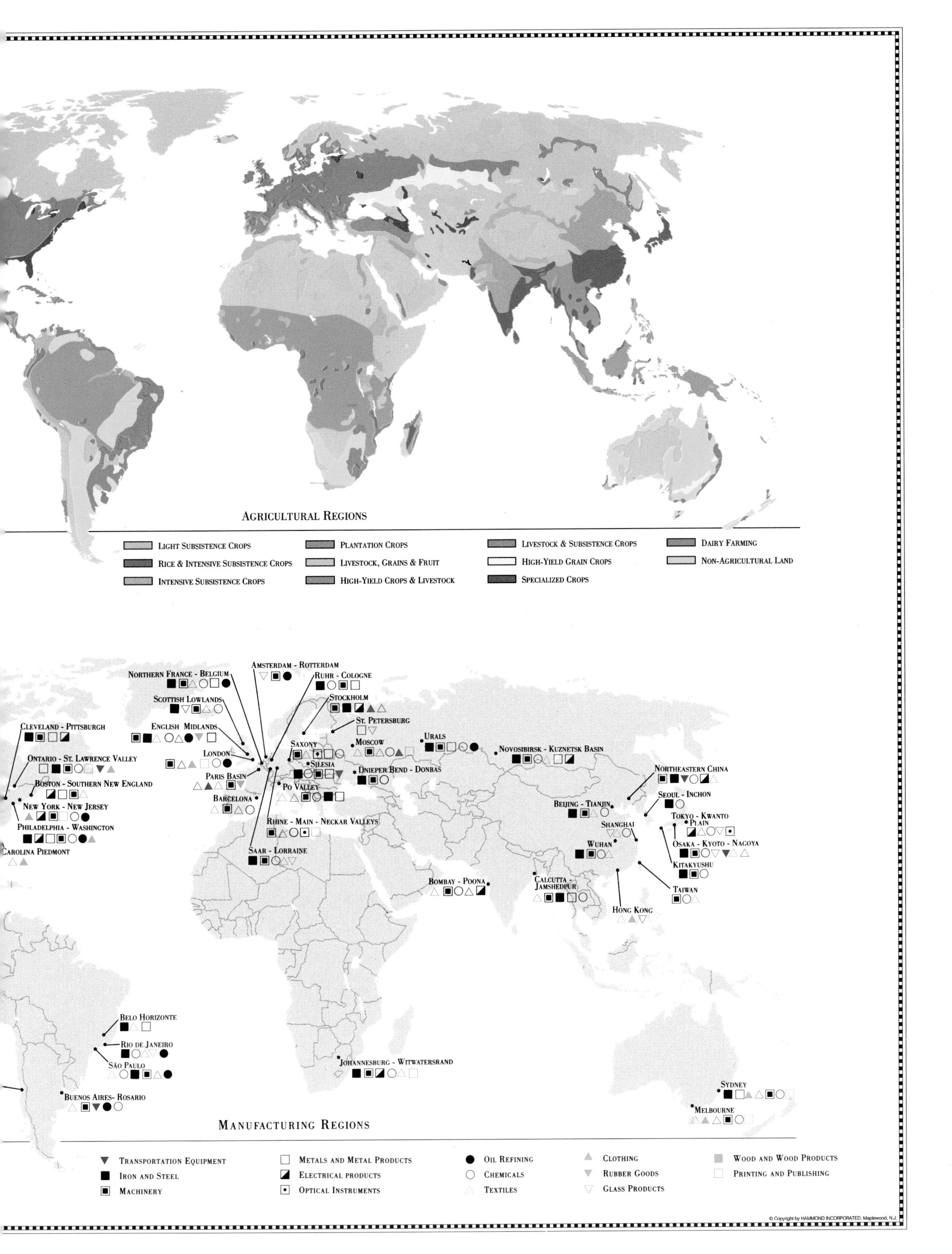
AGRICULTURAL REGIONS
LIGHT SUBSISTENCE CROPS
RICE & INTENSIVE SUBSISTENCE CROPS
INTENSIVE SUBSISTENCE CROPS
PLANTATION CROPS
LIVESTOCK, GRAINS & FRUIT
HIGH-YIELD CROPS & LIVESTOCK
LIVESTOCK & SUBSISTENCE CROPS
HIGH-YIELD GRAIN CROPS
SPECIALIZED CROPS
DAIRY FARMING
NON-AGRICULTURAL LAND
AMSTERDAM - ROTTERDAM
NORTHERN FRANCE - BELGIUM
RUHR - COLOGNE
SCOTTISH LOWLANDS
STOCKHOLM
ST. PETERSBURG
CLEVELAND - PITTSBURGH
ENGLISH MIDLANDS
URALS
SAXONY
MOSCOW
NOVOSIBIRSK - KUZNETSK BASIN
LONDON
ONTARIO - ST. LAWRENCE VALLEY
SILESIA
DNIEPER BEND - DONBAS
NORTHEASTERN CHINA
PARIS BASIN
BOSTON - SOUTHERN NEW ENGLAND
PO VALLEY
SEOUL - INCHON
BARCELONA
NEW YORK - NEW JERSEY
BEIJING - TIANJIN
TOKYO - KWANTO PLAIN
PHILADELPHIA - WASHINGTON
RHINE - MAIN - NECKAR VALLEYS
SHANGHAI
OSAKA - KYOTO - NAGOYA
WUHAN
CAROLINA PIEDMONT
SAAR - LORRAINE
KITAKYUSHU
BOMBAY - POONA
CALCUTTA - JAMSHEDPUR
TAIWAN
HONG KONG
BELO HORIZONTE
RIO DE JANEIRO
SÃO PAULO
JOHANNESBURG - WITWATERSRAND
SYDNEY
BUENOS AIRES- ROSARIO
MELBOURNE
MANUFACTURING REGIONS
TRANSPORTATION EQUIPMENT
IRON AND STEEL
MACHINERY
METALS AND METAL PRODUCTS
ELECTRICAL PRODUCTS
OPTICAL INSTRUMENTS
OIL REFINING
CHEMICALS
TEXTILES
CLOTHING
RUBBER GOODS
GLASS PRODUCTS
WOOD AND WOOD PRODUCTS
PRINTING AND PUBLISHING

Energy & Resources

Top Five World Producers of Selected Mineral Commodities

Mineral Fuels	1	2	3	4	5
Crude Oil	Saudi Arabia	Russia	United States	Iran	China
Gasoline	United States	Russia	Japan	China	United Kingdom
Natural Gas	Russia	United States	Canada	Netherlands	Turkmenistan
Coal (and Lignite)	China	United States	Russia	Germany	India
Uranium-Bearing Ores	Canada	Niger	Kazakstan	Russia	Uzbekistan
Metals					
Chromite	Kazakstan	South Africa	India	Finland	Turkey
Iron Ore	Brazil	Australia	China	Russia	Ukraine
Manganese Ore	Ukraine	China	South Africa	Australia	Brazil
Mine Nickel	Russia	Canada	New Caledonia	Indonesia	Australia
Mine Silver	Mexico	United States	Peru	Australia	Canada
Bauxite	Australia	Guinea	Jamaica	Brazil	Russia
Aluminum	United States	Russia	Canada	Australia	China
Mine Gold	South Africa	United States	Australia	China	Canada
Mine Copper	Chile	United States	Canada	Russia	Peru
Mine Lead	Australia	China	United States	Peru	Canada
Mine Tin	China	Indonesia	Brazil	Bolivia	Peru
Mine Zinc	Canada	Australia	China	Peru	United States
Nonmetals					
Natural Diamond	Australia	Botswana	Russia	Zaire	South Africa
Potash	Canada	Germany	Russia	Belarus	United States
Phosphate Rock	United States	China	Morocco	Russia	Kazakstan
Sulfur (All Forms)	United States	Canada	China	Japan	Poland

Names in Black Indicate More Than 10% of Total World Production

Commercial Energy Production/Consumption

Percentage of World Total

Production / Consumption

United States 20% / 25%

Russia 12% / 17.2%

China 9% / 8.9%

Saudi Arabia 5.8% / 0.9%

Canada 3.6% / 2.7%

United Kingdom 2.7% / 2.9%

Iran 2.5% / 0.9%

Mexico 2.4% / 1.5%

India 2.3% / 2.8%

Indonesia 2.0% / 0.7%

Germany 2.0% / 4.3%

Australia 2% / 1.2%

Venezuela 1.9% / 0.6%

Norway 1.8% / 0.3%

Nations With Highest Percentage of Nuclear Power Production

Nuclear / Thermal / Hydroelectric

Belgium 98% / 1% / 1%

France 75% / 11% / 14%

South Korea 71% / 21% / 8%

Japan 65% / 9% / 26%

Finland 58% / 42%

Sweden 43% / 57%

Spain 41% / 40% / 19%

Switzerland 39% / 61%

Germany 26% / 71% / 3%

Hungary 22% / 78%

Ukraine 21% / 77% / 2%

Bulgaria 17% / 80% / 3%

United Kingdom 11% / 88% / 1%

United States 10% / 86% / 4%

Oil Fields

Natural Gas Fields

● Major Coal Deposits

▲ Oil Sands

✦ Oil Shale

✶ Major Uranium Deposits

■ Important Peat Deposits

Iron and Ferroalloy Metals

1 Cobalt
2 Chromium
3 Iron Ore
4 Manganese
5 Molybdenum
6 Nickel
7 Vanadium
8 Tungsten

Other Metals

1 Silver
2 Bauxite
3 Gold
4 Copper
5 Mercury
6 Lead
7 Platinum
8 Antimony
9 Tin
10 Titanium
11 Zinc

Nonmetals

1 Asbestos
2 Borax
3 Diamonds
4 Emeralds
5 Fluorspar
6 Graphite
7 Iodine
8 Jade
9 Potash
10 Mica
11 Nitrates
12 Opals
13 Phosphates
14 Pearls
15 Rubies
16 Sulfur
17 Sapphires

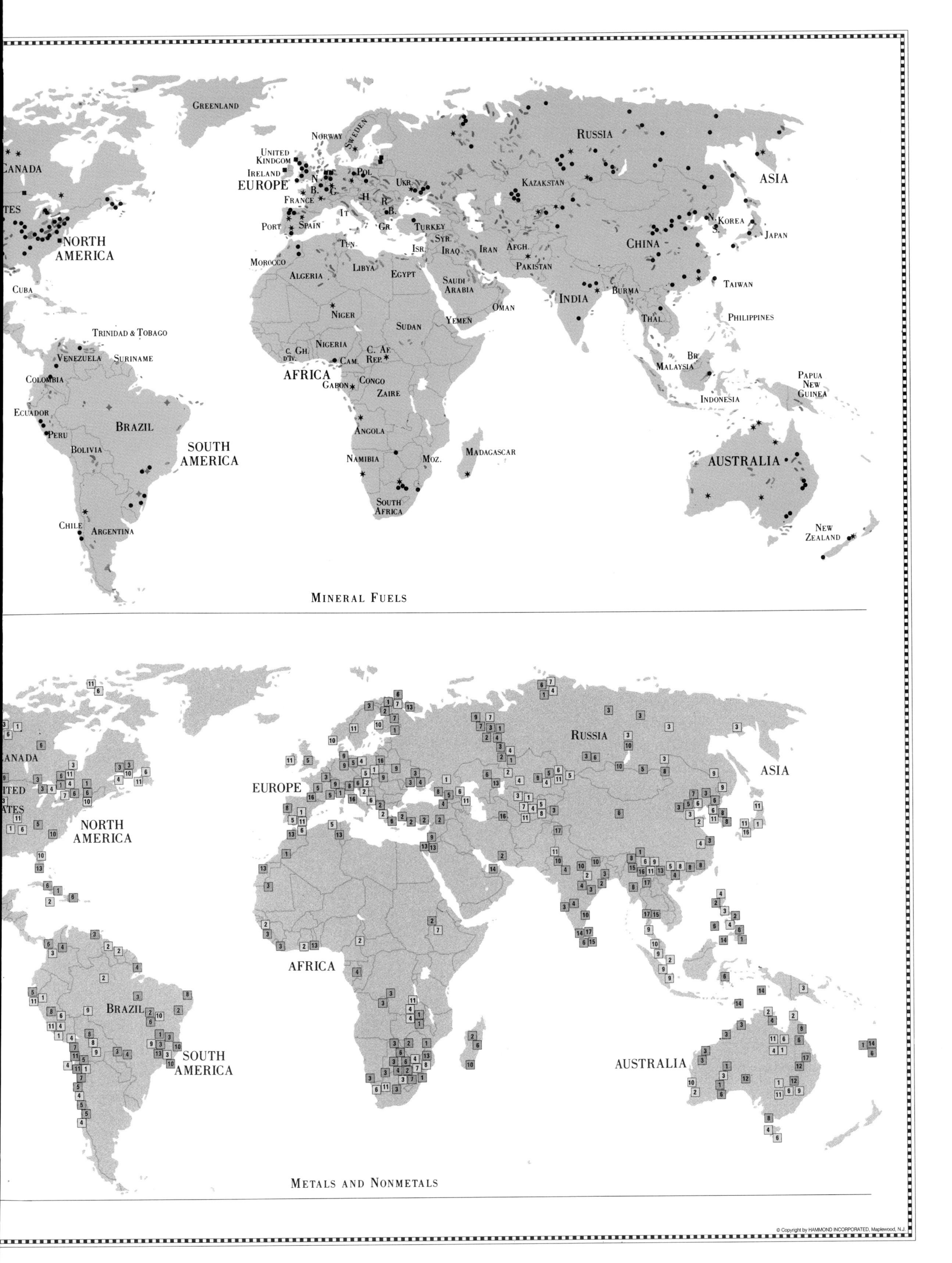
GREENLAND
NORWAY
SWEDEN
UNITED KINGDOM
IRELAND
EUROPE
N.
B.
G.
POL.
UKR.
FRANCE
H
R
B.
PORT.
SPAIN
IT.
GR.
TURKEY
SYR.
ISR.
IRAQ
IRAN
AFGH.
PAKISTAN
RUSSIA
KAZAKSTAN
ASIA
N.
KOREA
S.
JAPAN
CHINA
TAIWAN
INDIA
BURMA
THAI.
PHILIPPINES
BR.
MALAYSIA
INDONESIA
PAPUA NEW GUINEA
AUSTRALIA
NEW ZEALAND
MOROCCO
ALGERIA
TUN.
LIBYA
EGYPT
SAUDI ARABIA
OMAN
YEMEN
NIGER
SUDAN
NIGERIA
C. GH.
D'IV.
C. AF. REP.
CAM.
AFRICA
GABON
CONGO
ZAIRE
ANGOLA
NAMIBIA
MOZ.
MADAGASCAR
SOUTH AFRICA
CANADA
TES
NORTH AMERICA
CUBA
TRINIDAD & TOBAGO
VENEZUELA
SURINAME
COLOMBIA
ECUADOR
PERU
BRAZIL
BOLIVIA
SOUTH AMERICA
CHILE
ARGENTINA
MINERAL FUELS
RUSSIA
ASIA
EUROPE
ANADA
ITED
ATES
NORTH AMERICA
AFRICA
BRAZIL
SOUTH AMERICA
AUSTRALIA
METALS AND NONMETALS

Transportation & Trade

ANCHORAGE
SEATTLE
DENVER
SAN FRANCISCO
PHOENIX
LOS ANGELES
MEXICO CITY

World Exports by Regions

Percent (by Value) of Total Exports

To European Community · To United States · To Asia (excluding Japan) · To Japan · To European Free Trade Assn. · To Canada · To Latin America · To Africa · To Others

Region	Values (percent)
European Community	25 · 20 · 17 · 8 · 5 · 5 · 20
United States	24 · 20 · 20 · 15 · 12 · 9
Asia (excluding Japan)	33 · 25 · 22 · 20
Japan	37 · 29 · 19 · 4 · 11
European Free Trade Assn.	68 · 9 · 7 · 16
Canada	76 · 8 · 6 · 5 · 5
Latin America	43 · 30 · 8 · 7 · 12
Africa	62 · 20 · 6 · 12
Australia and New Zealand	35 · 28 · 13 · 11 · 13

Trade Balances of Leading Export Nations

Value in Billions of Dollars

Annual Exports · Annual Imports (Data based on average, 1992-1994)

Nation	Exports / Imports
United States	468 / 596
Germany	402 / 363
Japan	365 / 249
France	244 / 240
United Kingdom	192 / 215
Italy	179 / 175
Canada	140 / 131
Belgium	117 / 120
China	99 / 100
Taiwan	87 / 78
South Korea	85 / 88
Spain	69 / 95
Sweden	55 / 48
Mexico	46 / 64
Australia	45 / 44
Russia	43 / 33
Saudi Arabia	43 / 27
Brazil	39 / 26
Indonesia	36 / 28
Thailand	35 / 44
South Africa	24 / 19
India	22 / 24
Iran	16 / 21
Turkey	15 / 24
Venezuela	15 / 10
Argentina	14 / 17

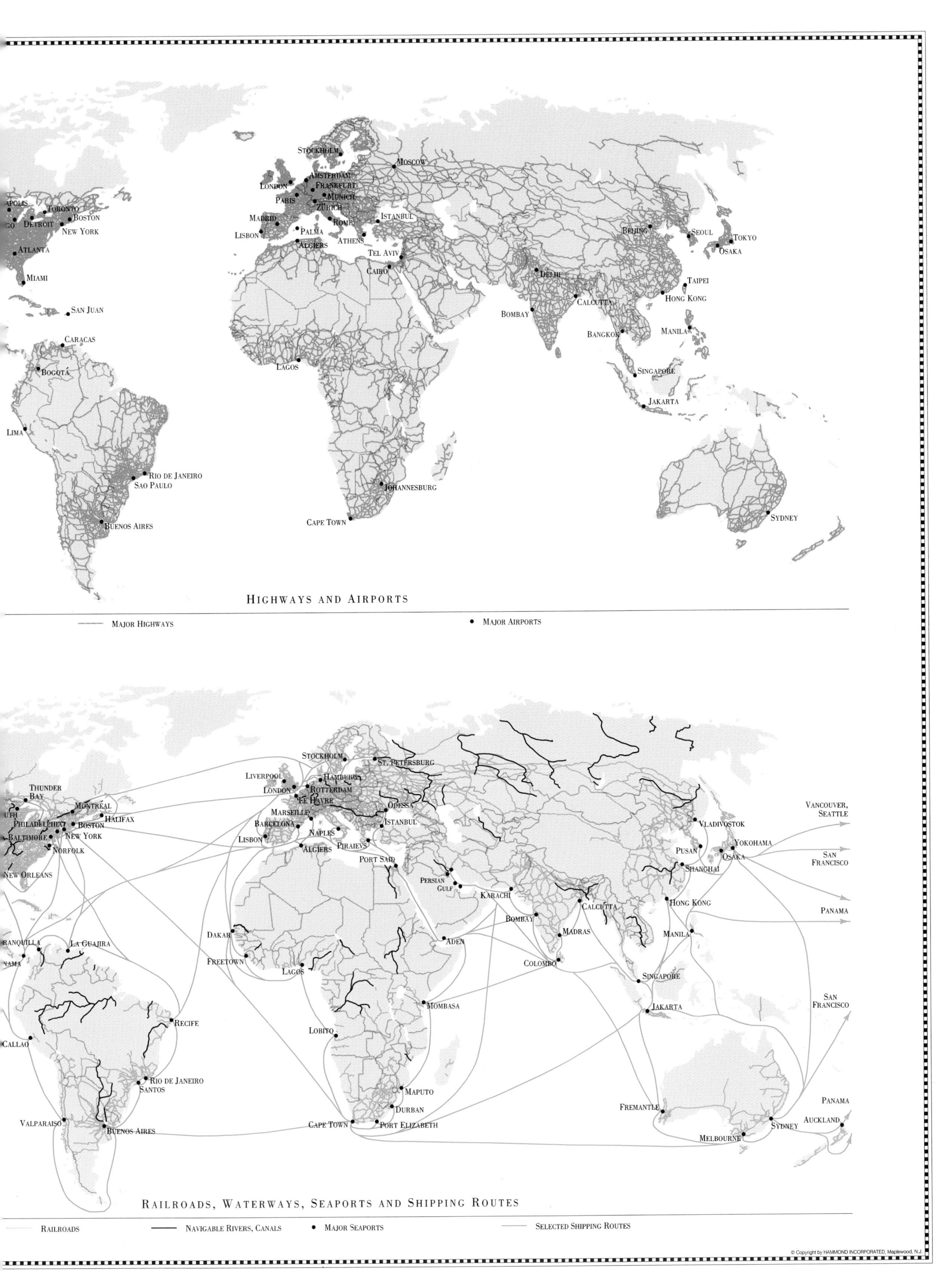

Stockholm
Moscow
London
Amsterdam
Frankfurt
Paris
Munich
Zurich
Madrid
Rome
Istanbul
Lisbon
Palma
Algiers
Athens
Tel Aviv
Cairo
Toronto
Boston
Detroit
New York
Atlanta
Miami
San Juan
Caracas
Bogotá
Lima
Rio de Janeiro
Sao Paulo
Buenos Aires
Lagos
Johannesburg
Cape Town
Beijing
Seoul
Tokyo
Osaka
Delhi
Taipei
Calcutta
Hong Kong
Bombay
Bangkok
Manila
Singapore
Jakarta
Sydney
Highways and Airports
Major Highways
Major Airports
Stockholm
St. Petersburg
Liverpool
Hamburg
London
Rotterdam
Le Havre
Odessa
Marseille
Barcelona
Istanbul
Lisbon
Naples
Piraievs
Algiers
Port Said
Thunder Bay
Montréal
Halifax
Philadelphia
Boston
Baltimore
New York
Norfolk
New Orleans
La Guajira
Persian Gulf
Karachi
Bombay
Calcutta
Madras
Colombo
Aden
Dakar
Freetown
Lagos
Mombasa
Lobito
Recife
Callao
Rio de Janeiro
Santos
Valparaiso
Buenos Aires
Cape Town
Maputo
Durban
Port Elizabeth
Vladivostok
Pusan
Yokohama
Osaka
Shanghai
Hong Kong
Manila
Singapore
Jakarta
Fremantle
Melbourne
Sydney
Auckland
Vancouver, Seattle
San Francisco
Panama
San Francisco
Panama
Railroads, Waterways, Seaports and Shipping Routes
Railroads
Navigable Rivers, Canals
Major Seaports
Selected Shipping Routes

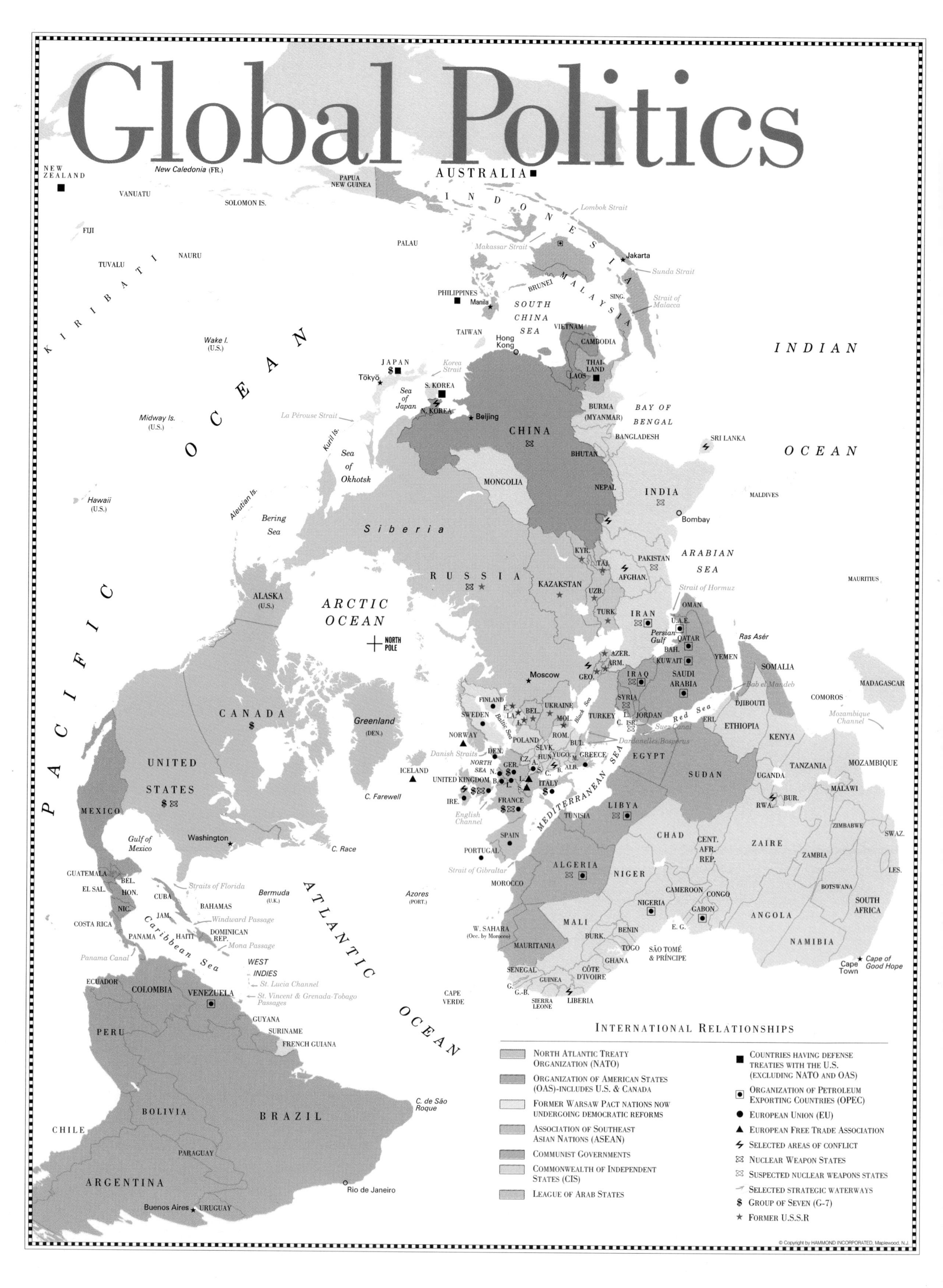
Global Politics
NEW ZEALAND
New Caledonia (FR.)
VANUATU
SOLOMON IS.
PAPUA NEW GUINEA
AUSTRALIA
INDONESIA
Lombok Strait
FIJI
TUVALU
NAURU
KIRIBATI
PALAU
Makassar Strait
Jakarta
Sunda Strait
BRUNEI
MALAYSIA
PHILIPPINES
Manila
SOUTH CHINA SEA
SING.
Strait of Malacca
TAIWAN
Hong Kong
VIETNAM
CAMBODIA
Wake I. (U.S.)
INDIAN
JAPAN
Tōkyō
Korea Strait
S. KOREA
Sea of Japan
N. KOREA
Beijing
THAILAND
LAOS
Midway Is. (U.S.)
La Pérouse Strait
Kuril Is.
BURMA (MYANMAR)
BAY OF BENGAL
CHINA
BANGLADESH
SRI LANKA
OCEAN
Sea of Okhotsk
BHUTAN
MONGOLIA
NEPAL
INDIA
MALDIVES
Hawaii (U.S.)
Aleutian Is.
Bering Sea
Siberia
Bombay
KYR.
PAKISTAN
ARABIAN SEA
TAJ.
AFGHAN.
RUSSIA
KAZAKSTAN
MAURITIUS
ALASKA (U.S.)
ARCTIC OCEAN
UZB.
Strait of Hormuz
OMAN
TURK.
IRAN
U.A.E.
Persian Gulf
QATAR
NORTH POLE
Ras Asér
BAH.
AZER.
ARM.
KUWAIT
YEMEN
SOMALIA
Moscow
GEO.
IRAQ
SAUDI ARABIA
Bab el Mandeb
MADAGASCAR
FINLAND
SYRIA
DJIBOUTI
COMOROS
E.
CANADA
UKRAINE
LA.
BEL.
Black Sea
SWEDEN
L.
JORDAN
Red Sea
Greenland (DEN.)
MOL.
TURKEY
C.
ISR.
Suez Canal
ERI.
ETHIOPIA
Mozambique Channel
Baltic Sea
ROM.
NORWAY
POLAND
BUL.
Dardanelles/Bosporus
KENYA
UNITED STATES
DEN.
SLVK.
Danish Straits
NORTH SEA
HUN.
YUGO.
GREECE
EGYPT
CZ.
GER.
A.
M.
B.
ALB.
TANZANIA
MOZAMBIQUE
ICELAND
N.
S.
SUDAN
UGANDA
UNITED KINGDOM
L.
ITALY
MEDITERRANEAN SEA
BUR.
MALAWI
C. Farewell
IRE.
FRANCE
LIBYA
RWA.
MEXICO
English Channel
TUNISIA
ZIMBABWE
SWAZ.
Gulf of Mexico
Washington
SPAIN
CHAD
CENT. AFR. REP.
ZAIRE
C. Race
PORTUGAL
ZAMBIA
Strait of Gibraltar
ALGERIA
NIGER
LES.
GUATEMALA
BEL.
Straits of Florida
MOROCCO
EL SAL.
HON.
CUBA
Bermuda (U.K.)
ATLANTIC
Azores (PORT.)
CAMEROON
CONGO
BOTSWANA
NIC.
BAHAMAS
NIGERIA
SOUTH AFRICA
JAM.
Windward Passage
GABON
ANGOLA
COSTA RICA
Caribbean Sea
DOMINICAN REP.
W. SAHARA (Occ. by Morocco)
MALI
BENIN
E. G.
PANAMA
HAITI
Mona Passage
BURK.
NAMIBIA
Panama Canal
MAURITANIA
TOGO
SÃO TOMÉ & PRÍNCIPE
WEST INDIES
GHANA
Cape Town
Cape of Good Hope
SENEGAL
CÔTE D'IVOIRE
ECUADOR
St. Lucia Channel
GUINEA
COLOMBIA
VENEZUELA
St. Vincent & Grenada-Tobago Passages
CAPE VERDE
G.
G.-B.
SIERRA LEONE
LIBERIA
GUYANA
OCEAN
SURINAME
PERU
FRENCH GUIANA
PACIFIC OCEAN
BOLIVIA
BRAZIL
C. de São Roque
CHILE
PARAGUAY
ARGENTINA
Rio de Janeiro
Buenos Aires
URUGUAY
INTERNATIONAL RELATIONSHIPS
NORTH ATLANTIC TREATY ORGANIZATION (NATO)
ORGANIZATION OF AMERICAN STATES (OAS)-INCLUDES U.S. & CANADA
FORMER WARSAW PACT NATIONS NOW UNDERGOING DEMOCRATIC REFORMS
ASSOCIATION OF SOUTHEAST ASIAN NATIONS (ASEAN)
COMMUNIST GOVERNMENTS
COMMONWEALTH OF INDEPENDENT STATES (CIS)
LEAGUE OF ARAB STATES
COUNTRIES HAVING DEFENSE TREATIES WITH THE U.S. (EXCLUDING NATO AND OAS)
ORGANIZATION OF PETROLEUM EXPORTING COUNTRIES (OPEC)
EUROPEAN UNION (EU)
EUROPEAN FREE TRADE ASSOCIATION
SELECTED AREAS OF CONFLICT
NUCLEAR WEAPON STATES
SUSPECTED NUCLEAR WEAPONS STATES
SELECTED STRATEGIC WATERWAYS
GROUP OF SEVEN (G-7)
FORMER U.S.S.R
© Copyright by HAMMOND INCORPORATED, Maplewood, N.J.

Regional Maps

Globe circa 1955

Europe - Physical

Europe - Political

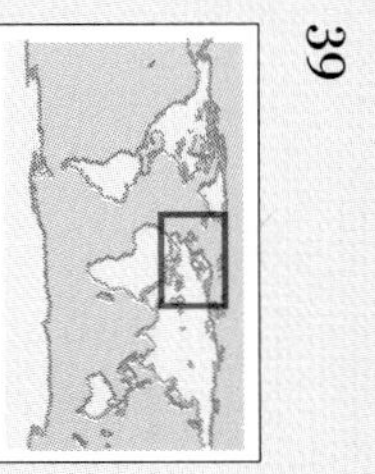

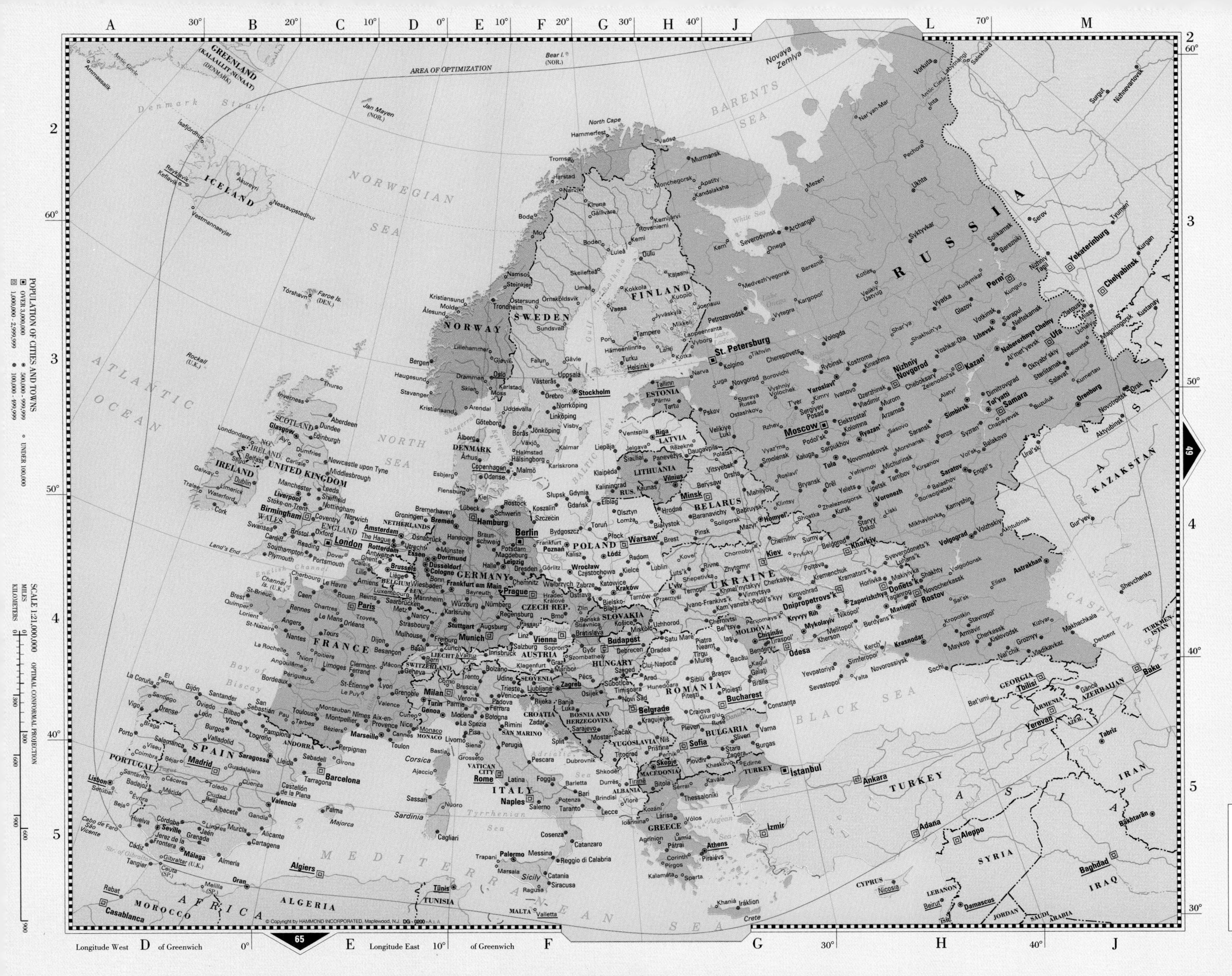

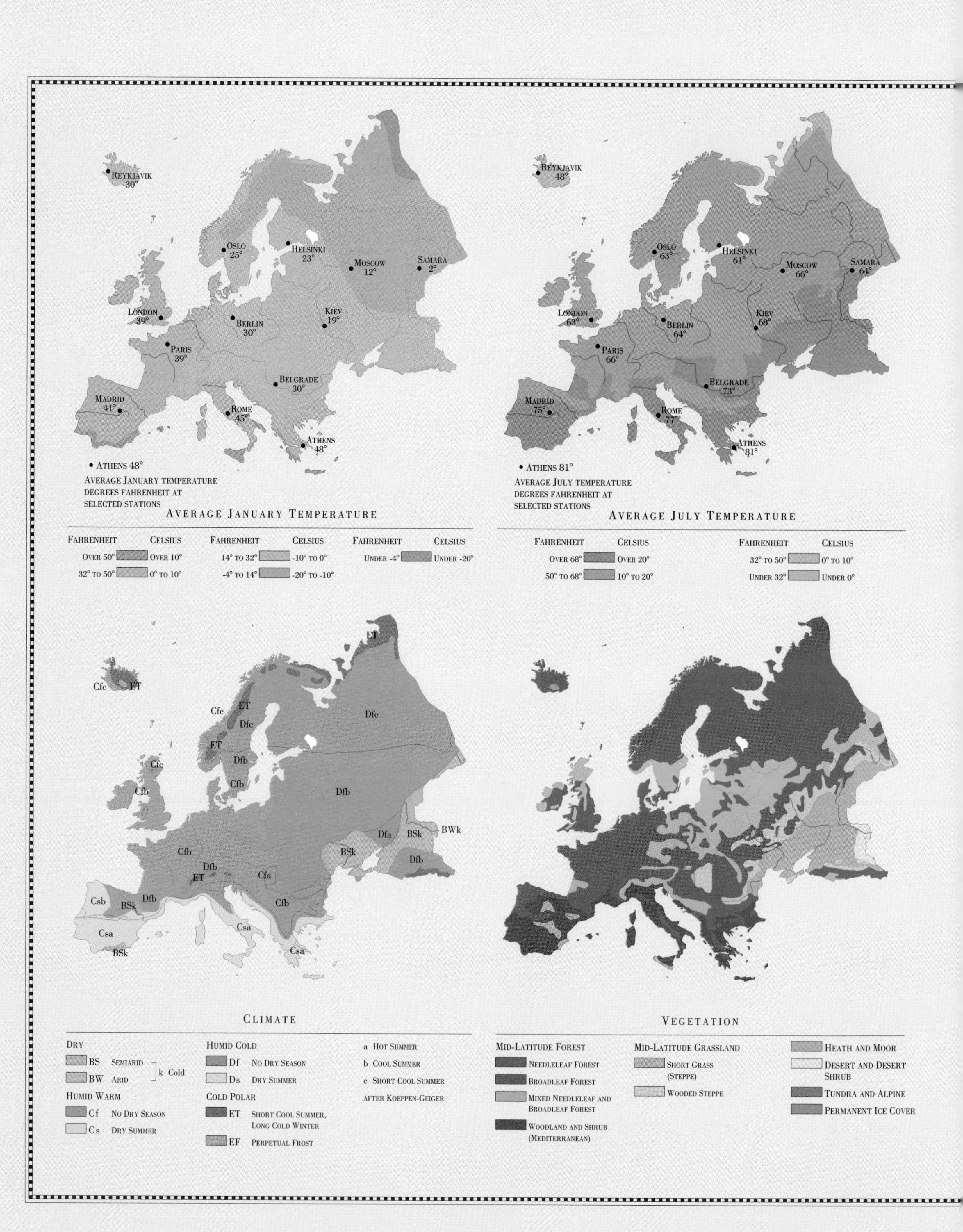
Reykjavik 30°
Oslo 25°
Helsinki 23°
Moscow 12°
Samara 2°
London 39°
Berlin 30°
Kiev 19°
Paris 39°
Belgrade 30°
Madrid 41°
Rome 45°
Athens 48°
• Athens 48°
Average January temperature degrees Fahrenheit at selected stations
Average January Temperature
Fahrenheit Celsius
Over 50° Over 10°
32° to 50° 0° to 10°
14° to 32° -10° to 0°
-4° to 14° -20° to -10°
Under -4° Under -20°
Reykjavik 48°
Oslo 63°
Helsinki 61°
Moscow 66°
Samara 64°
London 63°
Berlin 64°
Kiev 68°
Paris 66°
Belgrade 73°
Madrid 75°
Rome 77°
Athens 81°
• Athens 81°
Average July temperature degrees Fahrenheit at selected stations
Average July Temperature
Fahrenheit Celsius
Over 68° Over 20°
50° to 68° 10° to 20°
32° to 50° 0° to 10°
Under 32° Under 0°
Cfc ET Cfc ET Dfc Dfc ET Dfb Cfc Cfb Cfb Dfb Dfa BSk BWk BSk Dfb Cfb Dfb ET Cfa Csb BSk Dfb Cfb Csa Csa BSk Csa
Climate
Dry
BS Semiarid
BW Arid
k Cold
Humid Warm
Cf No Dry Season
Cs Dry Summer
Humid Cold
Df No Dry Season
Ds Dry Summer
Cold Polar
ET Short Cool Summer, Long Cold Winter
EF Perpetual Frost
a Hot Summer
b Cool Summer
c Short Cool Summer
After Koeppen-Geiger
Vegetation
Mid-Latitude Forest
Needleleaf Forest
Broadleaf Forest
Mixed Needleleaf and Broadleaf Forest
Woodland and Shrub (Mediterranean)
Mid-Latitude Grassland
Short Grass (Steppe)
Wooded Steppe
Heath and Moor
Desert and Desert Shrub
Tundra and Alpine
Permanent Ice Cover

Europe - Comparisons

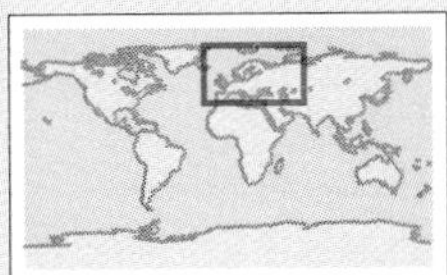

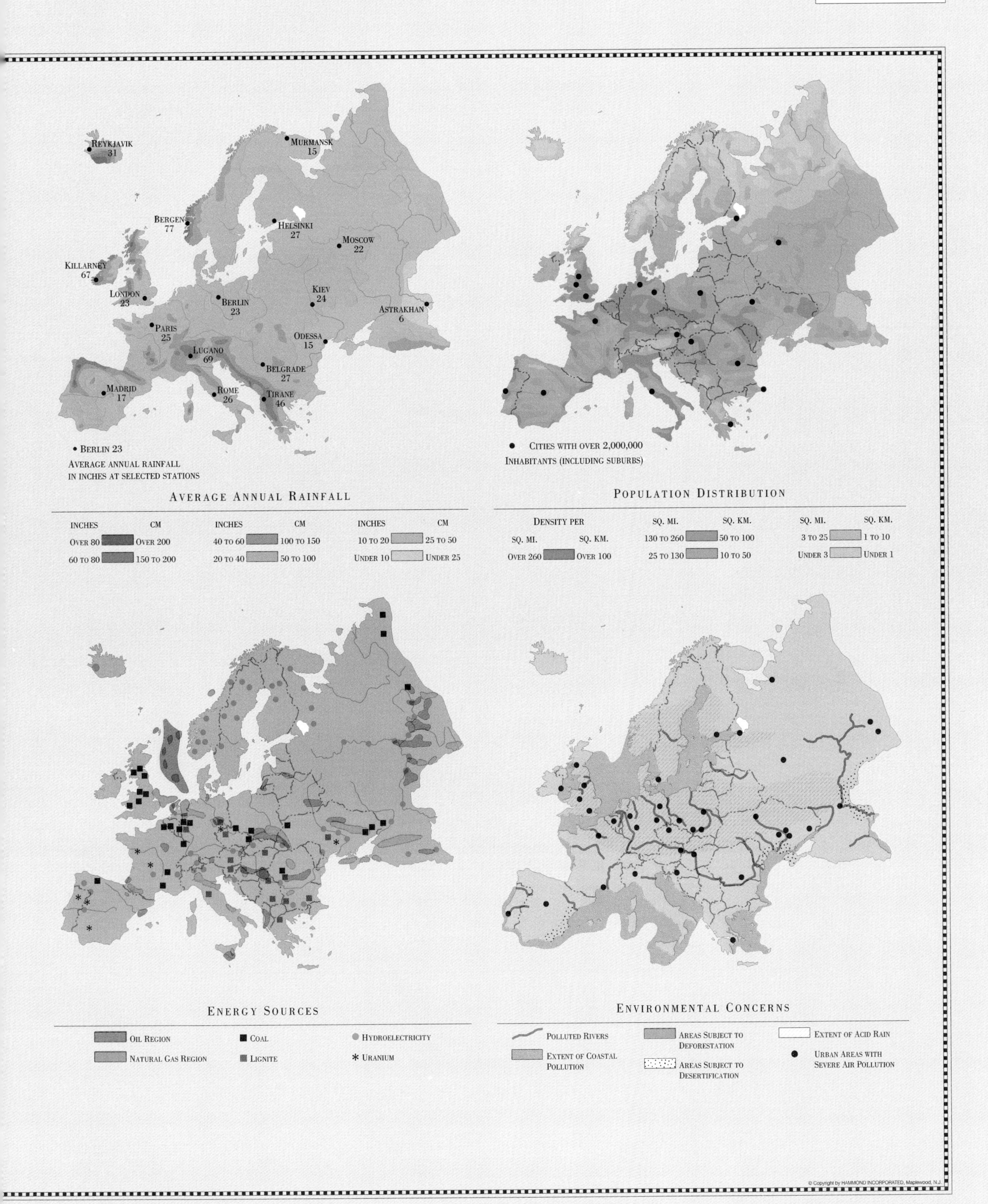

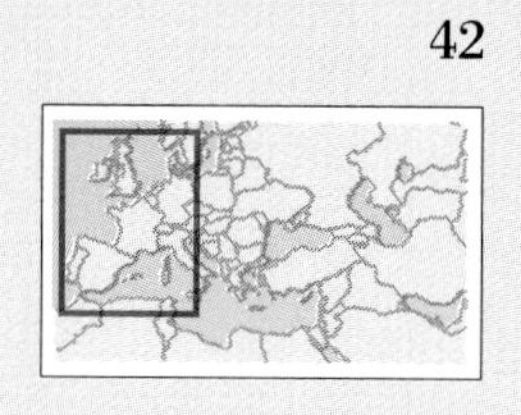

Western Europe

Northern Europe

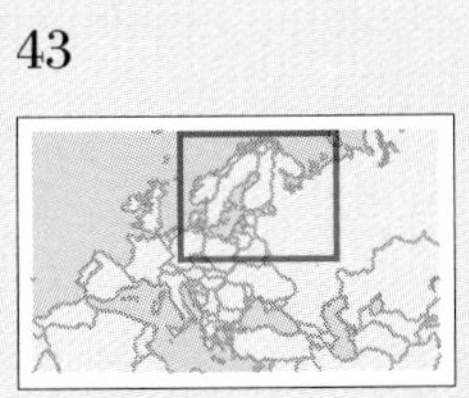

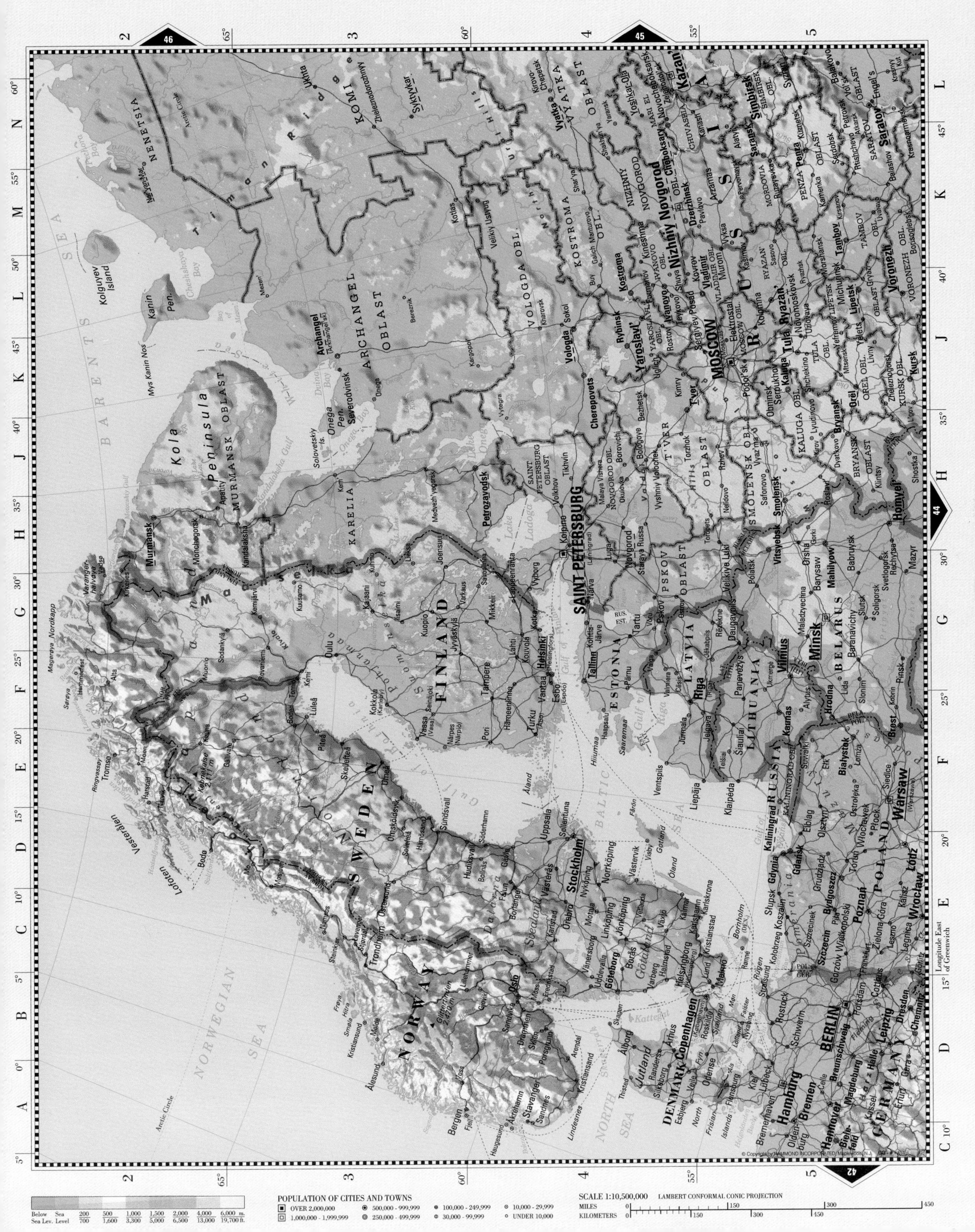

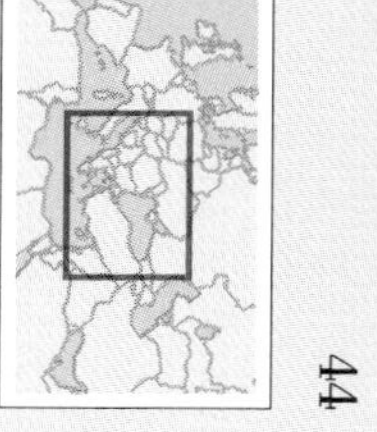

South Central Europe

Central Eurasia

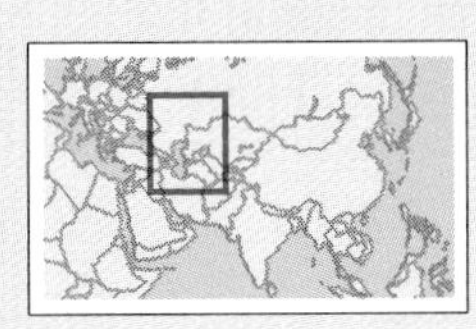

4
3
2
30°
B
C
D
E
F
G
H
J
SVALBARD
(NORWAY)
Spitsbergen
Northeast Land
Edge I.
Bear I. (NOR.)
FRANZ JOSEF LAND
George Land
Wiese I.
Pioner I.
SEVERNAYA ZEMYLA
Barents Sea
Norwegian Sea
North Sea
Novaya Zemlya
Kara Sea
Kola Pen.
White Sea
Yamal Pen.
Gyda Pen.
TAYMYRIA
NENETSIA
KOMI
Northern Uvals
Ural Mts.
YAMALIA
KHANTIA-MANSIA
West Siberian Plain
R U S S
London
U.K.
The Hague
Rotterdam
Amsterdam
Brussels
NETH.
Hamburg
Berlin
GERMANY
Frankfurt am Main
Cologne
Dortmund
Leipzig
Dresden
Prague
DENMARK
Copenhagen
NORWAY
Oslo
Bergen
SWEDEN
Stockholm
Göteborg
FINLAND
Helsinki
Tallinn
ESTONIA
LATVIA
Riga
LITH.
Vilnius
POLAND
Warsaw
Poznań
Łódź
Wrocław
Kraków
Budapest
HUNG.
ROMANIA
Minsk
UKRAINE
Kiev
Odesa
Kharkiv
Donetsk
St. Petersburg
Moscow
Nizhniy Novgorod
Kazan
Samara
Saratov
Volgograd
Rostov
Krasnodar
Archangel
Murmansk
Perm'
Yekaterinburg
Ufa
Chelyabinsk
Tyumen'
Omsk
Novosibirsk
Tomsk
Krasnoyarsk
Kemerovo
Novokuznetsk
Barnaul
Orenburg
Astrakhan'
Black Sea
Caspian Sea
Priksaspian Plain
Kirghiz Steppe
KAZAKSTAN
Kazakh Uplands
Qaraghandy
Aqmola
Pavlodar
Almaty
Bishkek
KYRGYZSTAN
Tashkent
UZBEKISTAN
TURKMENISTAN
Ashgabat
Dushanbe
TAJIKISTAN
AFGHANISTAN
Hindu Kush
Tehrān
IRAN
Zagros Mts.
Elburz Mts.
IRAQ
TURKEY
Tbilisi
Yerevan
Baku
Tian Shan
CHINA
Tarim Basin
Xinjiang
Dzungarian Basin
Ürümqi
Altay Mountains
MONGOLIA
ALTAY
TUVA
42
44
52
50°
40°
30°
5
6
7
F
G
H
J
K
60°
70°
80°
90°
Longitude East of Greenwich
Below Sea Lev.
Sea Level
200
700
500
1,600
1,000
3,300
1,500
5,000
2,000
6,500
4,000
13,000
6,000 m.
19,700 ft.

Russia and Neighboring Countries

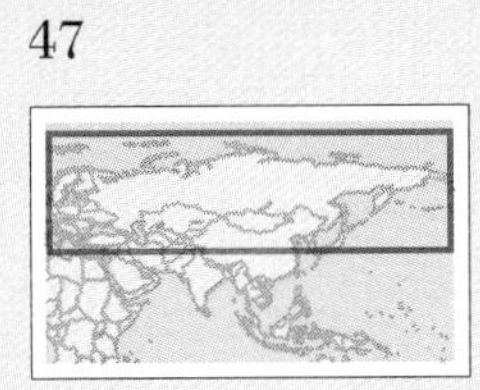

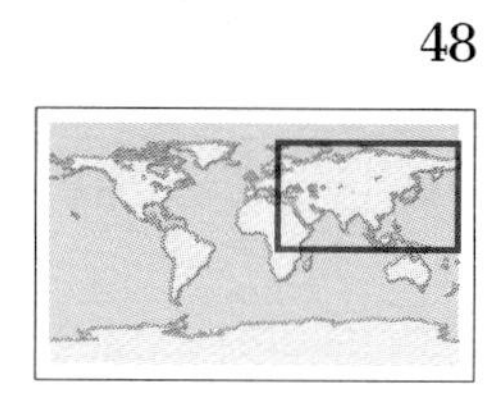

Asia-Physical

AREA OF OPTIMIZATION
The red band which surrounds these physical and political maps defines the "Area of Optimization." Within this bounding curve is the most accurate conformal map that can be made of the region. Outside the optimized area, distortion increases rapidly, and tears or other irregularities in the grid may occur.

Longitude East of Greenwich

SCALE 1:49,000,000 OPTIMAL CONFORMAL PROJECTION
MILES 0 700 1400 2100
KILOMETERS 0 700 1400 2100

POPULATION OF CITIES AND TOWNS
- OVER 3,000,000
- 1,000,000 - 2,999,999
- 500,000 - 999,999
- 100,000 - 499,999
- UNDER 100,000

Asia - Political

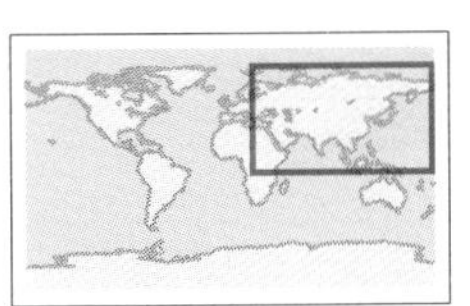

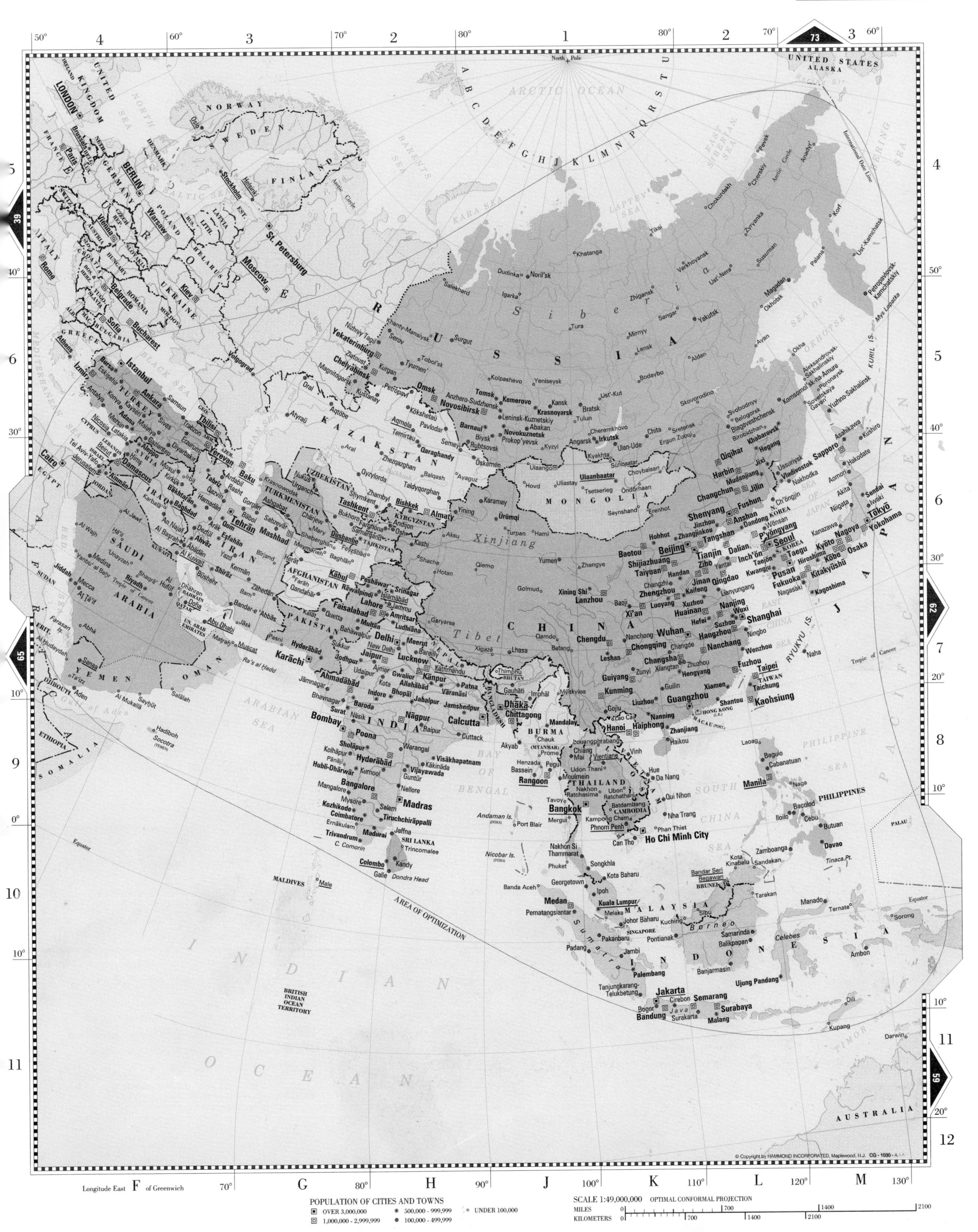

POPULATION OF CITIES AND TOWNS

- OVER 3,000,000
- 1,000,000 - 2,999,999
- 500,000 - 999,999
- 100,000 - 499,999
- UNDER 100,000

SCALE 1:49,000,000 OPTIMAL CONFORMAL PROJECTION

MILES 0 700 1400 2100

KILOMETERS 0 700 1400 2100

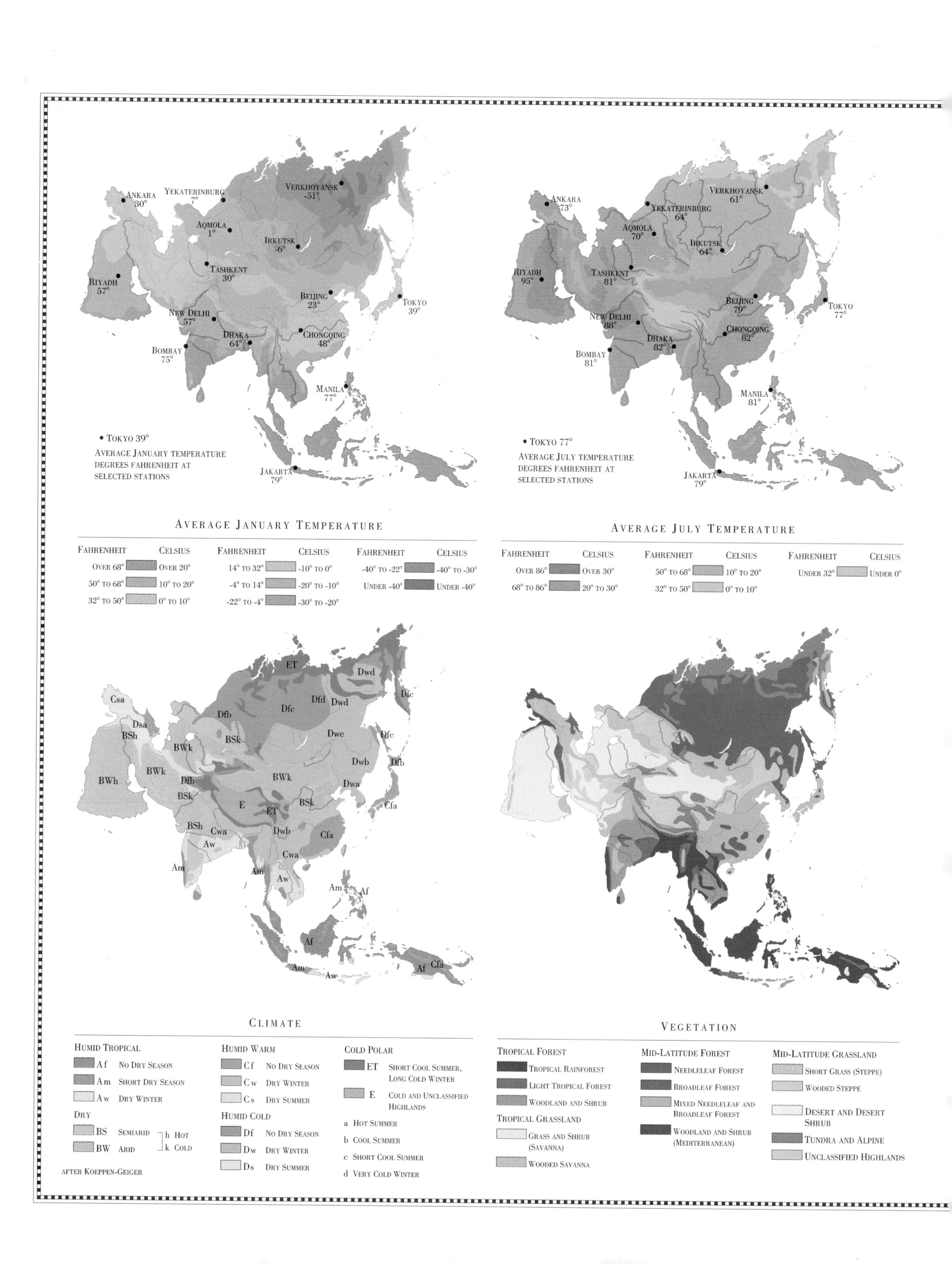
Ankara 30°
Yekaterinburg 7°
Verkhoyansk -51°
Aqmola 1°
Irkutsk -6°
Tashkent 30°
Riyadh 57°
Beijing 23°
Tokyo 39°
New Delhi 57°
Dhaka 64°
Chongqing 48°
Bombay 75°
Manila 77°
Jakarta 79°
• Tokyo 39°
Average January temperature degrees Fahrenheit at selected stations
Ankara 73°
Verkhoyansk 61°
Yekaterinburg 64°
Aqmola 70°
Irkutsk 64°
Riyadh 95°
Tashkent 81°
Beijing 79°
Tokyo 77°
New Delhi 88°
Chongqing 82°
Dhaka 82°
Bombay 81°
Manila 81°
Jakarta 79°
• Tokyo 77°
Average July temperature degrees Fahrenheit at selected stations
Average January Temperature
Fahrenheit Celsius
Over 68° Over 20°
50° to 68° 10° to 20°
32° to 50° 0° to 10°
14° to 32° -10° to 0°
-4° to 14° -20° to -10°
-22° to -4° -30° to -20°
-40° to -22° -40° to -30°
Under -40° Under -40°
Average July Temperature
Fahrenheit Celsius
Over 86° Over 30°
68° to 86° 20° to 30°
50° to 68° 10° to 20°
32° to 50° 0° to 10°
Under 32° Under 0°
ET
Dwd
Csa
Dfd
Dwd
Dfc
Dfb
Dfc
Dsa
BSh
BSk
Dwc
Dfc
BWk
Dwb
Dfb
BWk
Dfb
BWk
BWh
Dwa
BSk
E
ET
BSk
Cfa
BSh
Cwa
Dwb
Cfa
Aw
Cwa
Am
Am
Aw
Am
Af
Af
Am
Aw
Af
Cfa
Climate
Humid Tropical
Af No Dry Season
Am Short Dry Season
Aw Dry Winter
Dry
BS Semiarid
BW Arid
h Hot
k Cold
Humid Warm
Cf No Dry Season
Cw Dry Winter
Cs Dry Summer
Humid Cold
Df No Dry Season
Dw Dry Winter
Ds Dry Summer
Cold Polar
ET Short Cool Summer, Long Cold Winter
E Cold and Unclassified Highlands
a Hot Summer
b Cool Summer
c Short Cool Summer
d Very Cold Winter
After Koeppen-Geiger
Vegetation
Tropical Forest
Tropical Rainforest
Light Tropical Forest
Woodland and Shrub
Tropical Grassland
Grass and Shrub (Savanna)
Wooded Savanna
Mid-Latitude Forest
Needleleaf Forest
Broadleaf Forest
Mixed Needleleaf and Broadleaf Forest
Woodland and Shrub (Mediterranean)
Mid-Latitude Grassland
Short Grass (Steppe)
Wooded Steppe
Desert and Desert Shrub
Tundra and Alpine
Unclassified Highlands

Asia - Comparisons

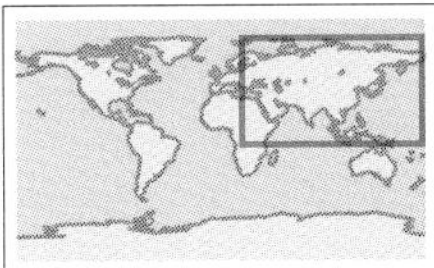

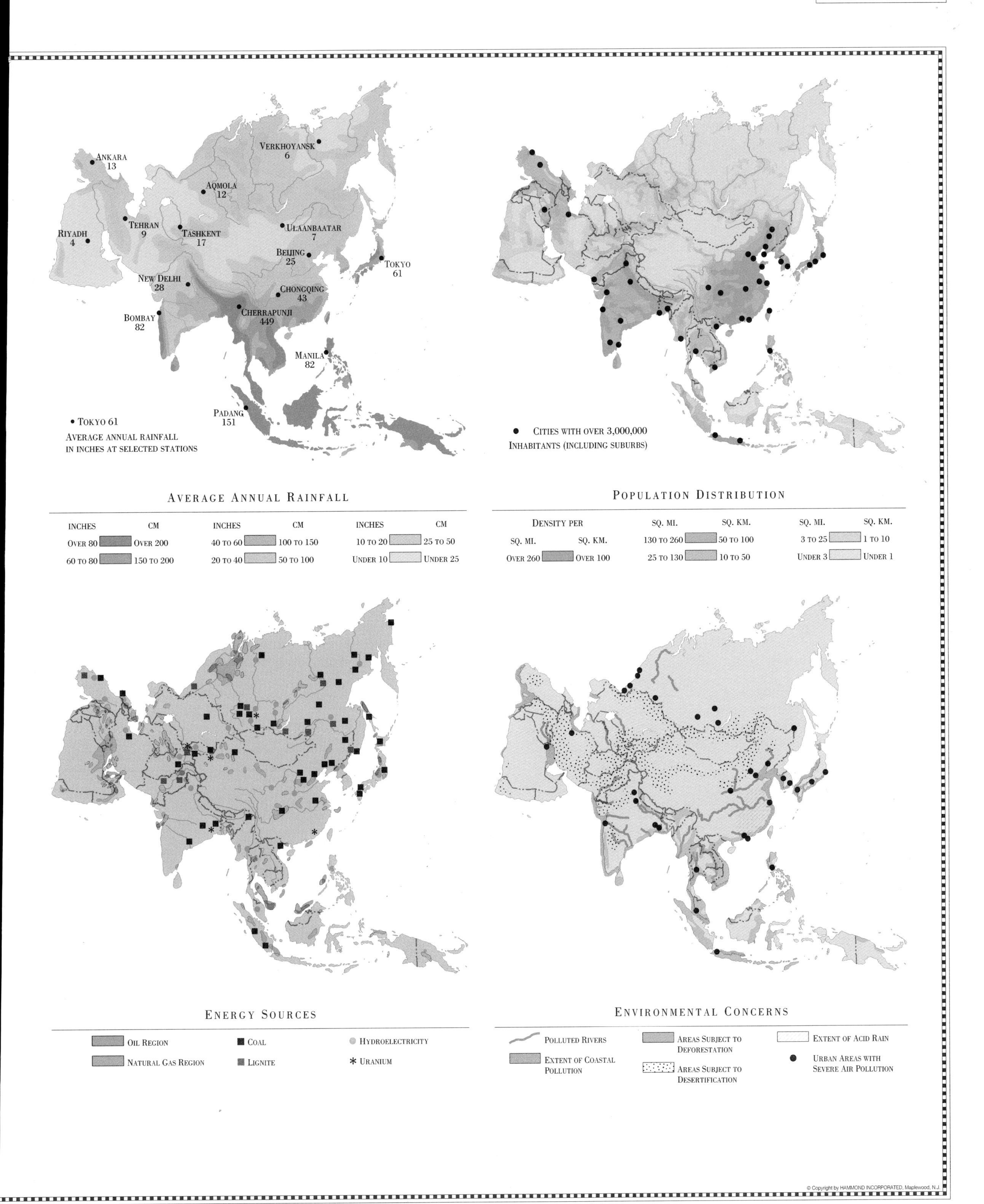

Southwestern Asia

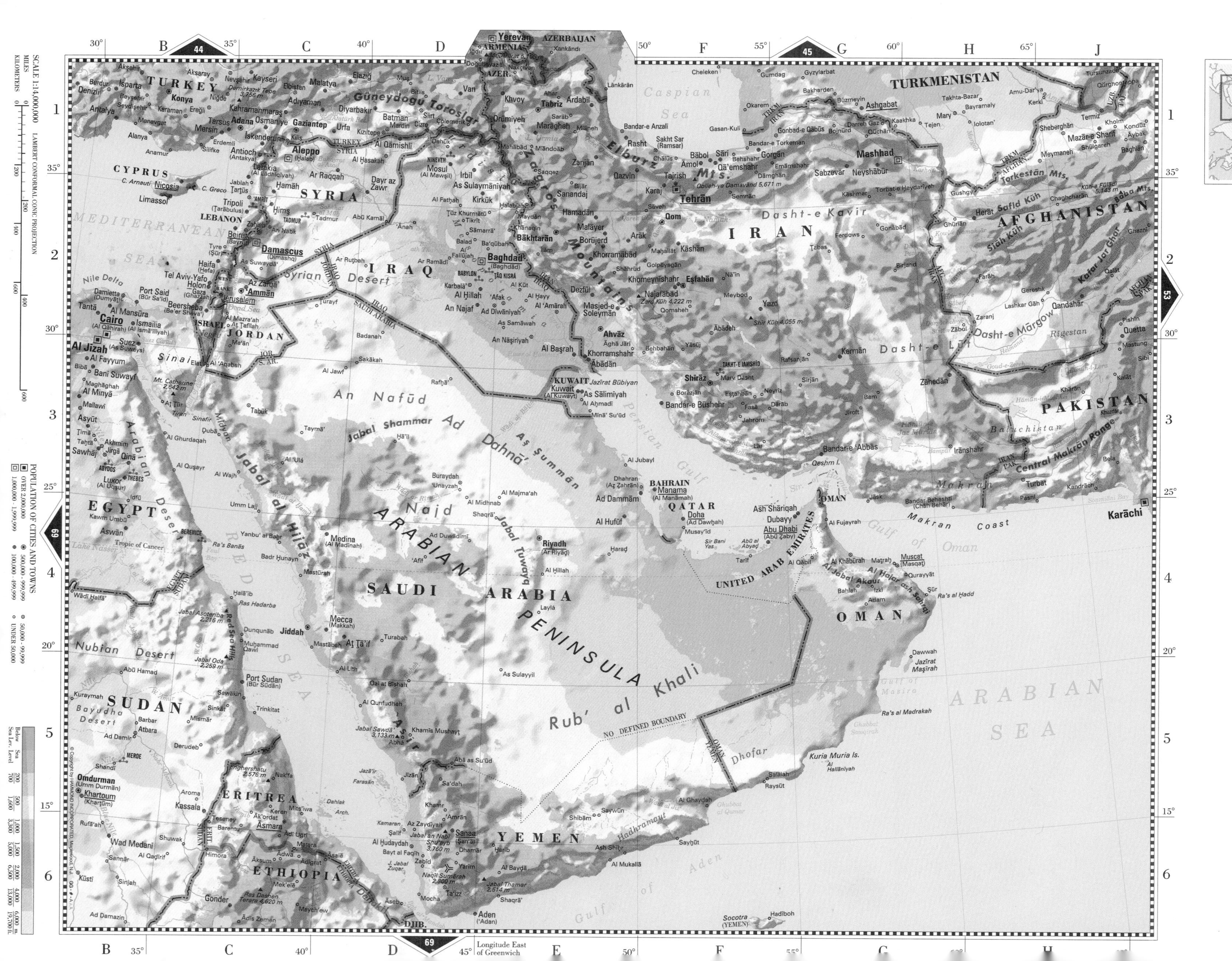
TURKEY
SYRIA
IRAQ
IRAN
AFGHANISTAN
PAKISTAN
TURKMENISTAN
SAUDI ARABIA
OMAN
YEMEN
QATAR
KUWAIT
BAHRAIN
UNITED ARAB EMIRATES
JORDAN
ISRAEL
LEBANON
CYPRUS
EGYPT
SUDAN
ERITREA
ETHIOPIA
ARABIAN SEA
Persian Gulf
Gulf of Oman
Gulf of Aden
RED SEA
MEDITERRANEAN SEA
Caspian Sea
ARABIAN PENINSULA
Rub' al Khali
NO DEFINED BOUNDARY
Longitude East of Greenwich
© Copyright by HAMMOND INCORPORATED, Maplewood, N.J.
SCALE 1:14,000,000 LAMBERT CONFORMAL CONIC PROJECTION
MILES 0 200 400 600
KILOMETERS 0 200 400 600
POPULATION OF CITIES AND TOWNS
OVER 2,000,000
1,000,000 - 1,999,999
500,000 - 999,999
100,000 - 499,999
50,000 - 99,999
UNDER 50,000
Below Sea Lev. Level 200 700 500 1,600 1,000 3,300 1,500 5,000 2,000 6,500 4,000 13,000 6,000 m. 19,700 ft.

Indian Subcontinent

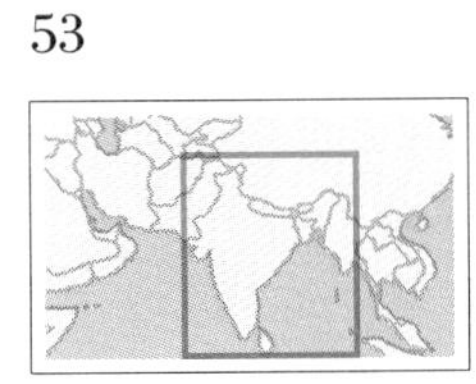

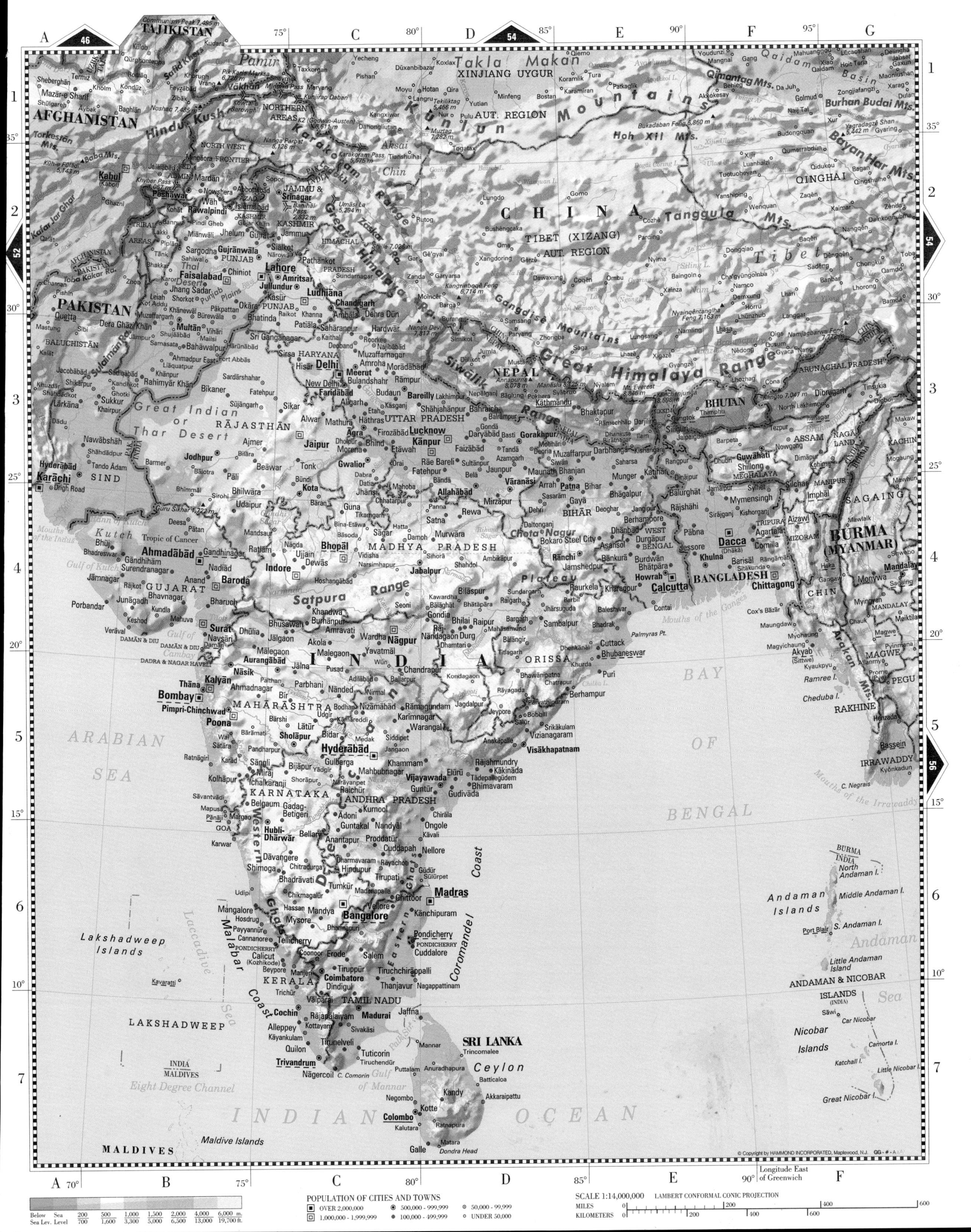

A
B
C
D
E
J
70°
75°
80°
85°
90°
105°
45°
40°
35°
30°
25°
20°
46
53
56
3
4
5
6
7
8
RUSSIA
KAZAKSTAN
KYRGYZSTAN
TAJIK.
AFGHAN.
PAKISTAN
INDIA
NEPAL
BHUTAN
BANGLADESH
BURMA
(MYANMAR)
THAILAND
LAOS
VIETNAM
MONGOLIA
CHINA
XINJIANG UYGUR
AUTONOMOUS REGION
TIBET (XIZANG)
AUT. REGION
QINGHAI
GANSU
SICHUAN
YUNNAN
GUIZHOU
SHAANXI
NINGXIA HU. Z.
UTTAR PRADESH
HIMACHAL PRADESH
MADHYA PRADESH
ANDHRA PRADESH
ORISSA
BIHAR
WEST BENGAL
ASSAM
MEGHALAYA
NAGALAND
MANIPUR
MIZORAM
ARUNACHAL PRADESH
JAMMU & KASHMIR
SAGAING
KACHIN
SHAN
CHIN
RAKHINE
MANDALAY
MAGWE
PEGU
KAYAH
Tian Shan
Tarim Basin
Takla Makan
Kunlun Mountains
Altun Mountains
Himalaya Range
Great Himalaya
Tanggula Mts.
Bayan Har Mountains
Qilian Shan
Gobi Desert
Altay
Altayn Mts.
Hangayn Mountains
Dzungarian Basin
Tarbagatay Mts.
Betpak-Dala
Moinkum Desert
Sary Ishikotrau Desert
Lake Balkhash
Tropic of Cancer
Mouths of the Ganges
BAY OF BENGAL
Gulf of Tonkin
Shan Plateau
Almaty
Bishkek
Ürümqi
Ulaanbaatar
Delhi
New Delhi
Kathmandu
Thimphu
Dacca
(Dhaka)
Calcutta
Lucknow
Patna
Chengdu
Chongqing
Kunming
Guiyang
Lanzhou
Xining
Hanoi
Haiphong
Mandalay
Chittagong
Visākhapatnam
Bhubaneswar
Kashi
Aksu
Hami
Golmud
Lhasa
Shigatse
Xi'an
Yinchuan
Baotou
Kānpur
Agra
Allahābād
Vārānasi
Jabalpur
Raipur
Cuttack
Jamshedpur
Rānchi
Guwāhati
Shillong
Imphāl
Aizawl
Agartala
Khulna
Jessore
Howrah
Akyab
(Sittwe)
Taunggyi
Lashio
Monywa
Kyaukpyu
Dali
Lijiang
Xichang
Zunyi
Yibin
Luzhou
Leshan
Ya'an
Pik Pobedy
7,439 m
K2 (Godwin-Austen)
8,611 m
Muztag
7,282 m
Annapurna
8,078 m
Mt. Everest
8,848 m
Kanchenjunga
8,598 m
Nanda Devi
7,817 m
Gongga Shan
7,556 m
Fan Si Pan
3,143 m
Below Sea Level
Sea
200
700
500
1,600
1,000
3,300
1,500
5,000
2,000
6,500
4,000
13,000
6,000 m.
19,700 ft.

Eastern Asia

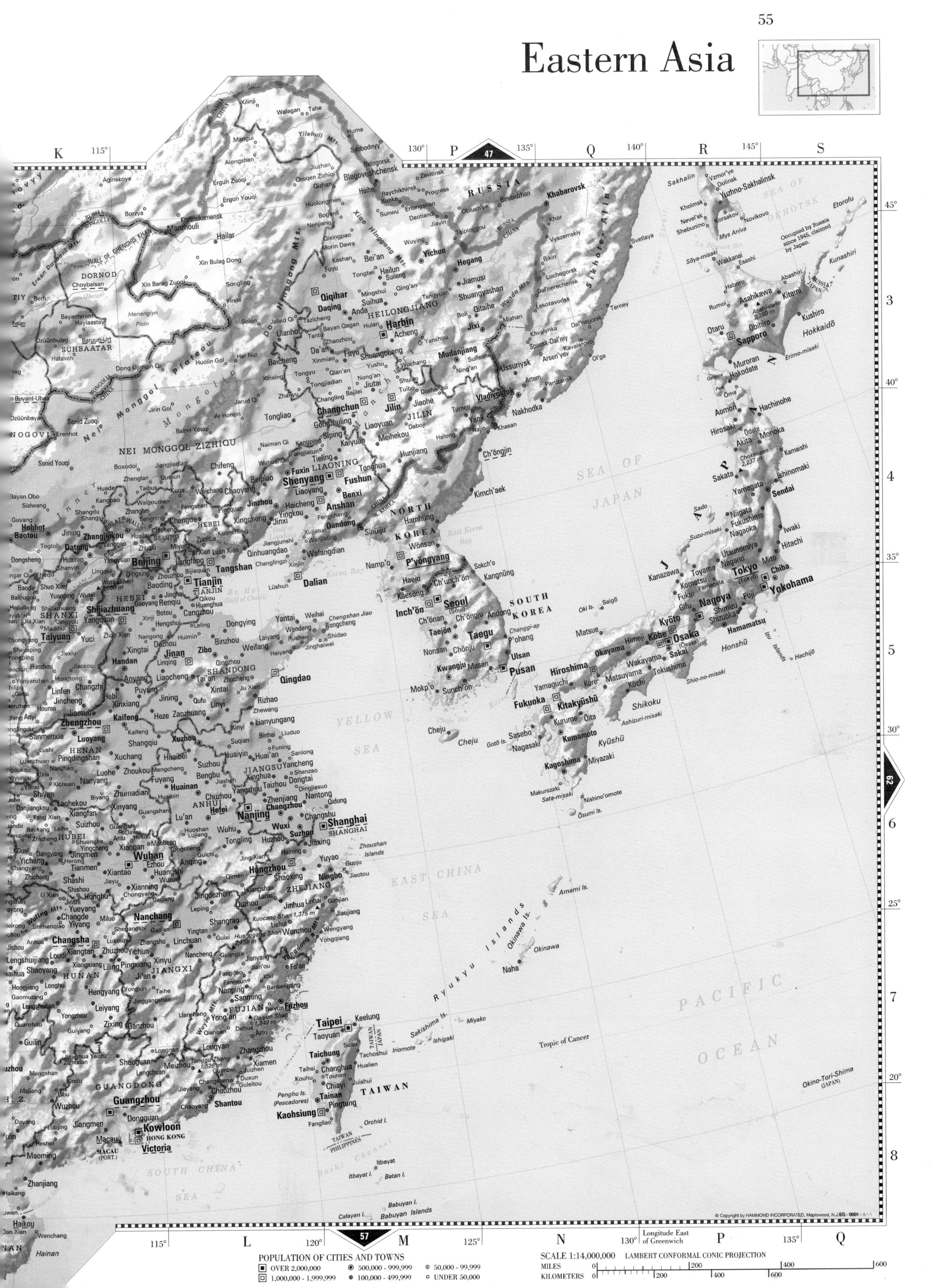

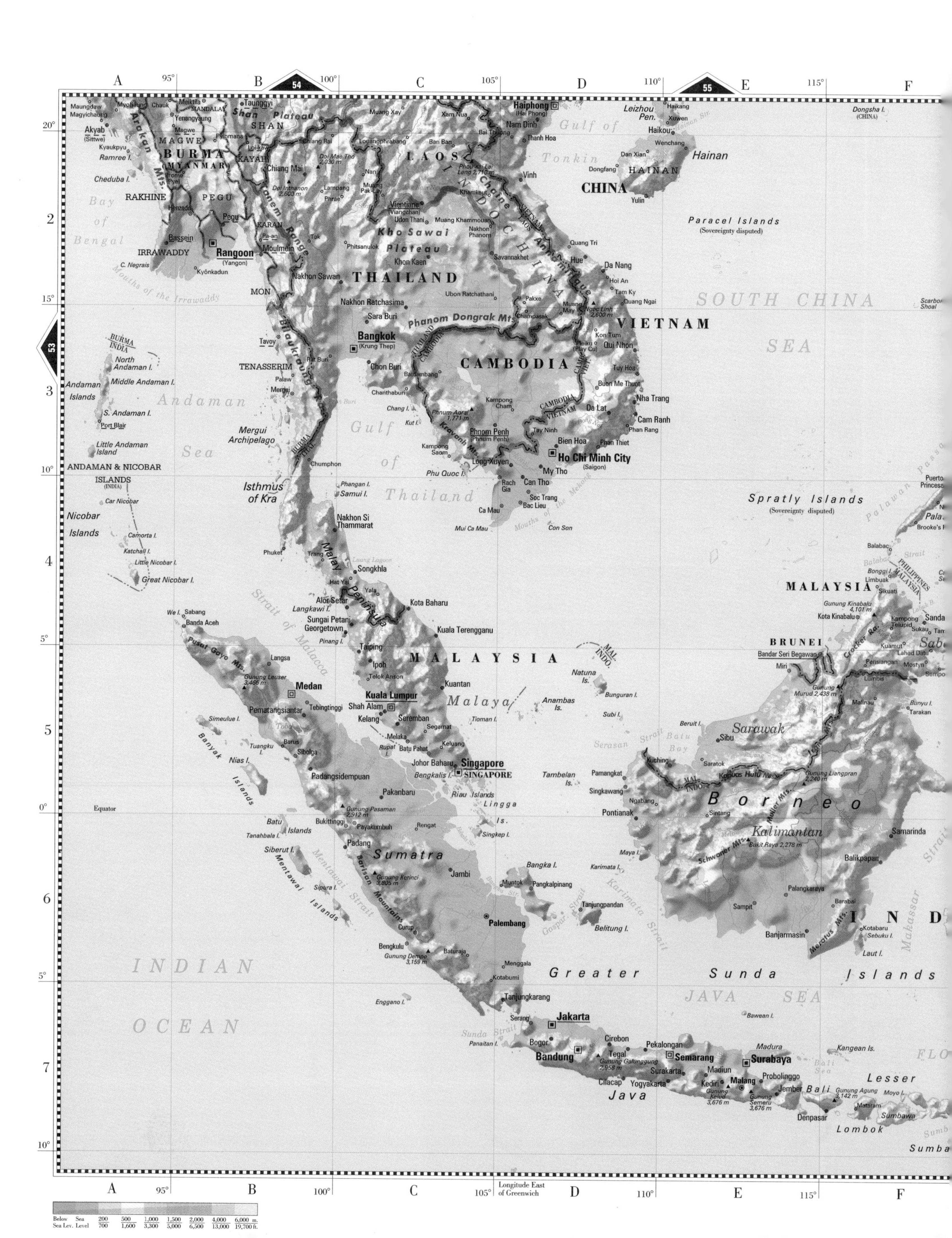

A
B
C
D
E
F
95°
100°
105°
110°
115°
54
55
53
20°
15°
10°
5°
0°
2
3
4
5
6
7
BURMA
(MYANMAR)
RAKHINE
PEGU
IRRAWADDY
MAGWE
MANDALAY
SHAN
KAYAH
KARAN
MON
TENASSERIM
Shan Plateau
Arakan Mts.
Akyab
(Sittwe)
Kyaukpyu
Ramree I.
Cheduba I.
Bay of Bengal
Bassein
Rangoon
(Yangon)
Pegu
Moulmein
C. Negrais
Mouths of the Irrawaddy
Taunggyi
Chiang Mai
Doi Inthanon
2,600 m
Tavoy
Mergui
Mergui Archipelago
Andaman Sea
North Andaman I.
Middle Andaman I.
Andaman Islands
S. Andaman I.
Port Blair
Little Andaman Island
ANDAMAN & NICOBAR ISLANDS
(INDIA)
Car Nicobar
Nicobar Islands
Camorta I.
Katchall I.
Little Nicobar I.
Great Nicobar I.
BURMA
INDIA
LAOS
Luang Prabang
Vientiane
(Viangchan)
Udon Thani
Khon Kaen
Kho Sawai Plateau
Savannakhet
Pakxe
THAILAND
Nakhon Sawan
Nakhon Ratchasima
Ubon Ratchathani
Sara Buri
Bangkok
(Krung Thep)
Phanom Dongrak Mts.
Chon Buri
Battambang
Chanthaburi
Chang I.
Kut I.
Gulf of Thailand
Chumphon
Isthmus of Kra
Phangan I.
Samui I.
Nakhon Si Thammarat
Phuket
Songkhla
Hat Yai
Yala
Malay Peninsula
Alor Setar
Langkawi I.
Sungai Petani
Georgetown
Pinang I.
Kota Baharu
Kuala Terengganu
Taiping
Ipoh
Telok Anson
Kuantan
Kuala Lumpur
Shah Alam
Kelang
Seremban
Segamat
Melaka
Batu Pahat
Keluang
Johor Baharu
Singapore
SINGAPORE
MALAYSIA
Malaya
Tioman I.
Strait of Malacca
Haiphong
(Hai Phong)
Nam Dinh
Thanh Hoa
Vinh
Gulf of Tonkin
Leizhou Pen.
Haikou
Hainan
HAINAN
CHINA
Yulin
Paracel Islands
(Sovereignty disputed)
INDOCHINA
Annamitique
Quang Tri
Hue
Da Nang
Hoi An
Tam Ky
Quang Ngai
Ngoc Linh
2,600 m
Kon Tum
Pleiku
(Play Cu)
Qui Nhon
Tuy Hoa
Buon Me Thuot
Nha Trang
Da Lat
Cam Ranh
Phan Rang
Phan Thiet
VIETNAM
CAMBODIA
Kampong Cham
Phnum Aoral
1,771 m
Phnom Penh
(Phnum Penh)
Kampong Saom
Kravanh Mts.
Phu Quoc I.
Tay Ninh
Bien Hoa
Ho Chi Minh City
(Saigon)
Long Xuyen
My Tho
Rach Gia
Can Tho
Soc Trang
Bac Lieu
Ca Mau
Mui Ca Mau
Con Son
Mouths of the Mekong
SOUTH CHINA SEA
Spratly Islands
(Sovereignty disputed)
Dongsha I.
(CHINA)
Natuna Is.
Bunguran I.
Anambas Is.
Subi I.
Tambelan Is.
Serasan Strait
Batu Bay
Beruit I.
Sarawak
Sibu
Kuching
Saratok
Pamangkat
Singkawang
Ngabang
Pontianak
Sintang
Borneo
Kalimantan
Schwaner Mts.
Muller Mts.
Bukit Raya 2,278 m
Gunung Liangpran
2,240 m
BRUNEI
Bandar Seri Begawan
Miri
MALAYSIA
Gunung Kinabalu
4,101 m
Kota Kinabalu
Sandakan
Gunung Murud 2,438 m
Malinau
Tarakan
Samarinda
Balikpapan
Palangkaraya
Sampit
Banjarmasin
Meratus Mts.
Kotabaru
Sebuku I.
Laut I.
Makassar
Balabac
PHILIPPINES
MALAYSIA
Banggi I.
Limbuak
Crocker Ra.
Maya I.
Karimata I.
Karimata Strait
Bangka I.
Muntok
Pangkalpinang
Tanjungpandan
Belitung I.
Gaspar Strait
Medan
Gunung Leuser
3,466 m
Pusat Gayo Mts.
Banda Aceh
We I.
Sabang
Langsa
Pematangsiantar
Tebingtinggi
Simeulue I.
Banyak Islands
Nias I.
Sibolga
Barus
Padangsidempuan
Pakanbaru
Riau Islands
Lingga Is.
Singkep I.
Bengkalis I.
Rupat I.
Gunung Pasaman
2,912 m
Bukittinggi
Payakumbuh
Rengat
Padang
Batu Islands
Tanahbala I.
Siberut I.
Mentawai Islands
Mentawai Strait
Sipura I.
Sumatra
Barisan Mountains
Gunung Kerinci
3,805 m
Jambi
Palembang
Curup
Bengkulu
Gunung Dempo
3,159 m
Baturaja
Menggala
Kotabumi
Tanjungkarang
Enggano I.
Equator
INDIAN OCEAN
Greater Sunda Islands
JAVA SEA
Bawean I.
Serang
Jakarta
Sunda Strait
Panaitan I.
Bogor
Bandung
Cirebon
Tegal
Gunung Galunggung
2,168 m
Pekalongan
Semarang
Surakarta
Cilacap
Yogyakarta
Java
Madiun
Kediri
Malang
Surabaya
Madura
Probolinggo
Jember
Gunung Semeru
3,676 m
Bali
Denpasar
Gunung Agung
3,142 m
Mataram
Lombok
Sumbawa
Moyo I.
Kangean Is.
Lesser
IND
Sumba
Longitude East of Greenwich
Below Sea Lev.
Sea Level
200
700
500
1,600
1,000
3,300
1,500
5,000
2,000
6,500
4,000
13,000
6,000 m.
19,700 ft.

Southeastern Asia

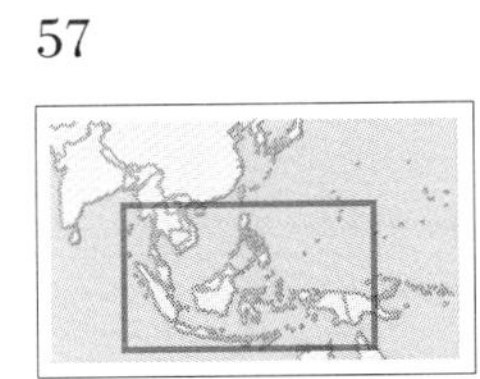

Australia, New Zealand - Physical

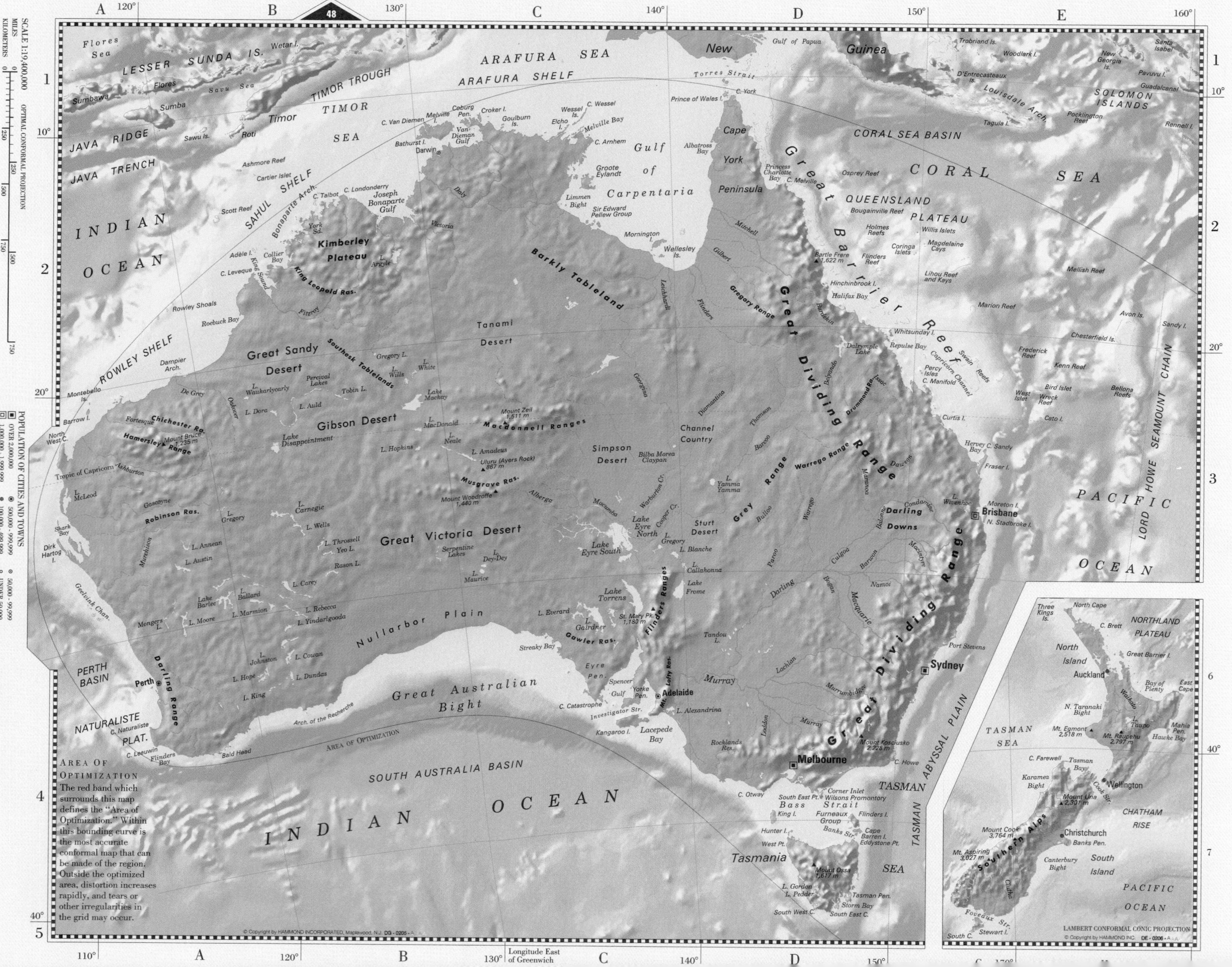

Australia, New Zealand - Political

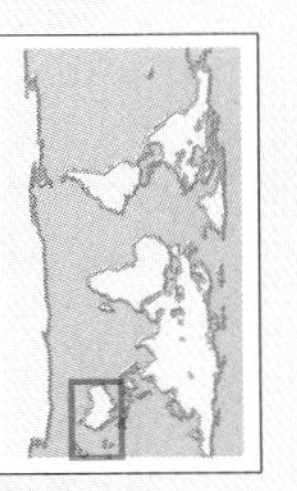

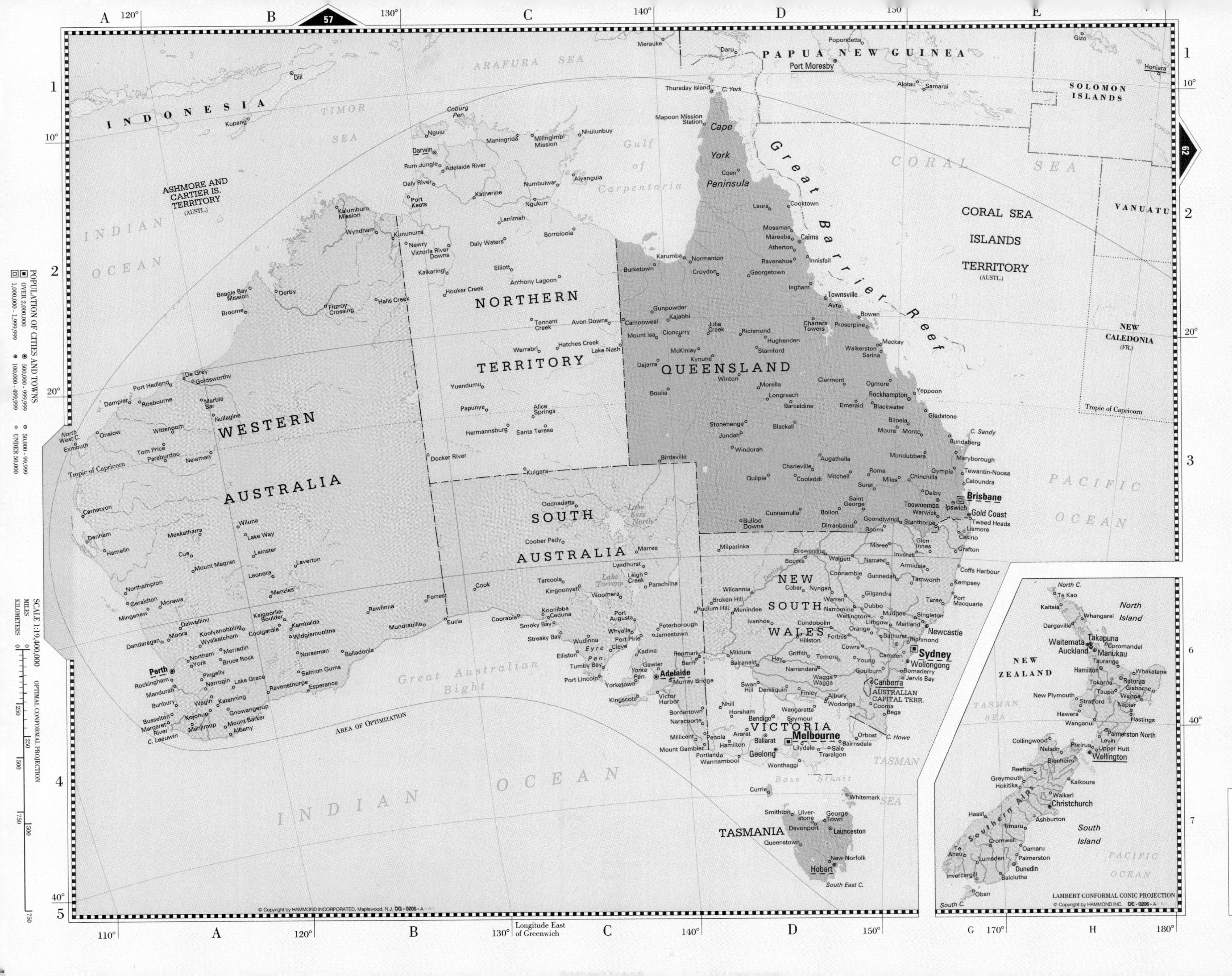

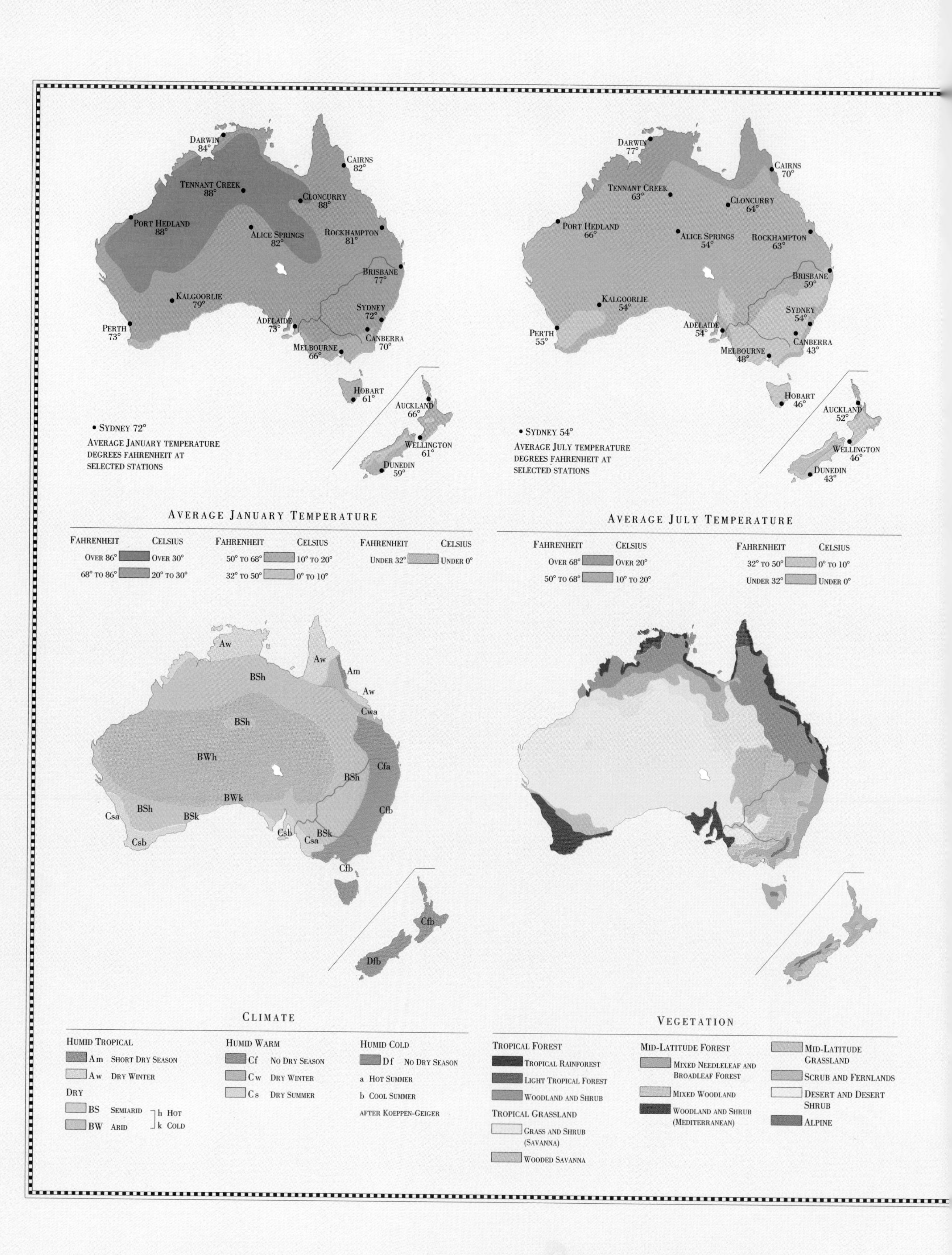

Darwin 84°
Cairns 82°
Tennant Creek 88°
Cloncurry 88°
Port Hedland 88°
Alice Springs 82°
Rockhampton 81°
Brisbane 77°
Kalgoorlie 79°
Sydney 72°
Perth 73°
Adelaide 73°
Canberra 70°
Melbourne 66°
Hobart 61°
Auckland 66°
Wellington 61°
Dunedin 59°
• Sydney 72°
Average January temperature degrees Fahrenheit at selected stations
Darwin 77°
Cairns 70°
Tennant Creek 63°
Cloncurry 64°
Port Hedland 66°
Alice Springs 54°
Rockhampton 63°
Brisbane 59°
Kalgoorlie 54°
Sydney 54°
Perth 55°
Adelaide 54°
Canberra 43°
Melbourne 48°
Hobart 46°
Auckland 52°
Wellington 46°
Dunedin 43°
• Sydney 54°
Average July temperature degrees Fahrenheit at selected stations
Average January Temperature
Fahrenheit Celsius
Over 86° Over 30°
68° to 86° 20° to 30°
50° to 68° 10° to 20°
32° to 50° 0° to 10°
Under 32° Under 0°
Average July Temperature
Fahrenheit Celsius
Over 68° Over 20°
50° to 68° 10° to 20°
32° to 50° 0° to 10°
Under 32° Under 0°
Aw
Aw
Am
Aw
BSh
Cwa
BSh
BWh
Cfa
BSh
BWk
Cfb
Csa
BSh
BSk
Csb
Csa
BSk
Csb
Cfb
Cfb
Dfb
Climate
Humid Tropical
Am Short Dry Season
Aw Dry Winter
Dry
BS Semiarid
BW Arid
h Hot
k Cold
Humid Warm
Cf No Dry Season
Cw Dry Winter
Cs Dry Summer
Humid Cold
Df No Dry Season
a Hot Summer
b Cool Summer
after Koeppen-Geiger
Vegetation
Tropical Forest
Tropical Rainforest
Light Tropical Forest
Woodland and Shrub
Tropical Grassland
Grass and Shrub (Savanna)
Wooded Savanna
Mid-Latitude Forest
Mixed Needleleaf and Broadleaf Forest
Mixed Woodland
Woodland and Shrub (Mediterranean)
Mid-Latitude Grassland
Scrub and Fernlands
Desert and Desert Shrub
Alpine

Australia, New Zealand - Comparisons

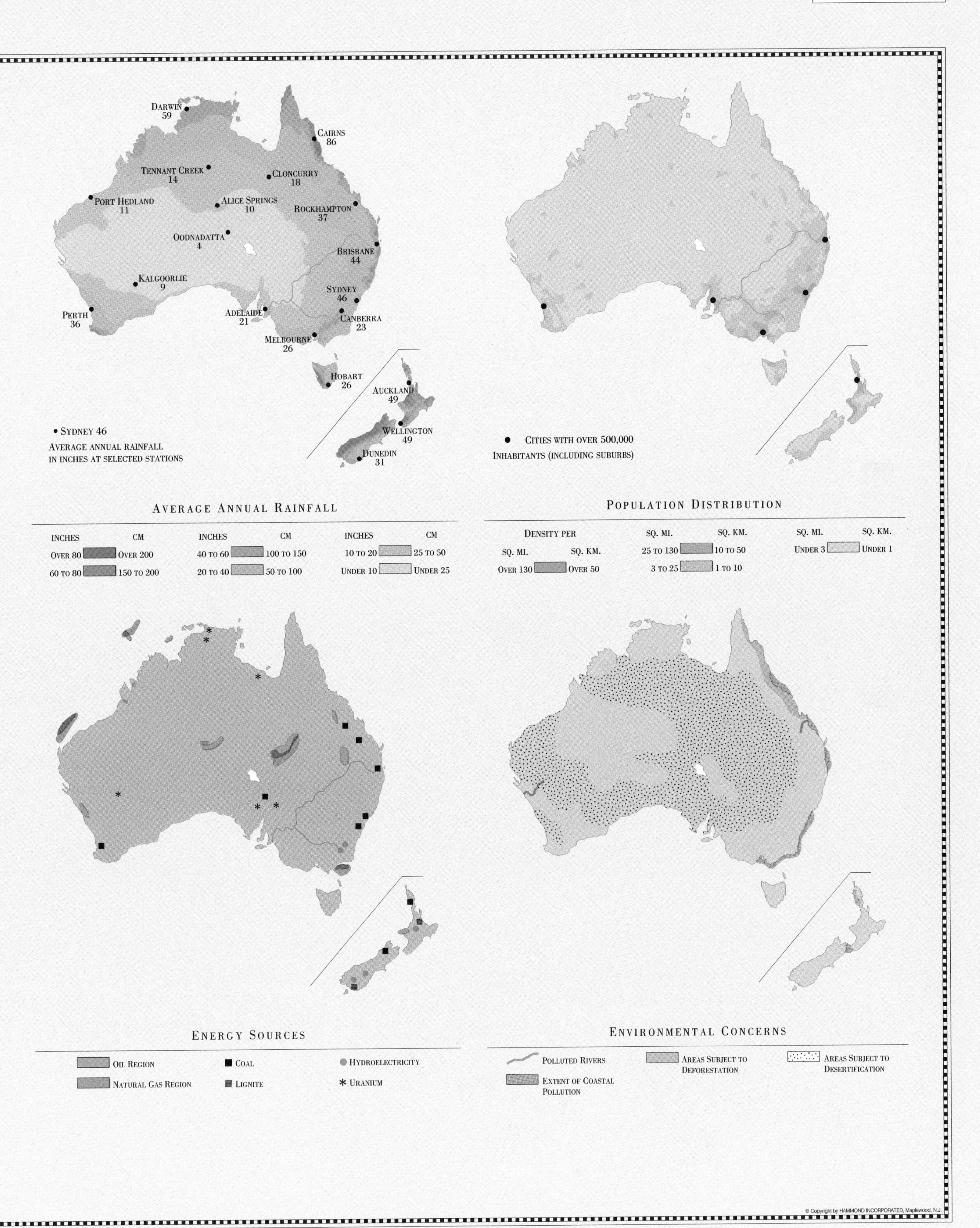

CHINA
Changsha
Nanchang
Jingdezhen
Ningbo
Wenzhou
Fuzhou
Xiamen
Guangzhou
Shantou
Kaohsiung
Taichung
Taipei
Tainan
Victoria
HONG KONG
(U.K.)
MACAU
(PORT.)
Macau
TAIWAN
EAST CHINA SEA
RYUKYU IS.
JAPAN
Kyūshū
Osumi Is.
Tokara Is.
Amami Is.
Okinawa Is.
Naha
Daito Is.
Sakishima Is.
Tori-Shima
(JAPAN)
Mukoshima Is.
Chichishima Is.
Hahashima Is.
Ogasawara
BONIN IS.
(JAPAN)
VOLCANO IS.
(JAPAN)
Iwo Jima
Minamiiō
Tropic of Cancer
Minami-Tori-Shima
(JAPAN)
Okino-Tori-Shima
(JAPAN)
Bashi Channel
Luzon Strait
Itbayat I.
Batan Is.
Calayan I.
Babuyan Is.
SOUTH CHINA SEA
PHILIPPINE SEA
Luzon
Laoag
Vigan
Dagupan
Baguio
Mt. Pinatubo
1,759 m
Cabanatuan
Manila
Quezon City
Lucena
Batangas
Mindoro
Catanduanes
Naga
Legazpi
Masbate
Samar
Panay
Iloilo
Bacolod
Cebu
Tacloban
Leyte
Bohol
Negros
Palawan
PHILIPPINES
Sulu Sea
Butuan
Mindanao
Cagayan de Oro
Davao
Zamboanga
Basilan
General Santos
Moro Gulf
Sandakan
Kudat
MALAYSIA
Sabah
Tawau
Sulu Archipelago
CELEBES SEA
Tarakan
Borneo
Talaud Is.
Sangihe Is.
Manado
Gorontalo
Gulf of Tomini
Morotai
Halmahera
Ternate
Samarinda
Palu
Celebes
Makassar Strait
Molucca Sea
Sula Is.
Obi
Misool
Waigeo
Sorong
Manokwari
Schouten Is.
Yapen
Ceram
Ceram Sea
Fakfak
Ambon
Buru
Kendari
Butung
Muna
Ujung Pandang
Gulf of Bone
Kabaena
INDONESIA
Salayar
BANDA SEA
Kai Is.
Aru Is.
Tanimbar Is.
FLORES SEA
Flores
Alor
Wetar
Ruteng
Sumbawa
Sumba
Savu Sea
Dili
Timor
Kupang
Leti Is.
Babar Is.
ARAFURA SEA
Timor Sea
Equator
Jayapura
Vanimo
Aitape
Wewak
Puncak Jaya
5,030 m
Maoke Mts.
New Guinea
Mt. Wilhelm
4,509 m
Mt. Hagen
Madang
Goroka
Kundiawa
Bulolo
Lae
Wau
PAPUA NEW GUINEA
Kolepom
Merauke
Daru
Gulf of Papua
Port Moresby
Popondetta
Torres Strait
C. York
Admiralty Islands
Manus
Lorengau
Mussau
St. Matthias Group
Ningingo Is.
BISMARCK ARCHIPELAGO
Bismarck Sea
Kavieng
New Ireland
New Hanover
Namatanai
Lyra Reef
Nuguria Is.
Karkar I.
Umboi
Rabaul
New Britain
Kimbe
Nissan I.
Buka
Bougainville
Kieta
Tulin Is.
Tauu Is.
Nukumanu Atoll
Ontong Java
Choiseul
Shortland I.
Arawa
Solomon Sea
Trobriand Is.
Woodlark I.
D'Entrecasteaux Is.
Normanby
Esa'ala
Alotau
Samarai
Tagula I.
Rossel I.
Louisiade Arch.
Milne Bay
Gizo
New Georgia Is.
Santa Isabel
Buala
Malaita
Auki
Honiara
Guadalcanal
Pocklington Reef
Kirakira
San Cristobal
Rennell I.
SOLOMON ISLANDS
Reef Is.
Lata
Ndende
Utupua
Vanikoro
SANTA CRUZ IS.
Duff Is.
Farallon de Pajaros
Maug Is.
Asuncion
Agrihan
Pagan
Alamagan
Guguan
Sarigan
Farallon de Medinilla
Anathan
NORTHERN MARIANAS
Saipan
Capitol Hill
Tinian
Aguijan
Rota
(U.S.)
Agaña
Guam
(U.S.)
Micronesia
Ulithi
Colonia
Yap Is.
Ngulu
Kavangel Is.
Babelthuap
Koror
PALAU
Sonsorol Is.
Sorol
Faraulep
Gaferut
Namonuito
Hall Is.
West Fayu
Pikelot
Olimarao
Woleai
Ifalik
Elato
Lamotrek
Eauripik
Pulap
Moen
Truk Is.
Puluwat
Oroluk
Senyavin Is.
Kolonia
Pohnpei
Ant
Mokil
Pingelap
Ngatik
Lelu
Kosrae
CAROLINE ISLANDS
Etal
Satawan
Lukunor
Nukuoro
FEDERATED STATES OF MICRONESIA
Kapingamarangi
Wake I.
(U.S.)
NORTH P
Enewetak
Bikini
Rongelap
Rongerik
Bikar
Utirik
Ailuk
Wotje
MARSHALL ISLANDS
Ujelang
Wotho
Kwajalein
Ujae
Lae
Erikub
RATAK CHAIN
RALIK CHAIN
Maloelap
Aur
Namu
Ailinglapalap
Majuro
Arno
Jaluit
Mili
Namorik
Ebon
Makin
Butaritari
Abaiang
Tarawa
Bairiki
Birkenebeu
Maiana
Abemama
Kuria
Aranuka
GILBERT ISLANDS
Banaba
Tabiang
Nonouti
Utiroa
Tabiteuea
Beru
Nikunau
Onotoa
Tamana
Arorae
NAURU
K
Melanesia
Lolua
Nanumea
Niutao
Nanumanga
Nui
Vaitupu
Nukufetau
Funafuti
Funafuti
Nukulaelae
TUVALU
Niulakita
Ahau
Rotuma I.
WALLIS & FUTUNA
(FR.)
Futuna
Torres Is.
Banks Is.
VANUATU
Espiritu Santo
Tabwemasana 1,879 m
Aoba
Maewo
Luganville
Pentecost
Norsup
Ambrym
Malekula
Epi
Shepherd Is.
Vila
Efate
NEW HEBRIDES
Erromango
Isangel
Tanna
Aneityum
NEW CALEDONIA
(FR.)
Chesterfield Is.
Koumac
Hienghène
LOYALTY IS.
Mont Panié 1,628 m
Wé
Thio
Humboldt 1,618 m
New Caledonia
Bourail
Nouméa
Ile des Pins
Bellona Reefs
FIJI
Vanua Levu
Yasawa Group
Lambasa
Savusavu
Lautoka
Nadi
Viti Levu
Suva
Vunisea
Kadavu
Moala Group
Lau
International Date Line
CORAL SEA
Great Barrier Reef
INDIAN OCEAN
Melville I.
Darwin
Bonaparte Arch.
Pine Creek
Katherine
Gulf of Carpentaria
Cape York Peninsula
Coen
Cooktown
Cairns
Wyndham
Daly Waters
Kimberley Plateau
Normanton
Townsville
Halls Creek
Broome
Tennant Creek
Camooweal
Bowen
Mackay
Cloncurry
Hughenden
Great Sandy Desert
Port Hedland
Marble Bar
Roebourne
Boulia
Clermont
Rockhampton
AUSTRALIA
Longreach
Barcaldine
Emerald
Exmouth
Onslow
Tropic of Capricorn
Mt. Bruce
1,235 m
Alice Springs
Bundaberg
Gibson Desert
Uluru (Ayers Rock)
867 m
Musgrave Ranges
Birdsville
Charleville
Roma
Gympie
Brisbane
Gold Coast
Toowoomba
Lismore
Great Dividing Range
Carnarvon
Wiluna
Oodnadatta
Cunnamulla
St. George
Grafton
Meekatharra
Great Victoria Desert
Coober Pedy
Marree
Moree
Armidale
Bourke
Tamworth
Port Macquarie
Leonora
Cobar
Dubbo
Newcastle
Northampton
Geraldton
Nullarbor Plain
Woomera
Broken Hill
Orange
Lithgow
Sydney
Kalgoorlie-Boulder
Port Augusta
Port Pirie
Whyalla
Wollongong
Merredin
Norseman
Great Australian Bight
Streaky Bay
Mildura
Cootamundra
Wagga Wagga
Canberra
Perth
Northam
Port Lincoln
Adelaide
Murray Bridge
Albury
Mt. Kosciusko
2,228 m
SOUTH
TASMAN SEA
Kingston
Norfolk I.
(AUSTL.)
Lord Howe I.
(AUSTL.)
Raoul I.
Macauley I.
Curtis I.
KERMADEC IS.
(N.Z.)
Three Kings Is.
North Cape
Whangarei
NEW ZEALAND
Auckland
Manukau
Tauranga
Hamilton
Rotorua
North I.
Longitude East of Greenwich
110°
120°
130°
140°
150°
160°
170°
180°
A
B
C
D
E
F
G
55
59
Below Sea Lev.
Sea Level
200
700
500
1,600
1,000
3,300
1,500
5,000
2,000
6,500
4,000
13,000
6,000 m.
19,700 ft.

Pacific Ocean

Africa - Physical

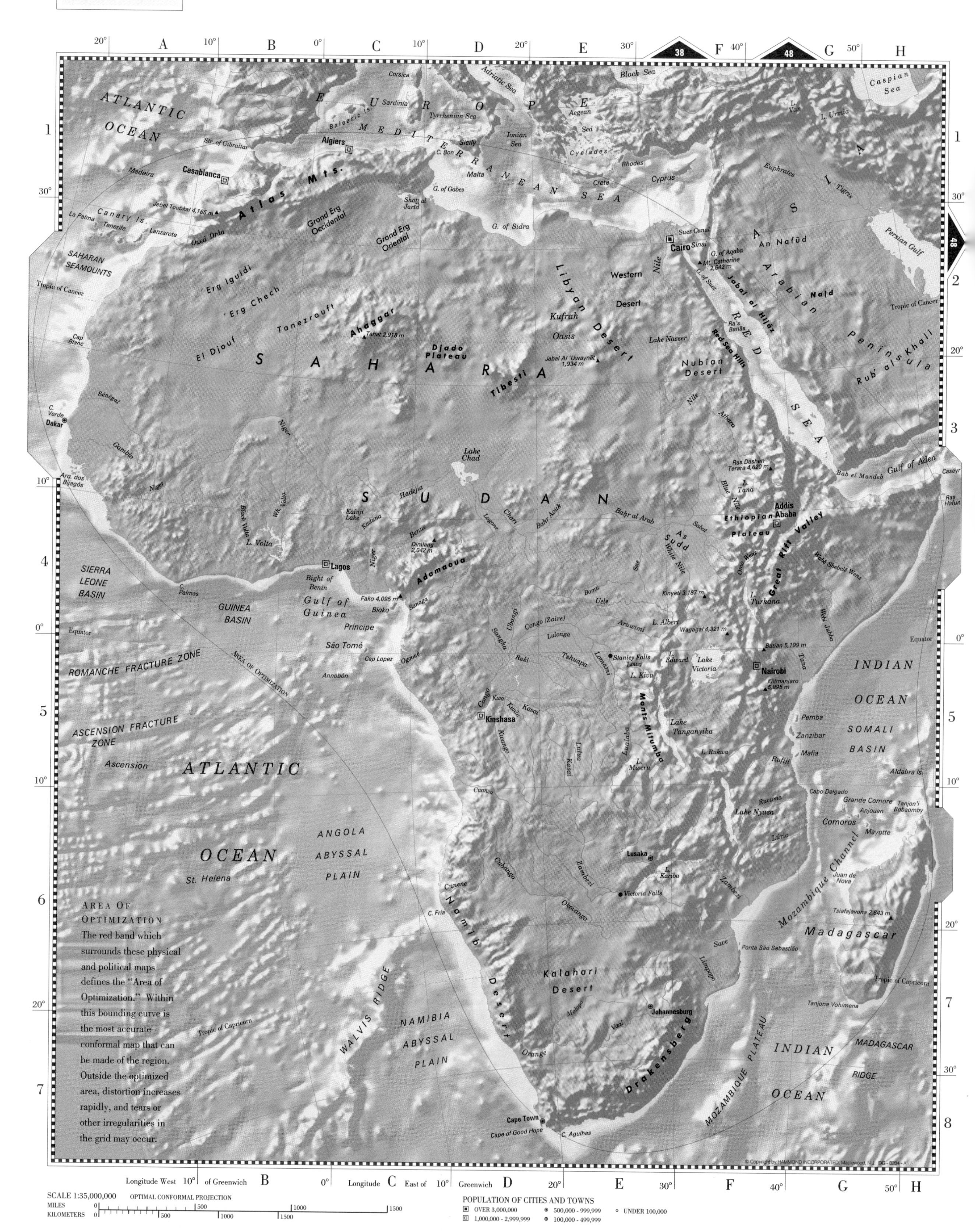

SCALE 1:35,000,000 OPTIMAL CONFORMAL PROJECTION

MILES 0 500 1000

KILOMETERS 0 500 1000 1500

POPULATION OF CITIES AND TOWNS

- OVER 3,000,000
- 1,000,000 - 2,999,999
- 500,000 - 999,999
- 100,000 - 499,999
- UNDER 100,000

Africa - Political

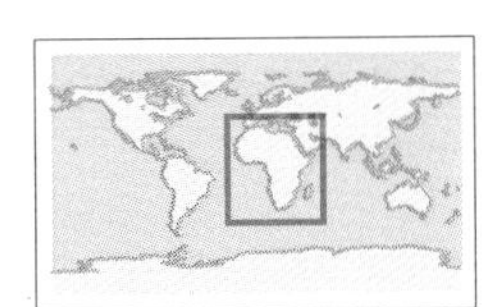

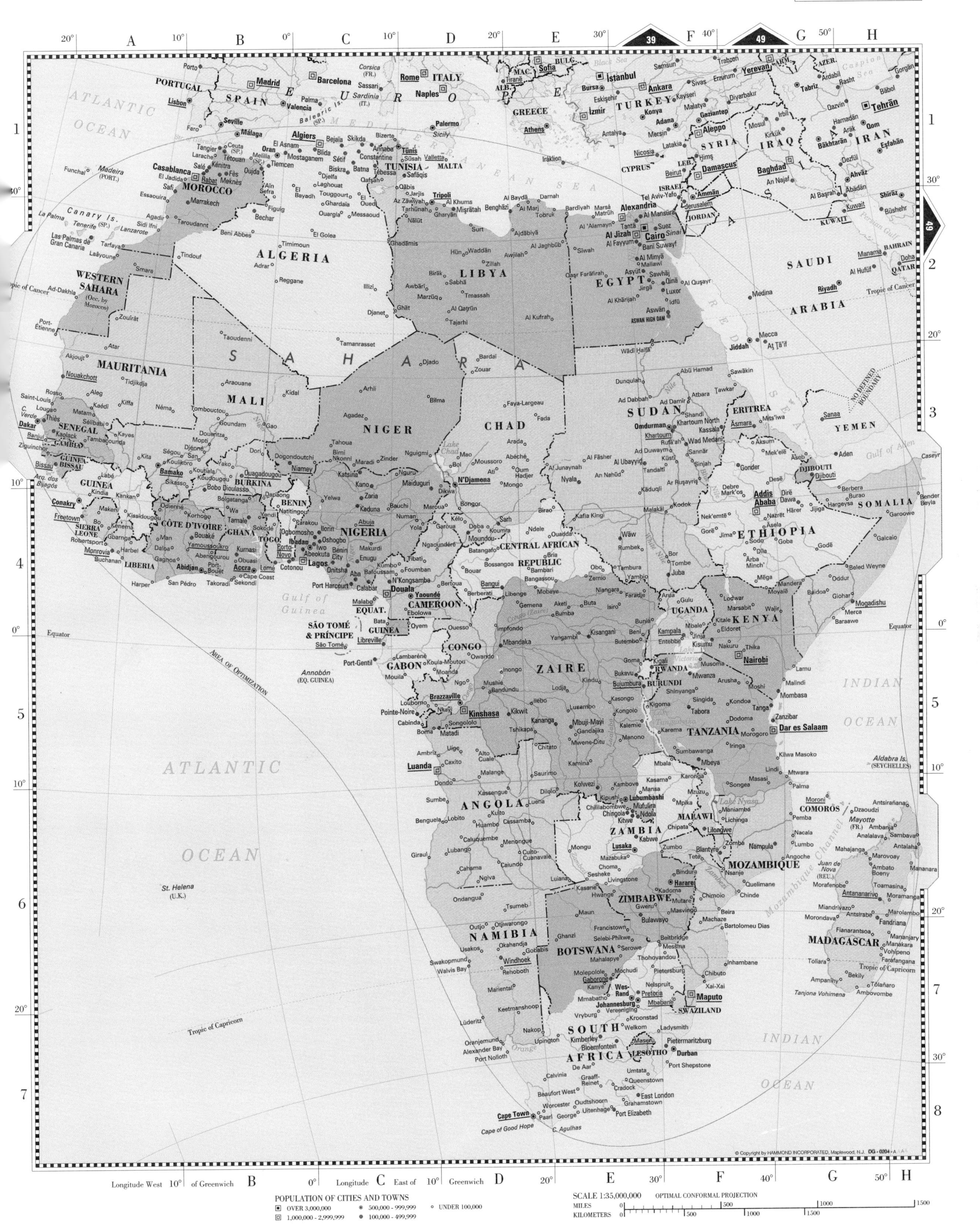

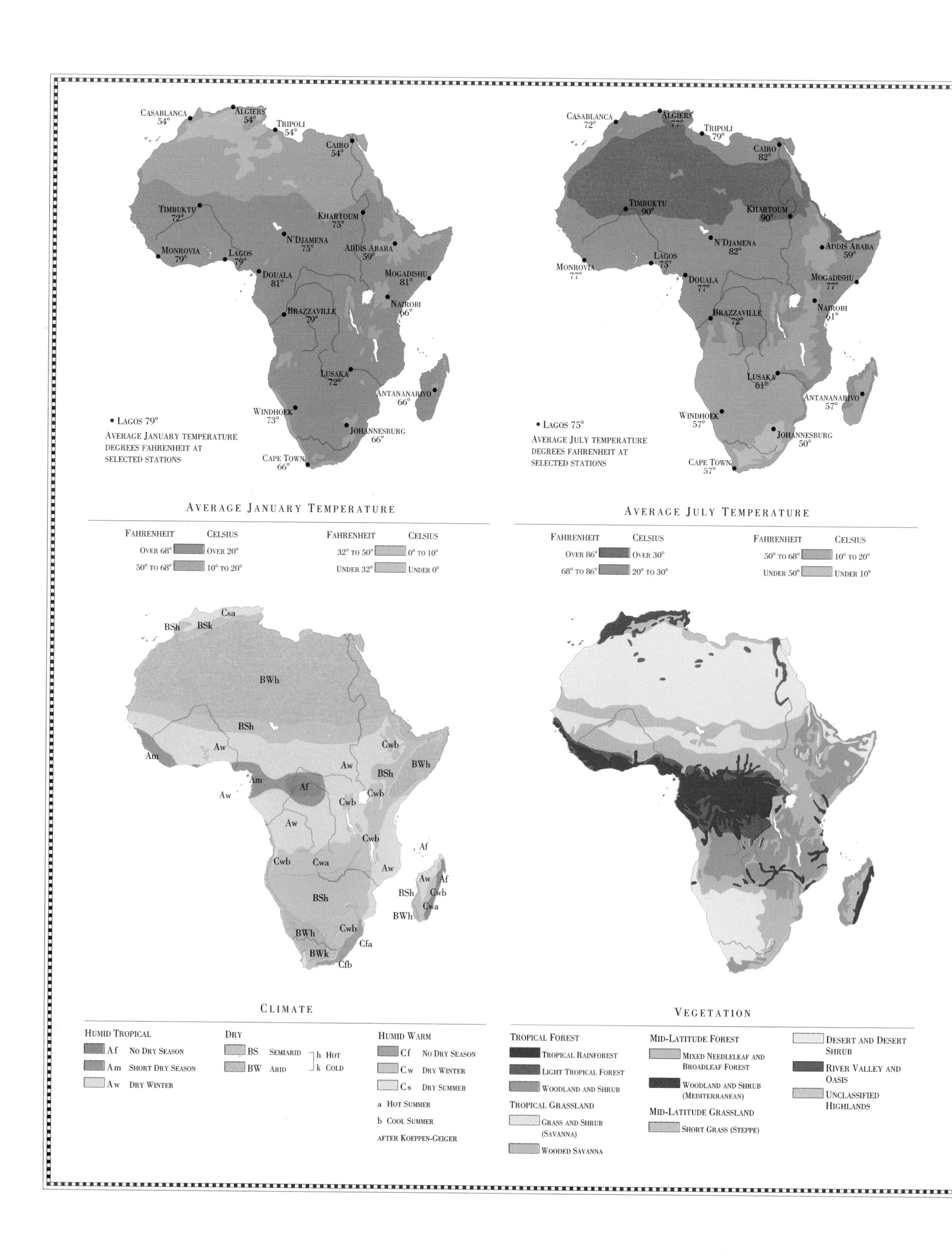
Casablanca 54°
Algiers 54°
Tripoli 54°
Cairo 54°
Timbuktu 72°
Khartoum 75°
N'Djamena 75°
Addis Ababa 59°
Monrovia 79°
Lagos 79°
Douala 81°
Mogadishu 81°
Nairobi 66°
Brazzaville 79°
Lusaka 72°
Antananarivo 66°
Windhoek 73°
Johannesburg 66°
Cape Town 66°
• Lagos 79°
Average January temperature degrees Fahrenheit at selected stations
Average January Temperature
Fahrenheit Celsius
Over 68° Over 20°
50° to 68° 10° to 20°
32° to 50° 0° to 10°
Under 32° Under 0°
Casablanca 72°
Algiers 77°
Tripoli 79°
Cairo 82°
Timbuktu 90°
Khartoum 90°
N'Djamena 82°
Addis Ababa 59°
Monrovia 77°
Lagos 75°
Douala 77°
Mogadishu 77°
Nairobi 61°
Brazzaville 72°
Lusaka 61°
Antananarivo 57°
Windhoek 57°
Johannesburg 50°
Cape Town 57°
• Lagos 75°
Average July temperature degrees Fahrenheit at selected stations
Average July Temperature
Fahrenheit Celsius
Over 86° Over 30°
68° to 86° 20° to 30°
50° to 68° 10° to 20°
Under 50° Under 10°
Csa
BSh
BSk
BWh
BSh
Aw
Am
Cwb
BWh
Aw
BSh
Am
Af
Cwb
Aw
Cwb
Aw
Cwb
Af
Cwb
Cwa
Aw
Aw
Af
BSh
BSh
Cwb
Cwa
BWh
BWh
Cwb
Cfa
BWk
Cfb
Climate
Humid Tropical
Af No Dry Season
Am Short Dry Season
Aw Dry Winter
Dry
BS Semiarid
BW Arid
h Hot
k Cold
Humid Warm
Cf No Dry Season
Cw Dry Winter
Cs Dry Summer
a Hot Summer
b Cool Summer
after Koeppen-Geiger
Vegetation
Tropical Forest
Tropical Rainforest
Light Tropical Forest
Woodland and Shrub
Tropical Grassland
Grass and Shrub (Savanna)
Wooded Savanna
Mid-Latitude Forest
Mixed Needleleaf and Broadleaf Forest
Woodland and Shrub (Mediterranean)
Mid-Latitude Grassland
Short Grass (Steppe)
Desert and Desert Shrub
River Valley and Oasis
Unclassified Highlands

Africa - Comparisons

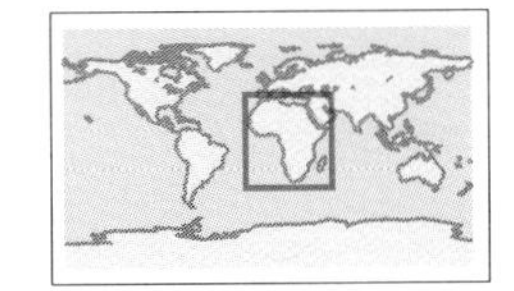

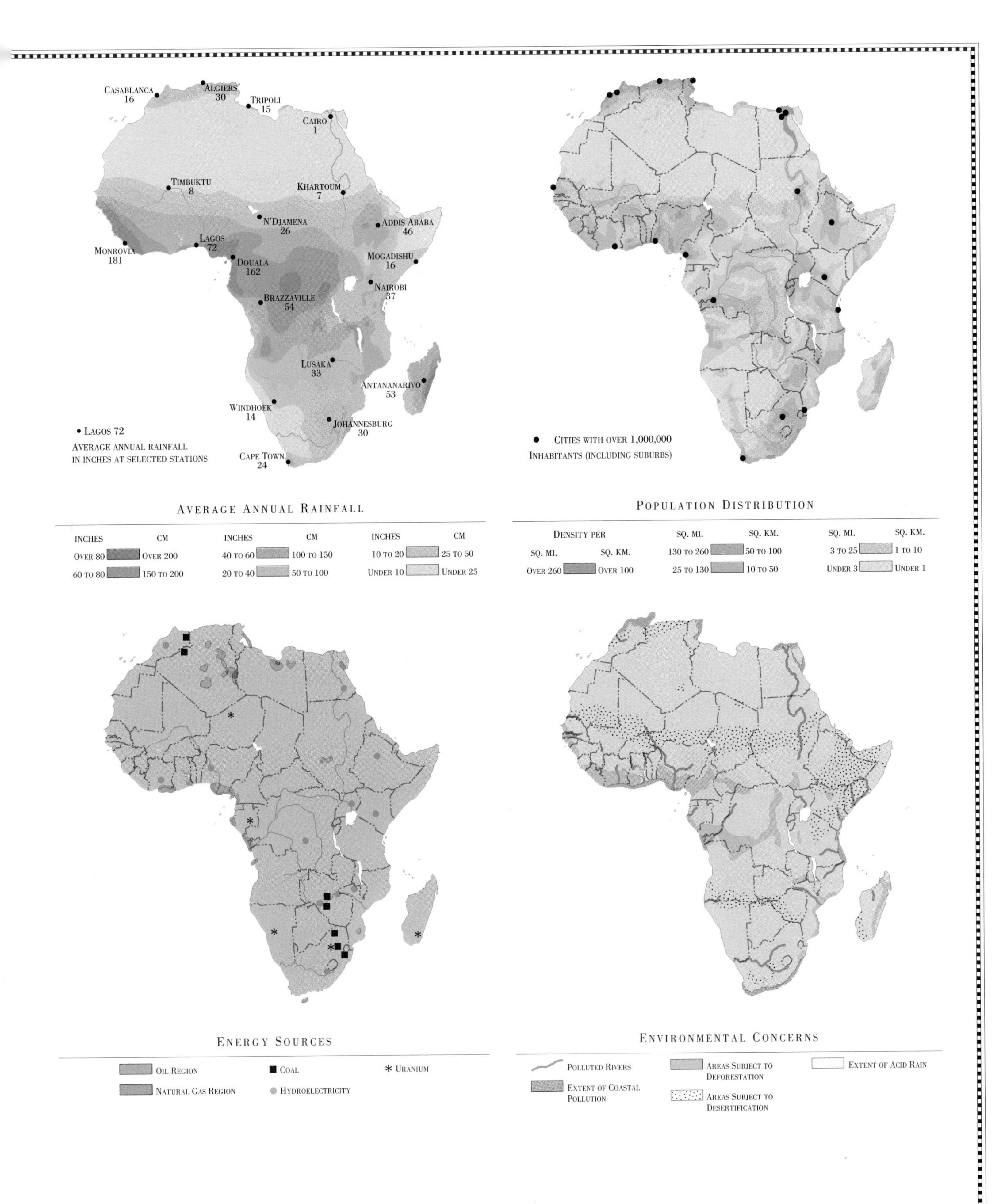

ATLANTIC OCEAN
Mediterranean Sea
Gulf of Guinea
Bight of Benin
MOROCCO
ALGERIA
TUNISIA
WESTERN SAHARA
(occ. by Morocco)
MAURITANIA
MALI
NIGER
SENEGAL
GAMBIA
GUINEA-BISSAU
GUINEA
SIERRA LEONE
LIBERIA
CÔTE D'IVOIRE
BURKINA
GHANA
TOGO
BENIN
NIGERIA
CAMEROON
EQUATORIAL GUINEA
SÃO TOMÉ AND PRÍNCIPE
GABON
CONGO
SPAIN
MALTA
Canary Is.
(SP.)
Madeira
(PORT.)
Algiers
Tūnis
Tripoli
Rabat
Casablanca
Marrakech
Fès
Meknès
Oran
Constantine
Tangier
Nouakchott
Dakar
Banjul
Bissau
Conakry
Freetown
Monrovia
Bamako
Ouagadougou
Niamey
Abidjan
Yamoussoukro
Accra
Lomé
Porto-Novo
Cotonou
Lagos
Ibadan
Abuja
Kano
Zaria
Kaduna
N'Djamena
Douala
Yaoundé
Malabo
Libreville
São Tomé
Timbouctou
(Timbuktu)
Gao
Agadez
Atlas Saharien
Haut Atlas
Anti-Atlas
Grand Erg Occidental
Grand Erg Oriental
Ahaggar
Tanezrouft
Tropic of Cancer
Equator
El Djouf
Sahara
Aïr
Ténéré
Lake Chad
Ivory Coast
Gold Coast
Grain Coast
Longitude West of Greenwich
Longitude East of Greenwich
Below Sea Lev.
Sea Level
200 700
500 1,600
1,000 3,300
1,500 5,000
2,000 6,500
4,000 13,000
6,000 m. 19,700 ft.

Northern Africa

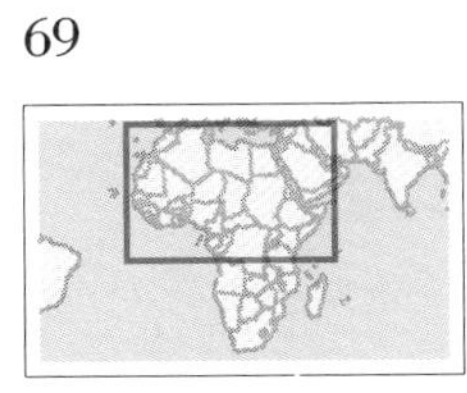

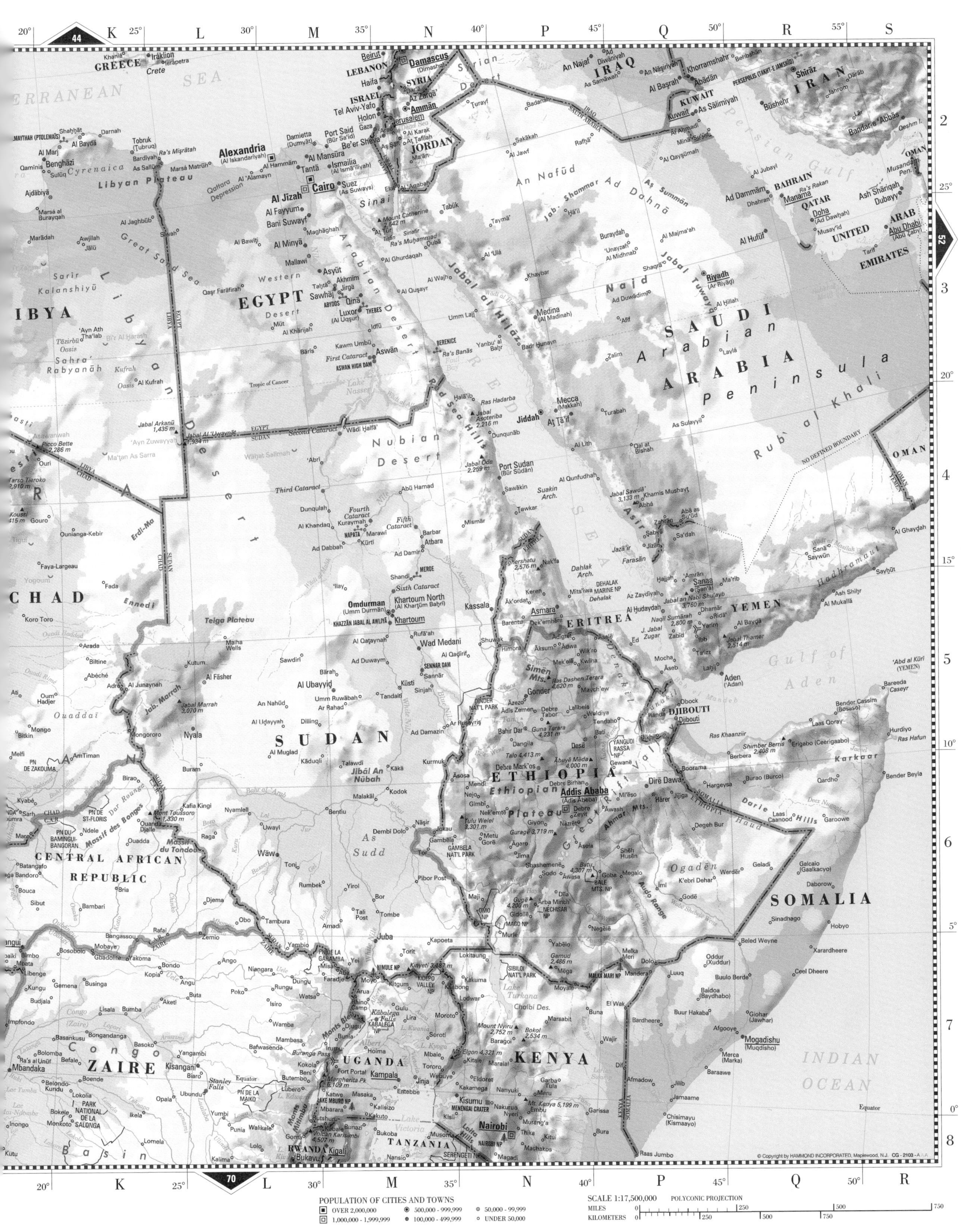

POPULATION OF CITIES AND TOWNS

▣ OVER 2,000,000	◉ 500,000 - 999,999	◎ 50,000 - 99,999
◻ 1,000,000 - 1,999,999	● 100,000 - 499,999	○ UNDER 50,000

SCALE 1:17,500,000 POLYCONIC PROJECTION

MILES 0 — 250 — 500 — 750

KILOMETERS 0 — 250 — 500 — 750

Southern Africa

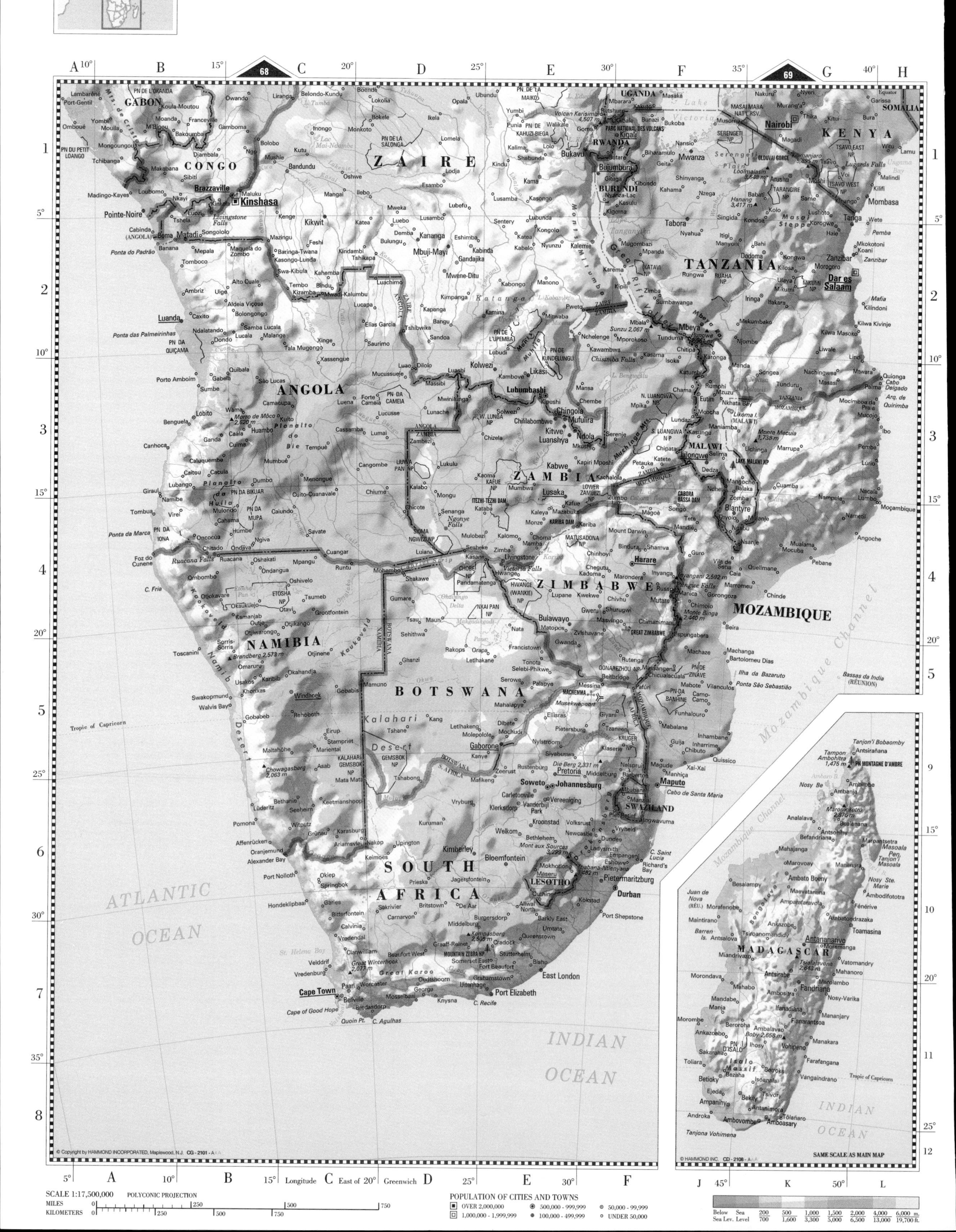

Arctic Regions, Antarctica

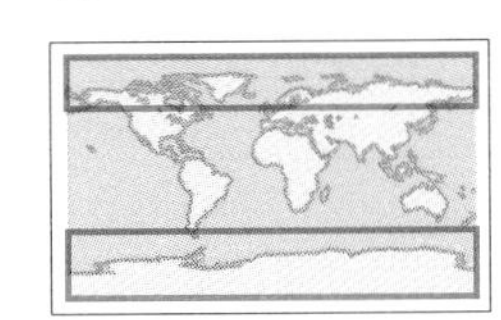

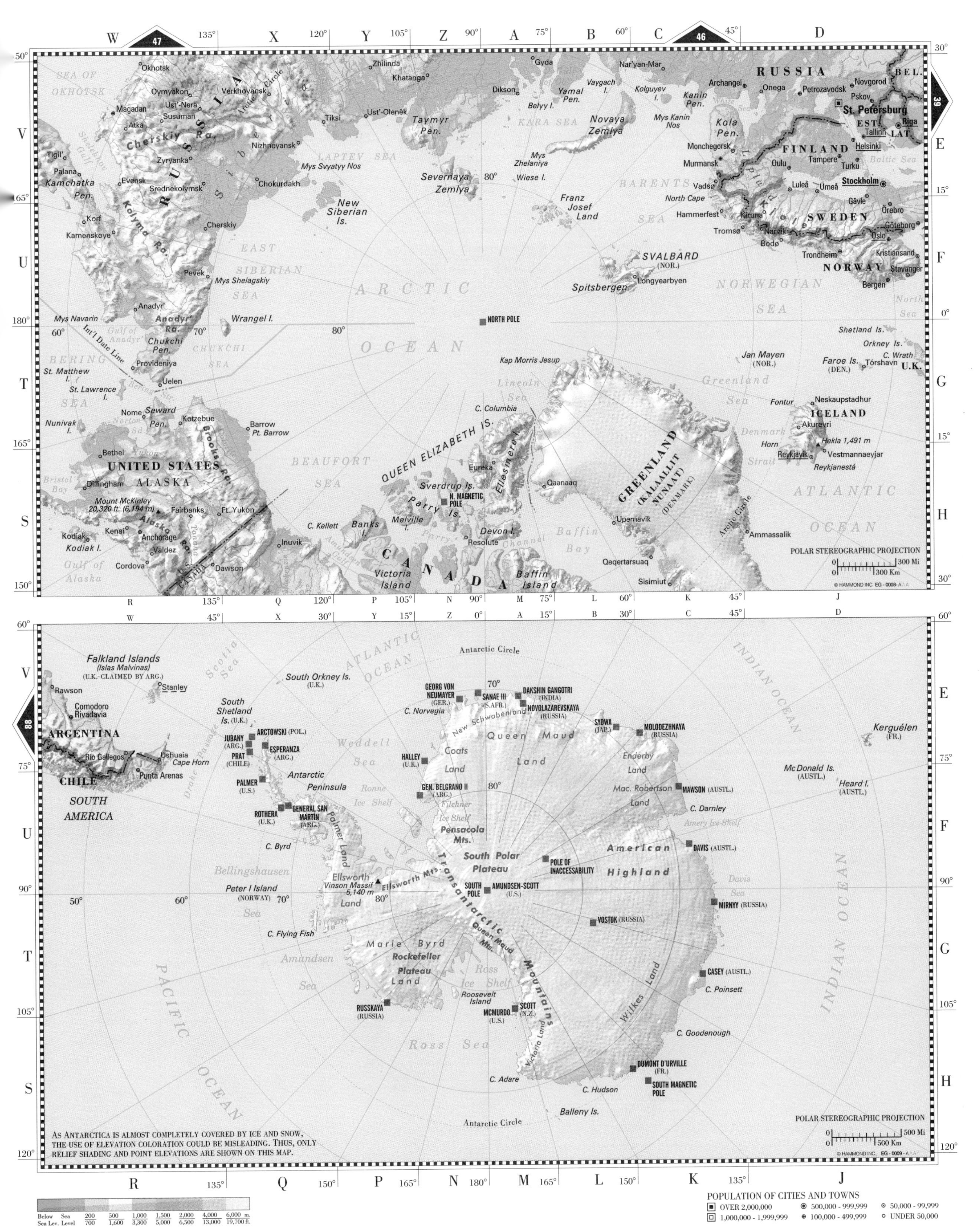

North America - Physical

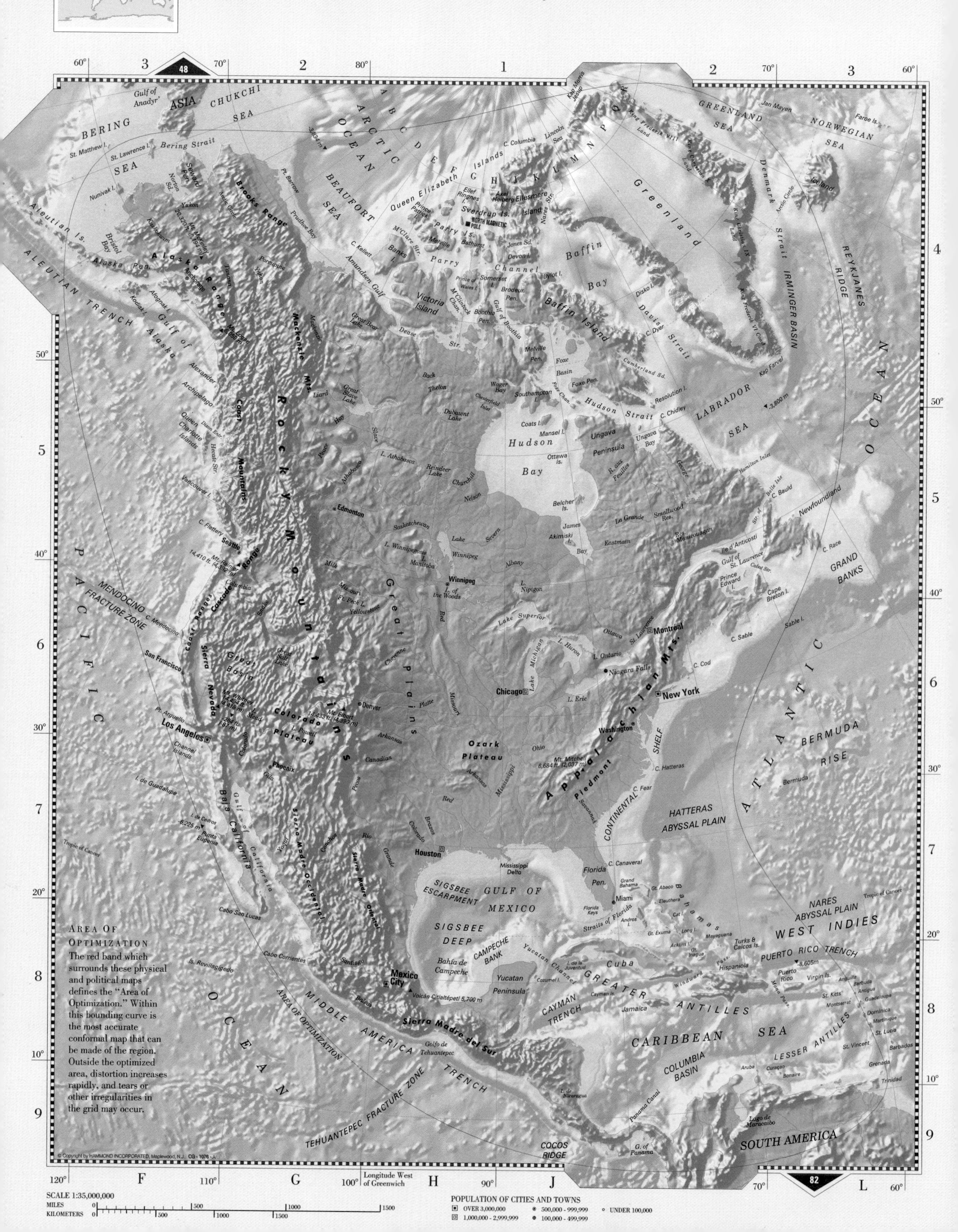

ARCTIC OCEAN
BEAUFORT SEA
CHUKCHI SEA
BERING SEA
Bering Strait
Gulf of Anadyr'
ASIA
GREENLAND SEA
NORWEGIAN SEA
Greenland
Baffin Bay
Baffin Island
Iceland
Jan Mayen
Faroe Is.
Denmark Strait
IRMINGER BASIN
REYKJANES RIDGE
Davis Strait
LABRADOR SEA
Hudson Bay
Hudson Strait
James Bay
Ungava Peninsula
Queen Elizabeth Islands
Ellesmere Island
Victoria Island
Banks I.
Brooks Range
Alaska Range
Aleutian Is.
ALEUTIAN TRENCH
Gulf of Alaska
Alaska Pen.
Mackenzie Mts.
Rocky Mountains
Coast Mountains
Cascade Range
Sierra Nevada
Great Basin
Colorado Plateau
Great Plains
Ozark Plateau
Appalachian Mts.
Piedmont
Great Slave Lake
Great Bear Lake
L. Athabasca
L. Winnipeg
Lake Superior
L. Michigan
L. Huron
L. Erie
L. Ontario
Edmonton
Winnipeg
Seattle
San Francisco
Los Angeles
Denver
Phoenix
Chicago
Montreal
New York
Washington
Houston
Miami
Mexico City
Newfoundland
Gulf of St. Lawrence
GRAND BANKS
ATLANTIC OCEAN
BERMUDA RISE
HATTERAS ABYSSAL PLAIN
CONTINENTAL SHELF
NARES ABYSSAL PLAIN
PUERTO RICO TRENCH
WEST INDIES
GULF OF MEXICO
SIGSBEE ESCARPMENT
SIGSBEE DEEP
CAMPECHE BANK
Yucatan Peninsula
Cuba
GREATER ANTILLES
LESSER ANTILLES
CARIBBEAN SEA
COLUMBIA BASIN
CAYMAN TRENCH
Sierra Madre Occidental
Sierra Madre Oriental
Sierra Madre del Sur
Baja California
Gulf of California
PACIFIC OCEAN
MENDOCINO FRACTURE ZONE
MIDDLE AMERICA TRENCH
TEHUANTEPEC FRACTURE ZONE
AREA OF OPTIMIZATION
COCOS RIDGE
SOUTH AMERICA
AREA OF OPTIMIZATION
The red band which surrounds these physical and political maps defines the "Area of Optimization." Within this bounding curve is the most accurate conformal map that can be made of the region. Outside the optimized area, distortion increases rapidly, and tears or other irregularities in the grid may occur.
© Copyright by HAMMOND INCORPORATED, Maplewood, N.J.
Longitude West of Greenwich
SCALE 1:35,000,000
MILES
KILOMETERS
POPULATION OF CITIES AND TOWNS
OVER 3,000,000
1,000,000 - 2,999,999
500,000 - 999,999
100,000 - 499,999
UNDER 100,000

North America - Political

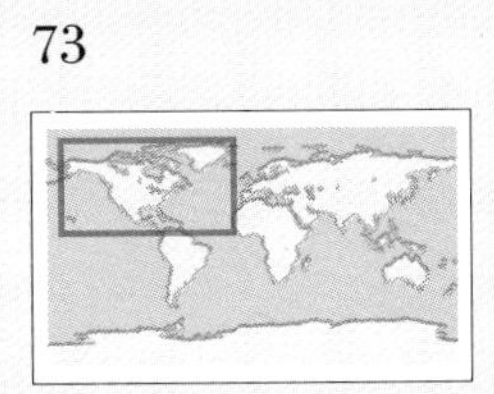

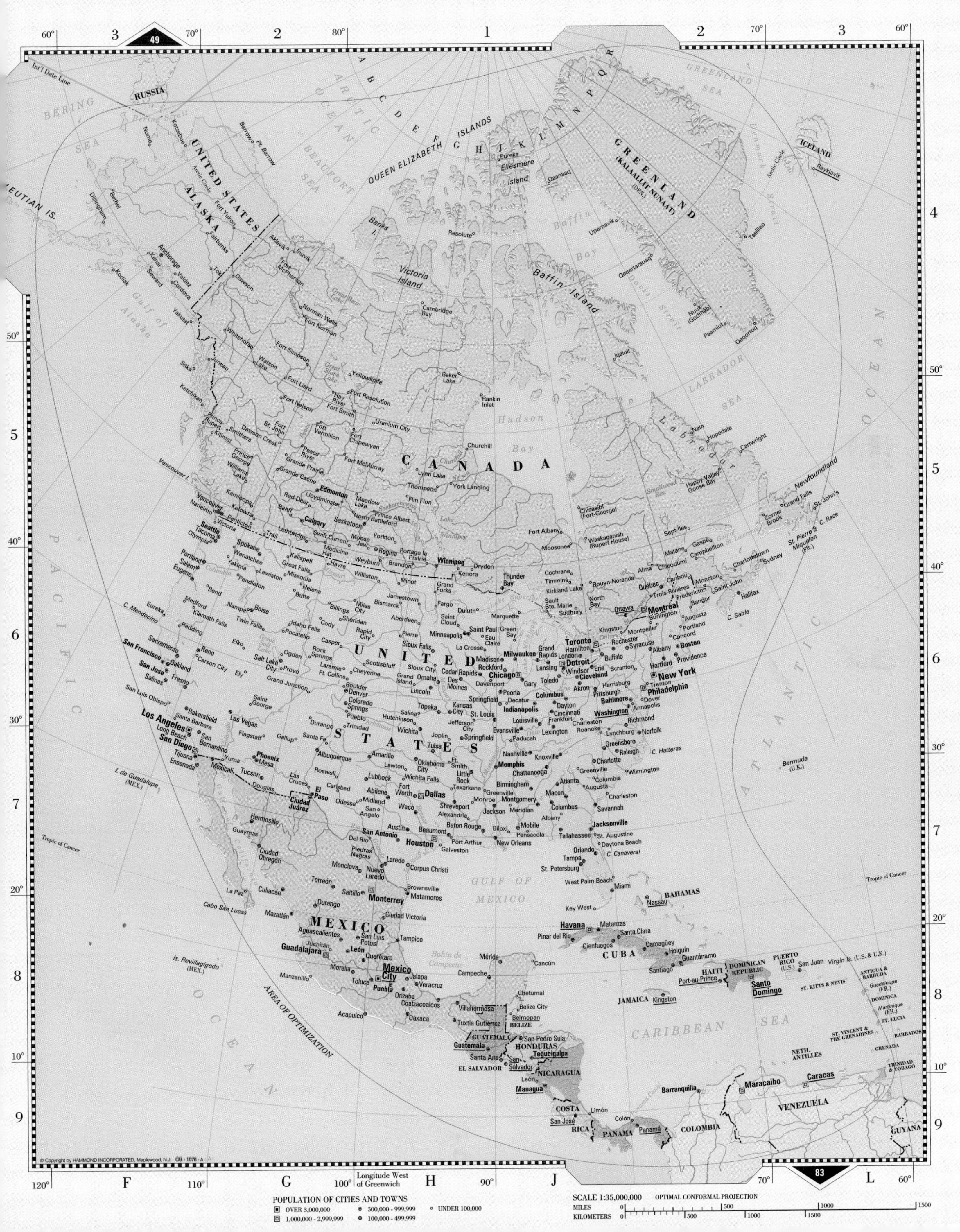

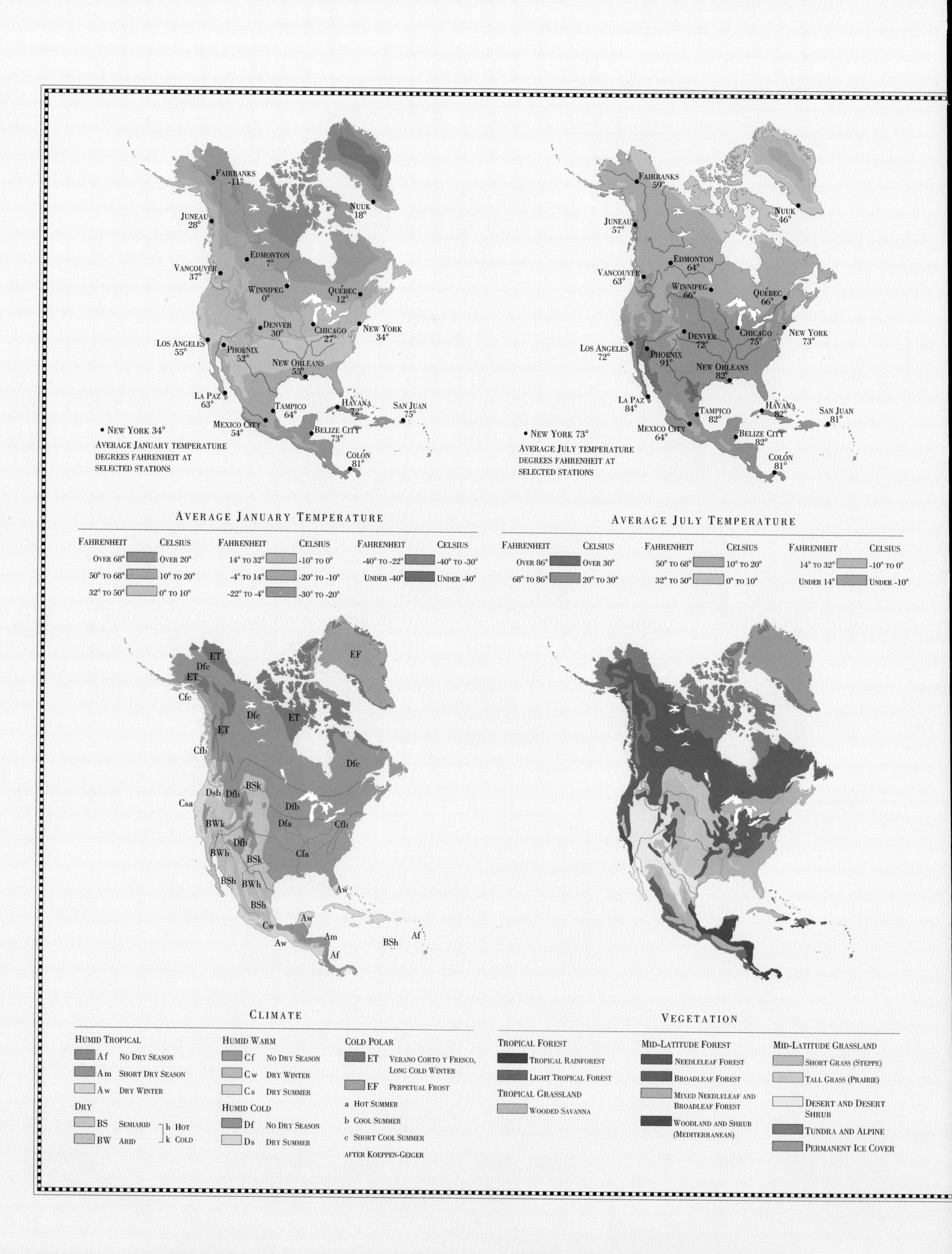

Fairbanks -11°
Juneau 28°
Nuuk 18°
Edmonton 7°
Vancouver 37°
Winnipeg 0°
Québec 12°
Denver 30°
Chicago 27°
New York 34°
Los Angeles 55°
Phoenix 52°
New Orleans 55°
La Paz 63°
Tampico 64°
Havana 72°
San Juan 75°
Mexico City 54°
Belize City 73°
Colón 81°
• New York 34°
Average January temperature degrees Fahrenheit at selected stations
Fairbanks 59°
Juneau 57°
Nuuk 46°
Edmonton 64°
Vancouver 63°
Winnipeg 66°
Québec 66°
Denver 72°
Chicago 75°
New York 73°
Los Angeles 72°
Phoenix 91°
New Orleans 82°
La Paz 84°
Tampico 82°
Havana 82°
San Juan 81°
Mexico City 64°
Belize City 82°
Colón 81°
• New York 73°
Average July temperature degrees Fahrenheit at selected stations
Average January Temperature
Fahrenheit Celsius
Over 68° Over 20°
50° to 68° 10° to 20°
32° to 50° 0° to 10°
14° to 32° -10° to 0°
-4° to 14° -20° to -10°
-22° to -4° -30° to -20°
-40° to -22° -40° to -30°
Under -40° Under -40°
Average July Temperature
Over 86° Over 30°
68° to 86° 20° to 30°
50° to 68° 10° to 20°
32° to 50° 0° to 10°
14° to 32° -10° to 0°
Under 14° Under -10°
ET
EF
Dfc
Cfc
Cfb
Csa
Dsb
Dfb
BSk
BWk
Dfa
Cfa
BWh
BSh
Aw
Cw
Am
Af
Climate
Humid Tropical
Af No Dry Season
Am Short Dry Season
Aw Dry Winter
Dry
BS Semiarid
BW Arid
h Hot
k Cold
Humid Warm
Cf No Dry Season
Cw Dry Winter
Cs Dry Summer
Humid Cold
Df No Dry Season
Ds Dry Summer
Cold Polar
ET Verano Corto y Fresco, Long Cold Winter
EF Perpetual Frost
a Hot Summer
b Cool Summer
c Short Cool Summer
after Koeppen-Geiger
Vegetation
Tropical Forest
Tropical Rainforest
Light Tropical Forest
Tropical Grassland
Wooded Savanna
Mid-Latitude Forest
Needleleaf Forest
Broadleaf Forest
Mixed Needleleaf and Broadleaf Forest
Woodland and Shrub (Mediterranean)
Mid-Latitude Grassland
Short Grass (Steppe)
Tall Grass (Prairie)
Desert and Desert Shrub
Tundra and Alpine
Permanent Ice Cover

North America - Comparisons

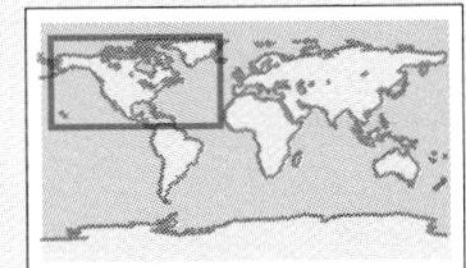

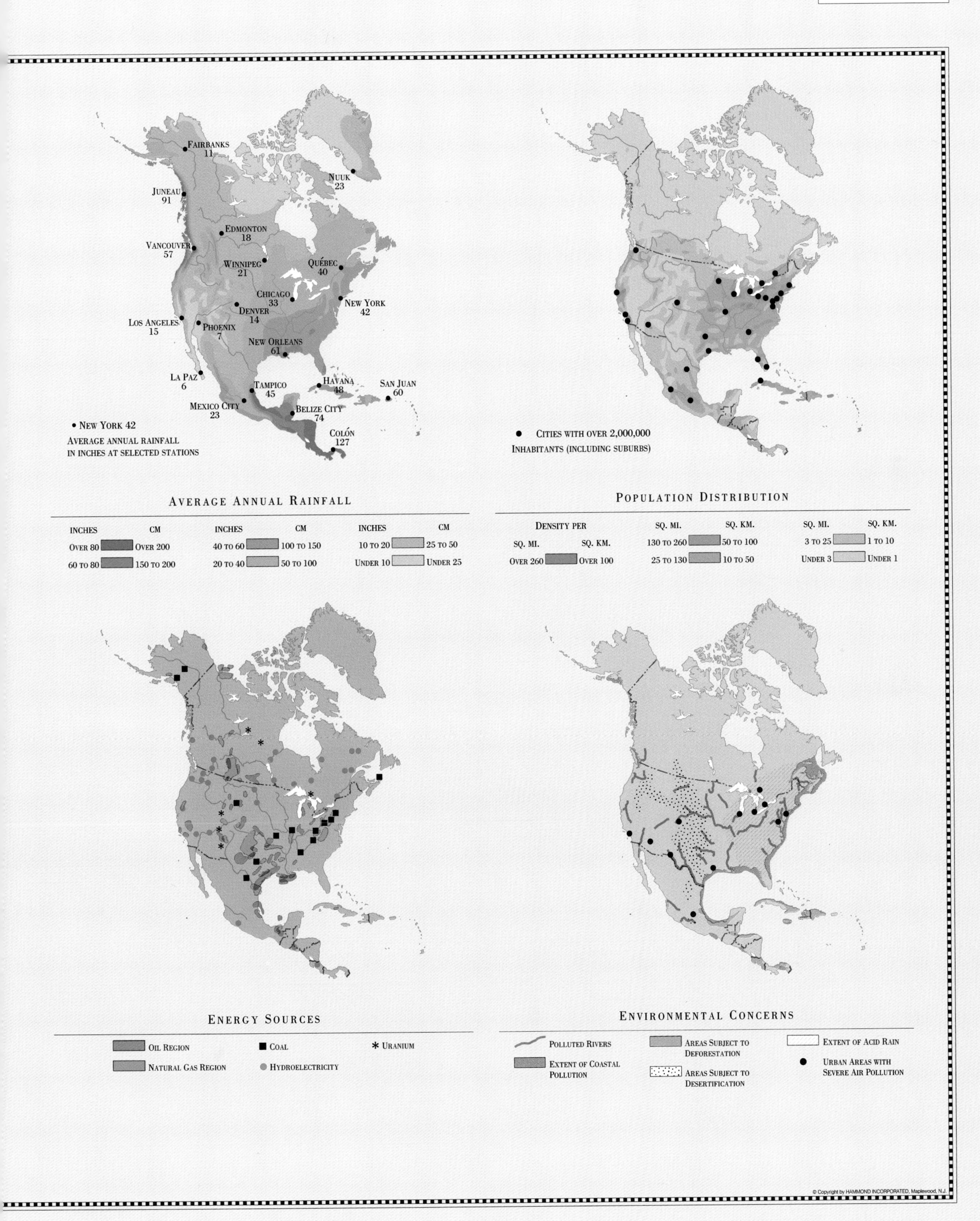

PACIFIC OCEAN
BRITISH COLUMBIA
ALBERTA
SASKATCHEWAN
WASHINGTON
MONTANA
NORTH DAKOTA
OREGON
IDAHO
SOUTH DAKOTA
WYOMING
NEBRASKA
NEVADA
UTAH
COLORADO
CALIFORNIA
ARIZONA
NEW MEXICO
TEXAS
SONORA
CHIHUAHUA
COAHUILA
NUEVO LEON
MEXICO
ZACATECAS
SAN LUIS POTOSÍ
JALISCO
GUANAJUATO
BAJA CAL. NORTE
CANADA
UNITED STATES
Great Basin
Great Salt Lake Desert
Painted Desert
Mojave Desert
Sierra Nevada
Coast Ranges
Rocky Mts.
Wasatch Ra.
Seattle
Portland
Salem
Spokane
Boise
Helena
Salt Lake City
Denver
Phoenix
Sacramento
San Francisco
Los Angeles
San Diego
Las Vegas
Reno
Albuquerque
Santa Fe
Cheyenne
Calgary
Regina
Vancouver
Victoria
Tijuana
Mexicali
Ciudad Juárez
El Paso
Tucson
Monterrey
Guadalajara
HAWAII
Kauai
Oahu
Molokai
Maui
Lanai
Kahoolawe
Hawaii
Niihau
Honolulu
Mauna Kea 13,796 ft. (4,205 m)
Mauna Loa 13,677 ft. (4,169 m)
Hilo
Kailua
Pahala
Ka Lae
PACIFIC OCEAN
100 Mi
100 Km
© HAMMOND INC. EG - 0003 - A
ALASKA
RUSSIA
ARCTIC OCEAN
CHUKCHI SEA
BERING SEA
Arctic Coastal Plain
Brooks Range
Alaska Range
Kuskokwim Mts.
Aleutian Ra.
Pt. Barrow
Barrow
Arctic Circle
Chukchi Pen.
Mys Dezhneva
Kotzebue
C. Prince of Wales
Nome
International Date Line
St. Lawrence Island
Norton Sound
St. Matthew I.
Nunivak I.
Bethel
Kuskokwim Bay
Dillingham
Bristol Bay
St. Paul I.
Pribilof Is.
St. George I.
Aleutian Islands
Umnak I.
Unalaska I.
Unimak I.
Fox Is.
Shumagin Is.
Kodiak I.
Afognak I.
Kodiak
Homer
Kenai
Seward
Anchorage
Palmer
Talkeetna
Mount McKinley 20,320 ft. (6,194 m)
DENALI NP
Fairbanks
Delta Junction
Tok
Fort Yukon
Glennallen
Valdez
Cordova
WRANGELL-ST. ELIAS NAT'L PARK
Mount Logan 6,050 m
C. St. Elias
Yakutat
Gulf of Alaska
GLACIER BAY NAT'L PARK
Juneau
Sitka
Petersburg
Wrangell
Ketchikan
Alexander Archipelago
C. Ommancy
Prince Rupert
Queen Charlotte Islands
Hecate Strait
Kitimat
YUKON TERRITORY
NORTHWEST TERRS.
BRITISH COLUMBIA
Mackenzie Mts.
Coast Mts.
Dawson
Whitehorse
Watson Lake
Fort Nelson
PACIFIC OCEAN
200 Mi
200 Km
© HAMMOND INC. EG - 0004 - A
BERING SEA
Aleutian Islands
Attu I.
Agattu I.
Near Is.
Kiska I.
Amchitka I.
Rat Is.
Tanaga I.
Andreanof Is.
Adak I.
Atka I.
Amlia I.
Seguam I.
Umnak I.
200 Mi
200 Km
© HAMMOND INC. EG - 0005 - A
79
80
Below Sea Level
Sea Level
200 / 700
500 / 1,600
1,000 / 3,300
1,500 / 5,000
2,000 / 6,500
4,000 / 13,000
6,000 m. / 19,700 ft.

United States

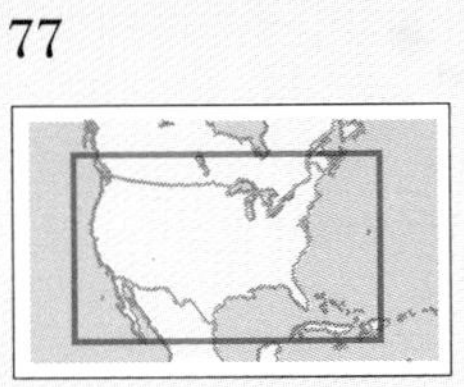

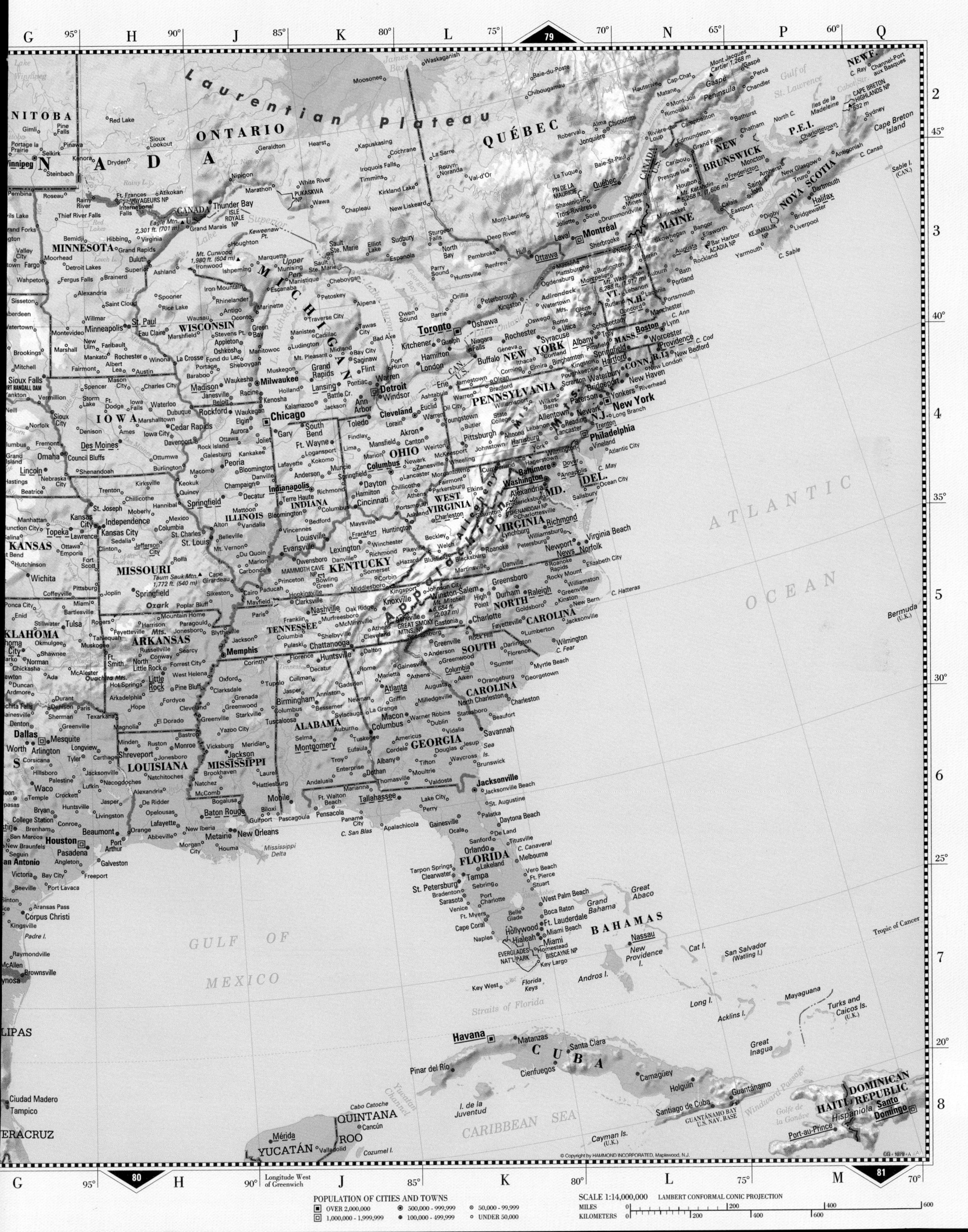

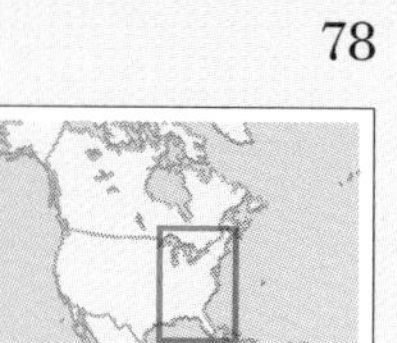

Eastern United States, Southeastern Canada

Canada

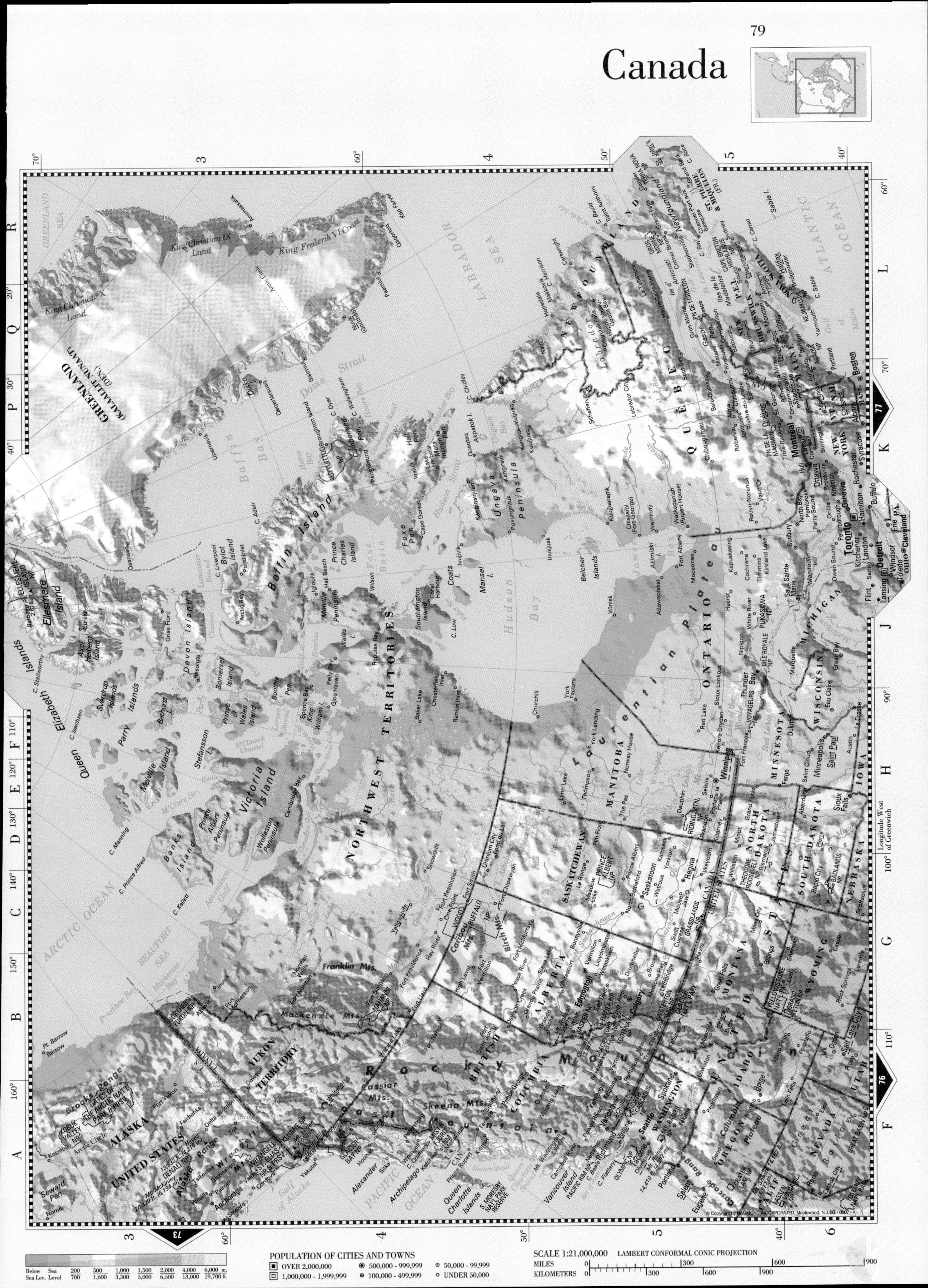

Below Sea Level | Sea Level | 200 m. 700 ft. | 500 m. 1,600 ft. | 1,000 m. 3,300 ft. | 1,500 m. 5,000 ft. | 2,000 m. 6,500 ft. | 4,000 m. 13,000 ft. | 6,000 m. 19,700 ft.

POPULATION OF CITIES AND TOWNS
- ■ OVER 2,000,000
- ▣ 1,000,000 - 1,999,999
- ◉ 500,000 - 999,999
- ● 100,000 - 499,999
- ⊙ 50,000 - 99,999
- ○ UNDER 50,000

SCALE 1:21,000,000 LAMBERT CONFORMAL CONIC PROJECTION
MILES 0 300 600 900
KILOMETERS 0 300 600 900

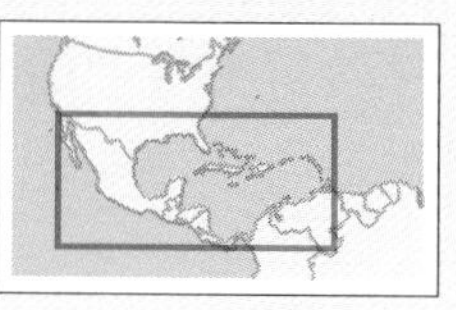

Mexico, Central America and West Indies

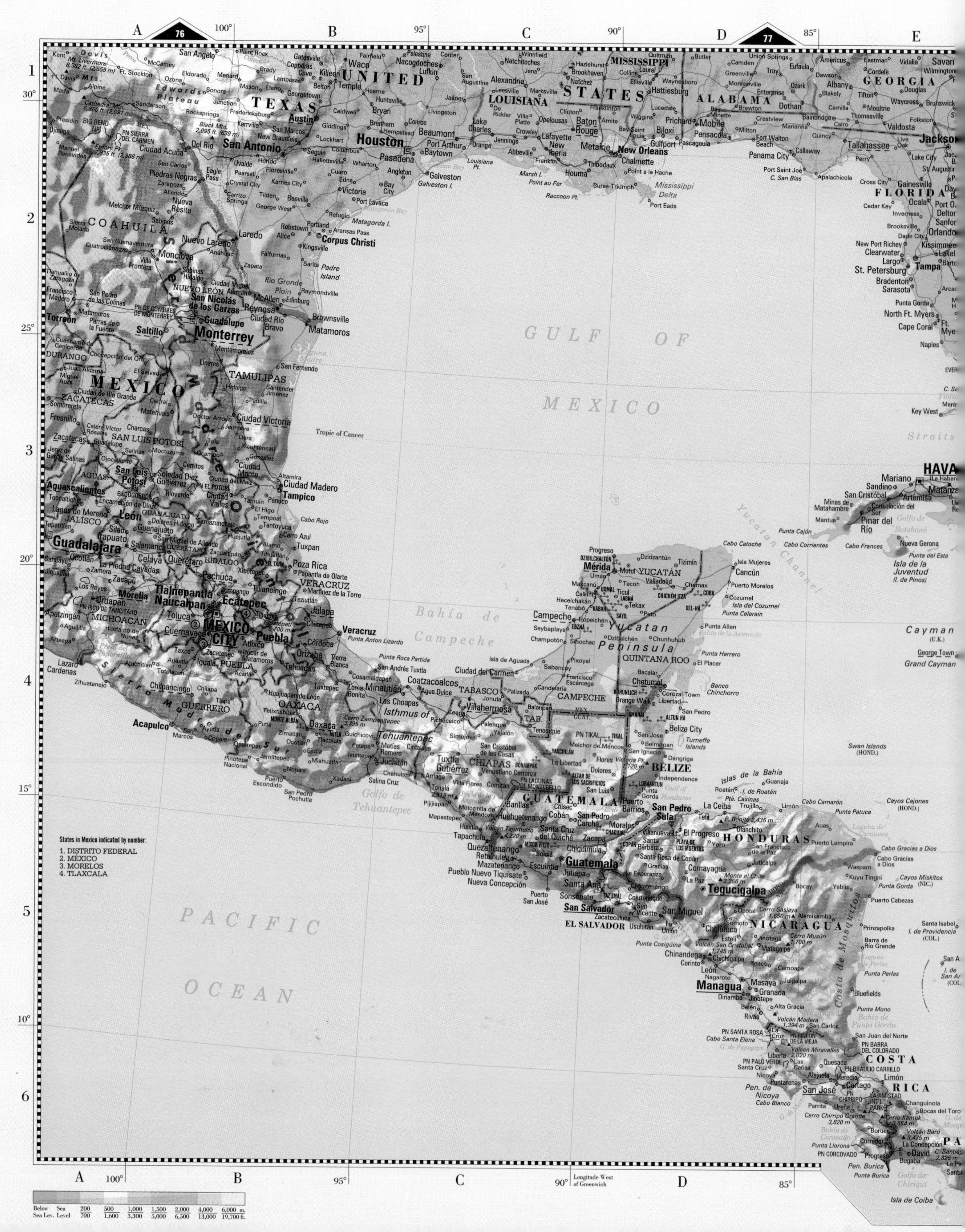

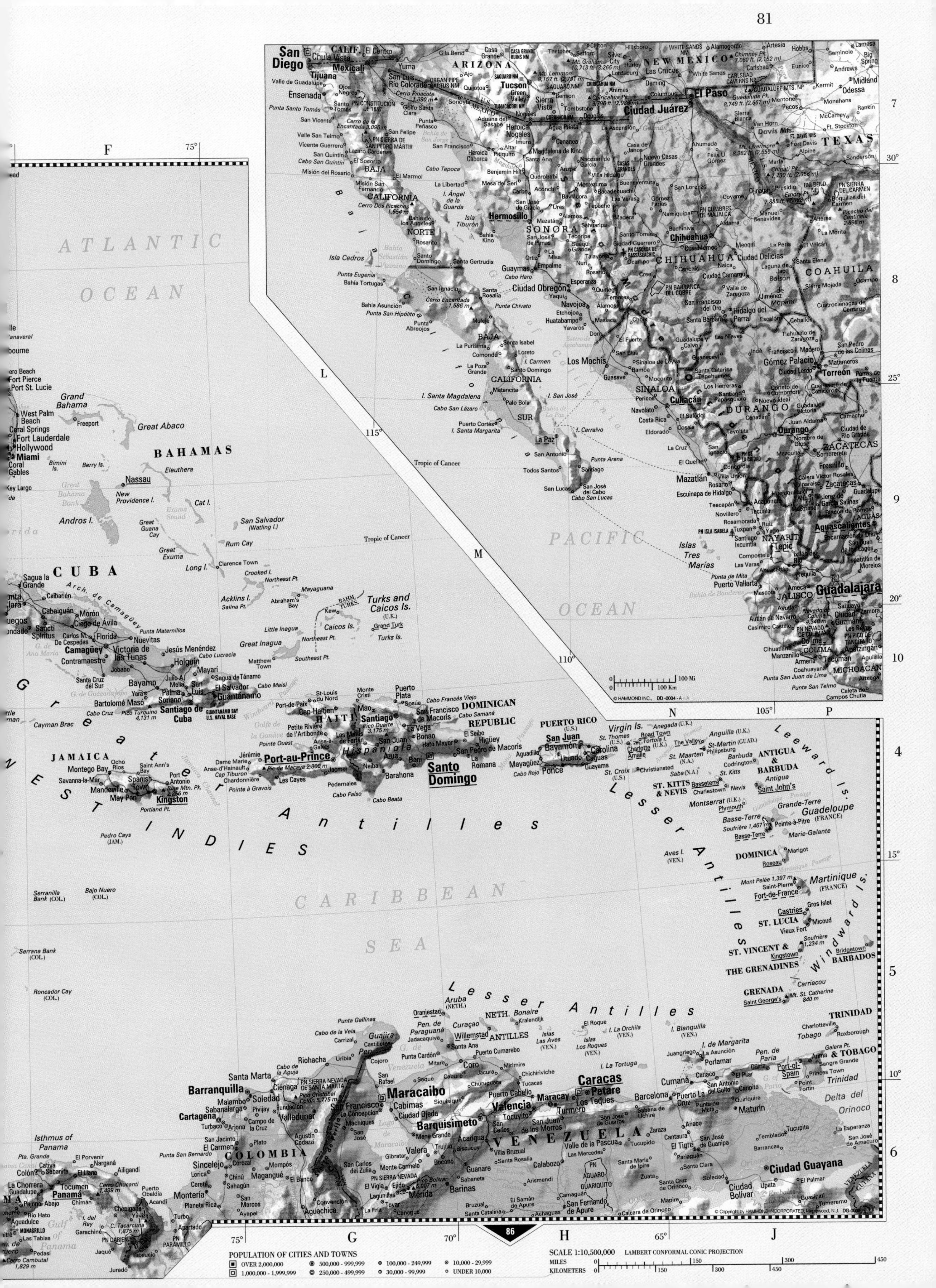
ATLANTIC OCEAN
PACIFIC OCEAN
CARIBBEAN SEA
Gulf of California
Baja California
Tropic of Cancer
BAHAMAS
CUBA
JAMAICA
HAITI
DOMINICAN REPUBLIC
Hispaniola
PUERTO RICO (U.S.)
Greater Antilles
WEST INDIES
Lesser Antilles
Leeward Is.
Windward Is.
Turks and Caicos Is. (U.K.)
Virgin Is.
NETH. ANTILLES
ST. KITTS & NEVIS
ANTIGUA & BARBUDA
Guadeloupe (FRANCE)
DOMINICA
Martinique (FRANCE)
ST. LUCIA
ST. VINCENT & THE GRENADINES
BARBADOS
GRENADA
TRINIDAD & TOBAGO
VENEZUELA
COLOMBIA
Gulf of Panama
Isthmus of Panama
ARIZONA
NEW MEXICO
TEXAS
CALIF.
SONORA
CHIHUAHUA
COAHUILA
DURANGO
SINALOA
ZACATECAS
NAYARIT
JALISCO
COLIMA
MICHOACAN
AGUAS CALIENTES
BAJA CALIFORNIA
BAJA CALIFORNIA SUR
San Diego
Tijuana
Mexicali
Tucson
El Paso
Ciudad Juárez
Chihuahua
Hermosillo
Ciudad Obregón
Los Mochis
Culiacán
Mazatlán
La Paz
Torreón
Durango
Guadalajara
Havana
Camagüey
Holguín
Santiago de Cuba
Guantánamo
Kingston
Port-au-Prince
Santo Domingo
San Juan
Nassau
Miami
Fort Lauderdale
Maracaibo
Barranquilla
Cartagena
Caracas
Valencia
Barquisimeto
Ciudad Guayana
Panamá
Port-of-Spain
© HAMMOND INC.
© Copyright by HAMMOND INCORPORATED, Maplewood, N.J.
F
G
H
J
L
M
N
P
75°
70°
65°
105°
110°
115°
30°
25°
20°
15°
10°
86
POPULATION OF CITIES AND TOWNS
OVER 2,000,000
1,000,000 - 1,999,999
500,000 - 999,999
250,000 - 499,999
100,000 - 249,999
30,000 - 99,999
10,000 - 29,999
UNDER 10,000
SCALE 1:10,500,000
LAMBERT CONFORMAL CONIC PROJECTION
MILES
KILOMETERS

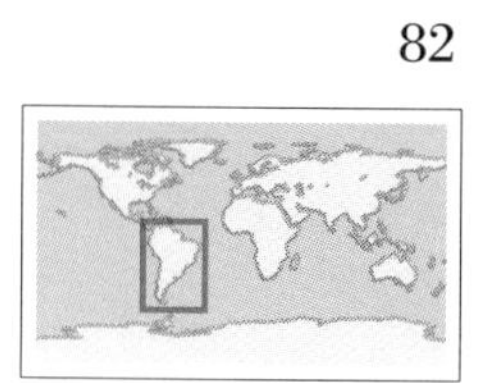

South America - Physical

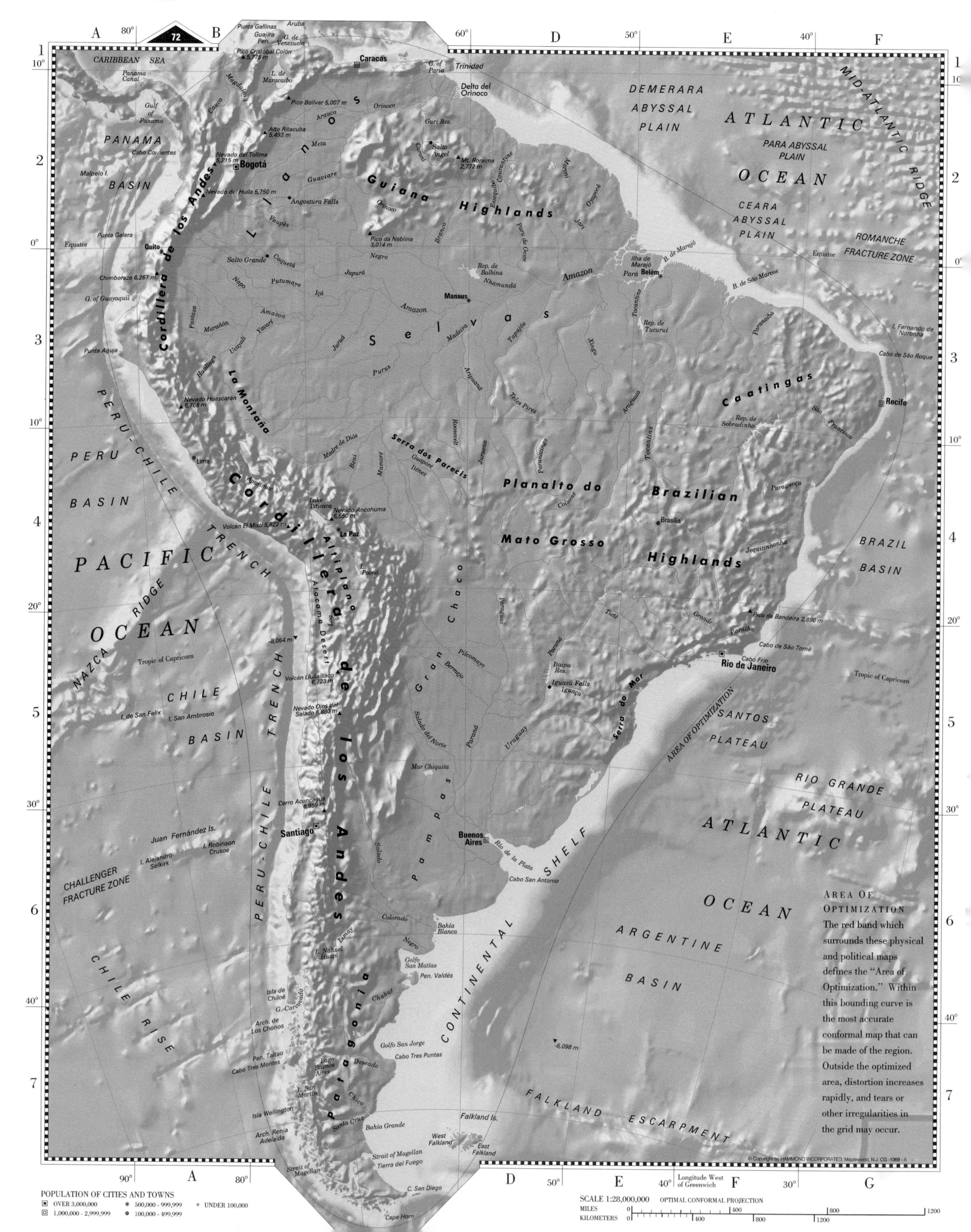

South America - Political

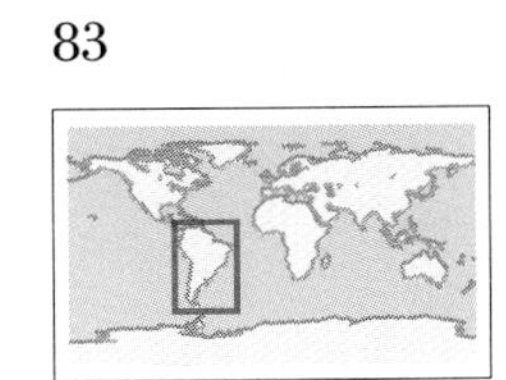

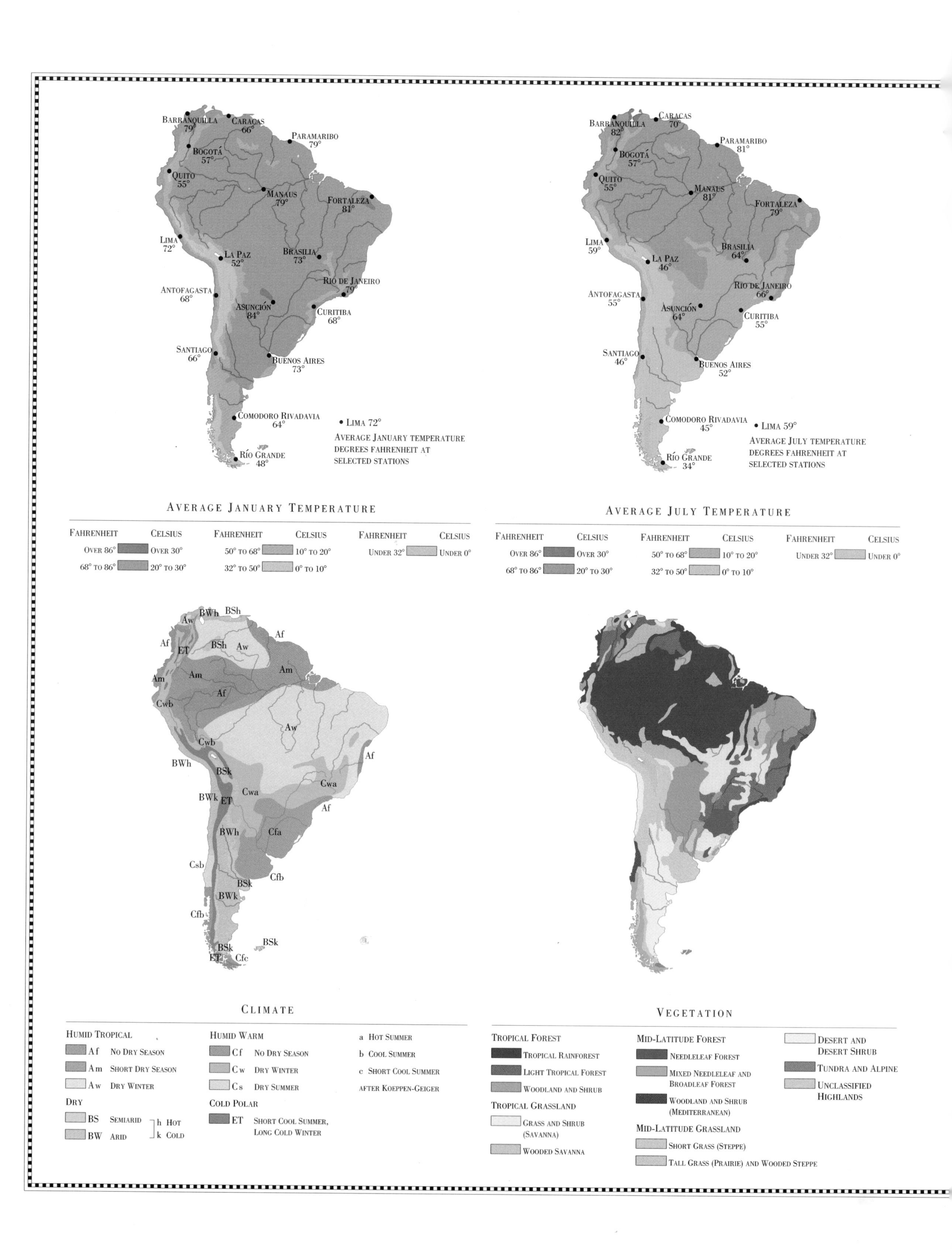

Barranquilla 79°
Caracas 66°
Paramaribo 79°
Bogotá 57°
Quito 55°
Manaus 79°
Fortaleza 81°
Lima 72°
La Paz 52°
Brasília 73°
Antofagasta 68°
Rio de Janeiro 79°
Asunción 84°
Curitiba 68°
Santiago 66°
Buenos Aires 73°
Comodoro Rivadavia 64°
Río Grande 48°
• Lima 72°
Average January temperature degrees Fahrenheit at selected stations
Barranquilla 82°
Caracas 70°
Paramaribo 81°
Bogotá 57°
Quito 55°
Manaus 81°
Fortaleza 79°
Lima 59°
Brasília 64°
La Paz 46°
Rio de Janeiro 66°
Antofagasta 55°
Asunción 64°
Curitiba 55°
Santiago 46°
Buenos Aires 52°
Comodoro Rivadavia 45°
Río Grande 34°
• Lima 59°
Average July temperature degrees Fahrenheit at selected stations
Average January Temperature
Fahrenheit Celsius
Over 86° Over 30°
68° to 86° 20° to 30°
50° to 68° 10° to 20°
32° to 50° 0° to 10°
Under 32° Under 0°
Average July Temperature
Fahrenheit Celsius
Over 86° Over 30°
68° to 86° 20° to 30°
50° to 68° 10° to 20°
32° to 50° 0° to 10°
Under 32° Under 0°
BWh BSh Aw Af ET BSh Aw Af Am Am Am Af Cwb Aw Cwb BWh BSk Af Cwa Cwa BWk ET Af BWh Cfa Csb BSk Cfb BWk Cfb BSk BSk ET Cfc
Climate
Humid Tropical
Af No Dry Season
Am Short Dry Season
Aw Dry Winter
Dry
BS Semiarid
BW Arid
h Hot
k Cold
Humid Warm
Cf No Dry Season
Cw Dry Winter
Cs Dry Summer
Cold Polar
ET Short Cool Summer, Long Cold Winter
a Hot Summer
b Cool Summer
c Short Cool Summer
after Koeppen-Geiger
Vegetation
Tropical Forest
Tropical Rainforest
Light Tropical Forest
Woodland and Shrub
Tropical Grassland
Grass and Shrub (Savanna)
Wooded Savanna
Mid-Latitude Forest
Needleleaf Forest
Mixed Needleleaf and Broadleaf Forest
Woodland and Shrub (Mediterranean)
Mid-Latitude Grassland
Short Grass (Steppe)
Tall Grass (Prairie) and Wooded Steppe
Desert and Desert Shrub
Tundra and Alpine
Unclassified Highlands

South America - Comparisons

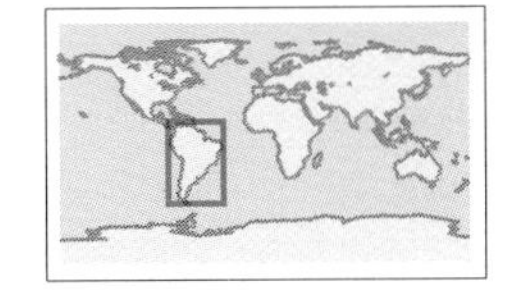

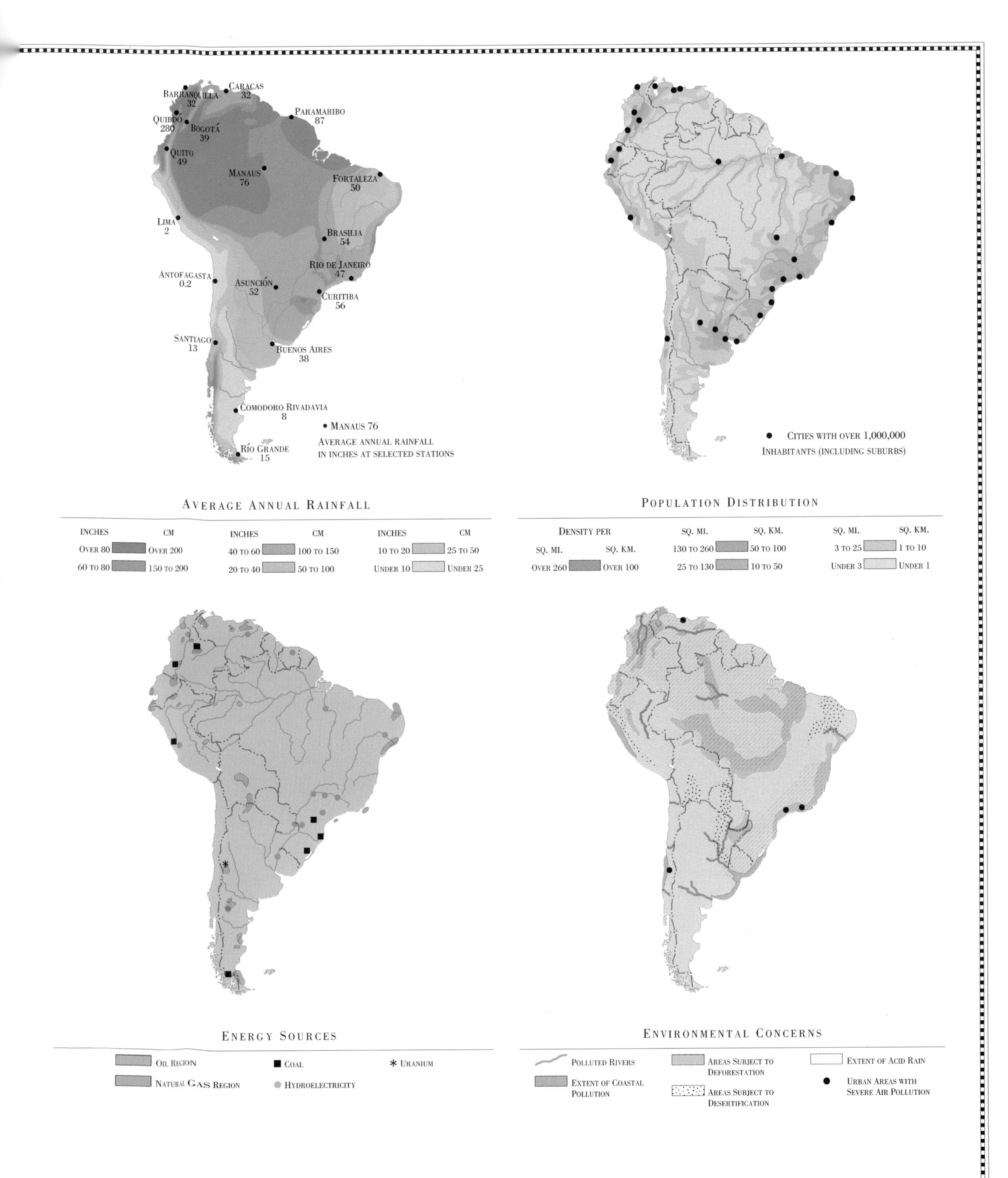

CARIBBEAN SEA
SAINT VINCENT AND THE GRENADINES
Kingstown
Carriacou
Saint George's
GRENADA
Tobago
TRINIDAD AND TOBAGO
Port-of-Spain
Trinidad
NETH. ANTILLES
Aruba (NETH.)
Oranjestad
Willemstad
Kralendijk
Curaçao
Bonaire
Punta Gallinas
Pen. de la Guajira
Pen. de Paraguaná
El Roque
Islas Los Roques
I. Blanquilla
I. La Tortuga
I. de Margarita
La Asunción
Porlamar
Cumaná
Carúpano
Barcelona
Caracas
Petare
Los Teques
Valencia
Maracay
Puerto Cabello
Coro
Maracaibo
Cabimas
Lake Maracaibo
Gulf of Venezuela
Barquisimeto
Mérida
Barinas
San Cristóbal
Ciudad Bolívar
Ciudad Guayana
Maturín
Delta del Orinoco
VENEZUELA
Llanos
Guiana Highlands
Serra Pacaraima
Georgetown
GUYAN
Barranquilla
Santa Marta
Cartagena
Valledupar
Sincelejo
Montería
Cúcuta
Bucaramanga
Medellín
Manizales
Pereira
Armenia
Ibagué
Bogotá
Villavicencio
Cali
Buenaventura
Popayán
Pasto
Neiva
COLOMBIA
Isla del Coco (COSTA RICA)
I. de Malpelo (COLOMBIA)
NICARAGUA
COSTA RICA
San José
Limón
PANAMA
Panamá
Colón
Isthmus of Panama
Gulf of Panama
Pen. de Nicoya
Pen. de Osa
Pen. de Azuero
I. de Coiba
Equator
Esmeraldas
Santo Domingo de los Colorados
Quito
ECUADOR
Manta
Portoviejo
Ambato
Riobamba
Guayaquil
Gulf of Guayaquil
Cuenca
Machala
Loja
Tumbes
Piura
Sullana
Chiclayo
Trujillo
Chimbote
Cajamarca
Iquitos
Pucallpa
PERU
La Montaña
Cordillera Central
Cordillera Occidental
Cordillera Oriental
Andes
Lima
Callao
Huancayo
Ayacucho
Cusco
Arequipa
Ica
Nazca
Puno
Lake Titicaca
Tacna
Arica
Iquique
Tocopilla
Punta Angamos
CHILE
Atacama Desert
La Paz
Cochabamba
Oruro
Sucre
Potosí
Santa Cruz
BOLIVIA
Altiplano
Llanos de Mojos
Trinidad
Riberalta
Tarija
ARGENTINA
PARAGUAY
Gran Chaco
Chaco Boreal
Tropic of Capricorn
Manaus
Porto Velho
Rio Branco
Selvas
Amazon (Solimões)
Tefé
Coari
Humaitá
Serra dos Parecis
Mato Grosso
Cáceres
BRA
Leticia
Benjamin Constant
Tabatinga
PACIFIC OCEAN
Longitude West of Greenwich
Below Sea Level
Sea Level
200 700
500 1,600
1,000 3,300
1,500 5,000
2,000 6,500
4,000 13,000
6,000 m. 19,700 ft.
80
88

Northern South America

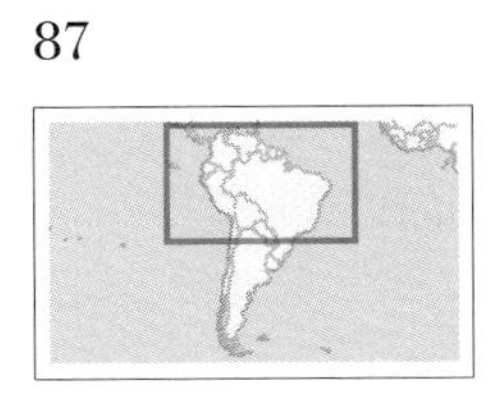

POPULATION OF CITIES AND TOWNS

- OVER 2,000,000
- 1,000,000 - 1,999,999
- 500,000 - 999,999
- 100,000 - 499,999
- 50,000 - 99,999
- UNDER 50,000

SCALE 1:15,000,000 LAMBERT CONFORMAL CONIC PROJECTION

MILES 0 200 400 600

KILOMETERS 0 200 400 600

Southern South America

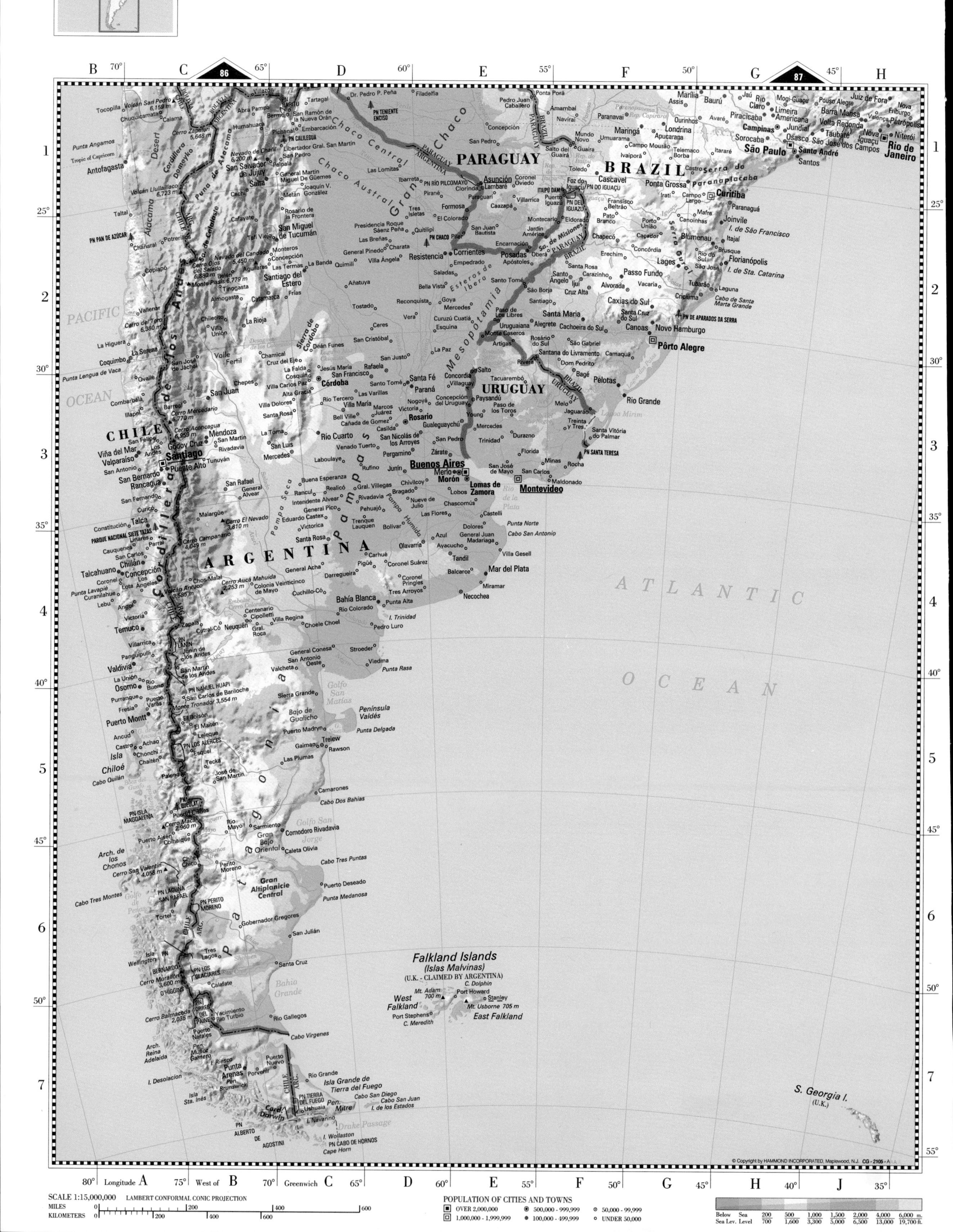

Population of Major World Cities

The following pages include population figures, given in thousands, for major cities in each country, and for all national capitals, regardless of size. Three dependencies, Hong Kong, Macau and Puerto Rico, follow the country listings. National capitals are indicated with an asterisk (*).

Country / City	Population in thousands
A **Afghanistan**	
Kābul*	1,424
Qandahar	226
Albania	
Tiranë*	239
Algeria	
Algiers*	1,688
Annaba	228
Constantine	450
Oran	599
Andorra	
Andorra la Vella*	12
Angola	
Luanda*	1,530
Antigua and Barbuda	
Saint John's*	36
Argentina	
Avellaneda	347
Bahía Blanca	240
Buenos Aires*	2,961
Córdoba	1,148
General San Martín	408
Lanús	467
La Plata	520
Lomas de Zamora	573
Mar del Plata	512
Morón	642
Qilmes	509
Rosario	895
San Miguel de Tucumán	471
Santa Fé	343
Armenia	
Yerevan*	1,199
Australia	
Adelaide	957
Brisbane	1,146
Canberra*	276
Hobart	127
Melbourne	2,762
Newcastle	262
Perth	1,019
Sydney	3,098
Austria	
Graz	238
Vienna*	1,540
Azerbaijan	
Baku*	1,150
B **Bahamas**	
Nassau*	172
Bahrain	
Manama*	143
Bangladesh	
Chittagong	1,388
Dhākā*	3,638
Khulna	623
Barbados	
Bridgetown*	7
Belarus	
Homyel'	500
Minsk*	1,589
Mahilyow	356
Vitsyebsk	350
Belgium	
Antwerp	468
Brussels*	954
Ghent	230
Liège	195
Belize	
Belmopan*	4
Benin	
Cotonou	383
Porto-Novo*	144
Bhutan	
Thimphu*	12
Bolivia	
Cochabamba	404
La Paz*	977
Santa Cruz	529
Sucre*	106
Bosnia & Herzegovina	
Banja Luka	142
Sarajevo*	416
Botswana	
Gaborone*	129
Brazil	
Aracaju	401
Belém	765
Belo Horizonte	2,206
Brasília*	1,493
Campinas	748
Campo Grande	516
Cuiabá	253
Curitiba	842
Florianópolis	192
Fortaleza	1,027
Goiânia	912
João Pessoa	497
Juiz de Fora	378
Maceió	555
Manaus	1,006
Natal	460
Niterói	401
Nova Iguaçu	562
Osasco	567
Porto Alegre	1,237
Recife	1,297
Ribeirão Preto	416
Rio de Janeiro	5,474
Salvador	2,070
Santo André	518
Santos	416
São Bernardo do Campo	550
São Luís	164
São Paulo	9,394
Teresina	556
Vitória	184
Brunei	
Bandar Seri Begawan*	64
Bulgaria	
Plovdiv	374
Sofia*	1,142
Varna	311
Burkina	
Ouagadougou*	442
Burma	
Mandalay	533
Moulmein	220
Rangoon*	2,513
Burundi	
Bujumbura*	215
C **Cambodia**	
Phnom Penh*	300
Cameroon	
Douala	1,030
Yaoundé*	654
Canada	
Calgary	711
Edmonton	617
Halifax	114
Hamilton	318
Laval	314
London	269
Mississauga	463
Montréal	1,018
Ottawa*	314
Québec	168
Regina	175
Saskatoon	201
Toronto	2,276
Vancouver	472
Windsor	193
Winnipeg	617
Cape Verde	
Praia*	57
Central African Republic	
Bangui*	474
Chad	
N'Djamena*	594
Chile	
Antofagasta	227
Concepción	327
Santiago*	4,298
Talcahuano	246
Valparaíso	282
Viña del Mar	306
China	
Anshan	1,215
Baotou	980
Beijing*	5,715
Benxi	767
Changchun	1,698
Changsha	1,077
Chengdu	1,719
Chongqing	2,265
Dalian	1,632
Dandong	525
Daqing	676
Datong	779
Fengcheng	996
Fushun	1,210
Fuxin	623
Fuzhou	890
Guangzhou	2,892
Guiyang	1,009
Handan	798
Hangzhou	1,119
Harbin	2,468
Hefei	733
Hegang	507
Hohhot	654
Huainan	674
Jilin	1,038
Jinan	1,361
Jinzhou	573
Jixi	638
Kaifeng	503
Kunming	1,108
Lanzhou	1,205
Lhasa	343
Liuzhou	602
Luoyang	730
Mudanjiang	562
Nanchang	1,026
Nanjing	2,114
Nanning	723
Ningbo	548
Qingdao	1,317
Qiqihar	1,066
Shanghai	7,551
Shantou	558
Shenyang	3,588
Shijiazhuang	1,065
Suzhou	697
Taiyuan	1,514
Tangshan	1,042
Tianjin	4,521
Ürümqi	1,071
Wuhan	3,177
Wuxi	806
Xi'an	1,954
Xining	559
Xuzhou	795
Yichun	787
Yinchuan	350
Zhangjiakou	525
Zhengzhou	1,139
Zibo	864
Colombia	
Barranquilla	1,000
Bogotá*	5,699
Bucaramanga	403
Cali	1,625
Cartagena	576
Cúcuta	462
Ibagué	336
Manizales	341
Medellín	1,485
Pereira	329
Comoros	
Moroni*	20
Congo	
Brazzaville*	596
Pointe-Noire	298
Costa Rica	
San José*	241
Côte d'Ivoire	
Abidjan	1,929
Yamoussoukro*	107
Croatia	
Rijeka	168
Split	189
Zagreb*	704
Cuba	
Camagüey	279
Guantánamo	198
Havana*	2,078
Holguín	223
Santiago de Cuba	397
Cyprus	
Nicosia*	167
Czech Republic	
Brno	388
Ostrava	328
Prague*	1,212
D **Denmark**	
Århus	182
Copenhagen*	618
Djibouti	
Djibouti*	200
Dominica	
Roseau*	6
Dominican Republic	
Santiago de los Caballeros	279
Santo Domingo*	1,313
E **Ecuador**	
Guayaquil	1,513
Quito*	1,113
Egypt	
Alexandria	3,295
Al Jīzah	2,096
Asyūt	313
Cairo*	6,663
Port Said	449
Shubrā al Khaymah	812
Tantā	285
El Salvador	
San Salvador*	498
Equatorial Guinea	
Malabo*	37
Eritrea	
Asmara*	344
Estonia	
Tallinn*	482
Ethiopia	
Addis Ababa*	1,739
F **Fiji**	
Suva*	70
Finland	
Helsinki*	492
Tampere	172
France	
Bordeaux	213
Le Havre	197
Lille	178
Lyon	422
Marseille	808
Montpellier	211
Nantes	252
Nice	346
Paris*	2,175
Rennes	204
Saint-Étienne	202
Strasbourg	256
Toulouse	366
G **Gabon**	
Libreville*	352
Gambia	
Banjul*	44
Georgia	
Tbilisi*	1,260
Germany	
Berlin*	3,434
Bochum	396
Bonn	292
Bremen	551
Chemnitz	294
Cologne	954
Dortmund	599
Dresden	491
Duisburg	535
Düsseldorf	576
Essen	627
Frankfurt am Main	645
Hamburg	1,652
Hannover	513
Kiel	246
Leipzig	511
Magdeburg	279
Mannheim	310
Munich	1,229
Münster	259
Nürnberg	494
Rostock	249
Saarbrücken	192
Stuttgart	563
Wiesbaden	254
Ghana	
Accra*	860
Kumasi	349
Greece	
Athens*	748
Piraiévs	170
Thessaloníki	406
Grenada	
Saint George's*	5
Guatemala	
Guatemala*	1,676
Guinea	
Conakry*	526
Guinea-Bissau	
Bissau*	109
Guyana	
Georgetown*	72
H **Haiti**	
Port-au-Prince*	690
Honduras	
San Pedro Sula	287
Tegucigalpa*	577
Hungary	
Budapest*	2,017
Debrecen	212
Miskolc	196
Szeged	175
I **Iceland**	
Reykjavík*	96
India	
Āgra	892
Ahmadābād	2,877
Allahābād	793
Amritsar	709
Aurangābād	573
Bangalore	2,660
Bareilly	587
Baroda	1,031
Bhopāl	1,063
Bombay	9,926
Calcutta	4,400
Chandigarh	504
Cochin	565
Coimbatore	816
Cuttack	403
Delhi	7,207
Farīdābād	618
Gwalior	691
Howrah	950
Hubli-Dhārwār	648
Hyderābād	3,044
Indore	1,092
Jabalpur	742
Jaipur	1,458
Jammu	206
Jamshedpur	461
Jodhpur	666
Jullundur	510
Kalyān	1,015
Kānpur	1,874
Kota	537
Kozhikode	420
Lucknow	1,619
Ludhiāna	1,043
Madras	3,841
Madurai	940
Meerut	754
Mysore	481
Nāgpur	1,625
Nāsik	657
New Delhi*	301
Patna	917
Poona	1,567
Rānchī	599
Sholāpur	604
Srīnagar	606
Surat	1,499
Thāna	803
Tiruchchirāppalli	387
Trivandrum	524
Vārānasi	929
Vijayawada	702
Visākhapatnam	752
Indonesia	
Bandung	2,027
Banjarmasin	381
Jakarta*	8,259
Malang	512
Medan	1,379
Padang	481
Palembang	787
Pontianak	305
Semarang	1,027
Surabaya	2,421
Surakarta	470
Ujung Pandang	709
Yogyakarta	399
Iran	
Ābādān	296
Ahvāz	580
Bākhtarān	561
Eşfahān	987
Mashhad	1,464
Qom	543
Rasht	291
Shīrāz	848
Tabrīz	971
Tehrān*	6,043
Zāhedān	282
Iraq	
Al Başrah	334
Baghdad*	1,984
Mosul	310
Ireland	
Cork	127
Dublin*	478
Israel	
Jerusalem*	499
Tel Aviv-Yafo	320
Italy	
Bari	353
Bologna	411
Catania	364
Florence	408
Genoa	701
Messina	275
Milan	1,432
Naples	1,206
Palermo	734
Rome*	2,693
Taranto	244
Trieste	231
Turin	992
Venice	110
Verona	259
J **Jamaica**	
Kingston*	104
Japan	
Amagasaki	499
Chiba	829
Fukuoka	1,237
Funabashi	533
Hamakita	811
Hamamatsu	535
Higashi-Ōsaka	518
Hiroshima	1,086
Kagoshima	536
Kawasaki	1,157
Kitakyūshū	1,034
Kōbe	1,477
Kumamoto	575
Kyōto	1,471
Nagoya	2,155
Niigata	485
Okayama	591
Ōsaka	2,624
Sakai	814
Sapporo	1,672
Sendai	910
Shizuoka	473
Tōkyō*	8,164
Toyonaka	414
Utsunomiya	423
Wakayama	399
Yokohama	3,220
Yokosuka	434

Country / City	Population in thousands
Jordan	
'Ammān*	936
K	
Kazakstan	
Almaty	1,128
Aqmola*	277
Öskemen	324
Pavlodar	331
Qaraghandy	614
Semey	334
Shymkent	393
Zhambyl	307
Kenya	
Mombasa	442
Nairobi*	1,162
Kiribati	
Bairiki*	2
Korea, North	
Ch'ŏngjin	306
Hamhŭng	484
P'yŏngyang*	1,250
Wŏnsan	275
Korea, South	
Chŏnju	426
Inch'ŏn	1,387
Kwangju	906
Pusan	3,798
Seoul*	10,613
Taegu	2,229
Taejŏn	886
Kuwait	
Al Kuwait*	182
Kyrgyzstan	
Bishkek*	616
L	
Laos	
Vientiane*	377
Latvia	
Riga*	915
Lebanon	
Beirut*	475
Lesotho	
Maseru*	13
Liberia	
Monrovia*	421
Libya	
Benghāzī	287
Tripoli*	550
Liechtenstein	
Vaduz*	5
Lithuania	
Kaunas	423
Vilnius*	582
Luxembourg	
Luxembourg*	75
M	
Macedonia	
Skopje*	563
Madagascar	
Antananarivo*	452
Malawi	
Blantyre	332
Lilongwe*	234
Malaysia	
Ipoh	383
Kuala Lumpur*	1,145
Maldives	
Male*	55
Mali	
Bamako*	658
Malta	
Valletta*	9
Marshall Islands	
Majuro*	9
Mauritania	
Nouakchott*	135
Mauritius	
Port Louis*	134
Mexico	
Acapulco de Juárez	515
Aguascalientes	440
Chihuahua	516
Ciudad Juárez	790
Culiacán	415
Ecatepec de Morelos	1,218
Guadalajara	1,650
Guadalupe	535
Hermosillo	406
León	758
Mérida	529
Mexicali	439
Mexico City*	8,237
Monterrey	1,069
Morelia	429
Netzahualcóyotl	1,255
Puebla de Zaragoza	1,007
Saltillo	421
San Luis Potosí	489
Tijuana	699
Tlalnepantla de Galeana	702
Torreón	439
Veracruz Llave	439
Zapopan	668
Micronesia, Federated States of	
Kolonia*	6
Moldova	
Chişinău*	665
Monaco	
Monaco*	27
Mongolia	
Ulaanbaatar*	515
Morocco	
Casablanca	2,263
Fès	449
Marrakech	440
Rabat*	368
Mozambique	
Maputo*	1,007
N	
Namibia	
Windhoek*	115
Nepal	
Kāthmāndu*	423
Netherlands	
Amsterdam*	714
Eindhoven	194
Groningen	169
Rotterdam	590
The Hague*	445
Utrecht	233
New Zealand	
Auckland	316
Christchurch	293
Wellington*	150
Nicaragua	
Managua*	608
Niger	
Niamey*	225
Nigeria	
Abeokuta	308
Abuja*	306
Ibadan	1,060
Ilorin	282
Kano	399
Lagos	1,097
Ogbomosho	432
Oshogbo	345
Port Harcourt	242
Zaria	224
Norway	
Bergen	218
Oslo*	457
O	
Oman	
Muscat*	67
P	
Pakistan	
Faisalabad	1,104
Gujrānwāla	659
Hyderābād	752
Islāmābād*	204
Karāchi	5,076
Lahore	2,953
Multān	732
Peshāwar	566
Quetta	286
Rāwalpindi	795
Sargodha	291
Siālkot	302
Palau	
Koror*	9
Panama	
Panamá*	389
Papua New Guinea	
Port Moresby*	124
Paraguay	
Asunción*	502
Peru	
Callao	515
Chiclayo	280
Comas	287
Lima*	376
Trujillo	355
Philippines	
Caloocan	616
Cebu	627
Davao	844
Makati	409
Manila*	1,876
Quezon	1,587
Zamboanga	443
Poland	
Białystok	268
Bydgoszcz	380
Gdańsk	462
Gdynia	251
Katowice	366
Kraków	746
Łódź	849
Lublin	349
Poznań	587
Szczecin	411
Warsaw*	1,651
Wrocław	641
Portugal	
Lisbon*	678
Porto	311
Q	
Qatar	
Doha*	217
R	
Romania	
Braşov	324
Bucharest*	2,068
Cluj-Napoca	329
Constanţa	351
Iaşi	344
Ploieşti	253
Timisoara	334
Russia	
Archangel	416
Astrakhan'	509
Barnaul	602
Bryansk	452
Cheboksary	420
Chelyabinsk	1,143
Groznyy	401
Irkutsk	626
Ivanovo	481
Izhevsk	635
Kazan'	1,094
Kemerovo	520
Khabarovsk	601
Krasnodar	620
Krasnoyarsk	912
Kursk	424
Lipetsk	450
Magnitogorsk	440
Moscow*	8,769
Murmansk	468
Naberezhnye Chelny	501
Nizhniy Novgorod	1,438
Nizhniy Tagil	440
Novokuznetsk	600
Novosibirsk	1,436
Omsk	1,148
Orenburg	547
Penza	483
Perm'	1,091
Rostov	1,020
Ryazan'	515
Saint Petersburg	4,456
Samara	1,257
Saratov	905
Simbirsk	625
Tol'yatti	630
Tomsk	502
Tula	540
T'ver	451
Tyumen'	477
Ufa	1,083
Vladivostok	648
Volgograd	999
Voronezh	887
Vyatka	441
Yaroslavl'	633
Yekaterinburg	1,367
Rwanda	
Kigali*	118
S	
Saint Kitts and Nevis	
Basseterre*	14
Saint Lucia	
Castries*	56
Saint Vincent and the Grenadines	
Kingstown*	17
San Marino	
San Marino*	4
Sao Tome and Principe	
São Tomé*	8
Saudi Arabia	
Jiddah	561
Mecca	367
Riyadh*	667
Senegal	
Dakar*	799
Seychelles	
Victoria*	16
Sierra Leone	
Freetown*	470
Singapore	
Singapore*	2,704
Slovak Republic	
Bratislava*	442
Košice	235
Slovenia	
Ljubljana*	287
Solomon Islands	
Honiara*	30
Somalia	
Mogadishu*	500
South Africa	
Cape Town*	855
Durban	716
Johannesburg	714
Port Elizabeth	303
Pretoria*	526
Soweto	597
Spain	
Alicante	266
Barcelona	1,668
Bilbao	351
Córdoba	305
Granada	262
Las Palmas de Gran Canaria	354
Madrid*	2,991
Málaga	605
Murcia	315
Palma	297
Saragossa	574
Seville	654
Valencia	719
Valladolid	332
Vigo	262
Sri Lanka	
Colombo*	609
Sudan	
Khartoum*	474
Omdurman	526
Suriname	
Paramaribo*	68
Swaziland	
Mbabane*	38
Sweden	
Göteborg	431
Malmö	232
Stockholm*	669
Switzerland	
Bern*	136
Zürich	365
Syria	
Aleppo	1,355
Damascus*	1,378
Ḩimş	481
T	
Taiwan	
Kaohsiung	1,227
Keelung	348
Taichung	607
Tainan	582
Taipei*	2,268
Tajikistan	
Dushanbe*	595
Tanzania	
Dar es Salaam*	1,096
Thailand	
Bangkok*	5,876
Thon Buri	628
Togo	
Lomé*	370
Tonga	
Nuku'alofa*	21
Trinidad and Tobago	
Port-of-Spain*	51
Tunisia	
Tūnis*	597
Turkey	
Adana	916
Ankara*	2,559
Antalya	378
Bursa	835
Diyarbakır	381
Eskişehir	413
Gaziantep	603
İstanbul	6,620
İzmir	1,757
Kayseri	421
Konya	513
Malatya	281
Mersin	422
Turkmenistan	
Ashgabat*	398
Tuvalu	
Funafuti*	2
U	
Uganda	
Kampala*	458
Ukraine	
Chernihiv	296
Dniprodzerzhyns'k	282
Dnipropetrovs'k	1,179
Donets'k	1,110
Horlivka	337
Kharkiv	1,611
Kherson	355
Kiev*	2,587
Kryvyy Rih	713
Luhans'k	497
L'viv	790
Makiyivka	430
Mariupol'	517
Mykolayiv	503
Odesa	1,115
Poltava	315
Sevastopol'	356
Simferopol'	344
Sumy	291
Vinnytsya	374
Zaporizhzhya	884
Zhytomyr	292
United Arab Emirates	
Abu Dhabi*	243
Dubayy	266
United Kingdom	
Belfast	295
Birmingham	1,014
Bradford	293
Bristol	414
Cardiff	262
Coventry	319
Edinburgh	420
Glasgow	765
Hull	322
Leeds	452
Leicester	324
Liverpool	539
London*	6,680
Manchester	449
Nottingham	273
Plymouth	239
Sheffield	471
Stoke-on-Trent	272
Wolverhampton	264
United States	
Albuquerque	385
Atlanta	394
Austin	466
Baltimore	736
Boston	574
Buffalo	328
Charlotte	396
Chicago	2,784
Cincinnati	364
Cleveland	506
Columbus (Ohio)	633
Dallas	1,007
Denver	468
Detroit	1,028
El Paso	515
Fort Worth	448
Fresno	354
Honolulu	365
Houston	1,631
Indianapolis	742
Jacksonville	635
Kansas City (Mo.)	435
Long Beach	429
Los Angeles	3,485
Memphis	610
Miami	359
Milwaukee	628
Minneapolis	368
Nashville	488
New Orleans	497
New York	7,323
Oakland	372
Oklahoma City	445
Omaha	336
Philadelphia	1,586
Phoenix	983
Pittsburgh	370
Portland	437
Sacramento	369
Saint Louis	397
San Antonio	936
San Diego	1,111
San Francisco	724
San Jose	782
Seattle	516
Toledo	333
Tucson	405
Tulsa	367
Virginia Beach	393
Washington*	607
Wichita	304
Uruguay	
Montevideo*	1,252
Uzbekistan	
Andijon	293
Namangan	308
Samarqand	366
Tashkent*	2,073
V	
Vanuatu	
Vila*	19
Venezuela	
Barquisimeto	625
Caracas*	1,822
Ciudad Guayana	453
Maracaibo	1,124
Maracay	354
Petare	338
Valencia	903
Vietnam	
Đà Nang	319
Haiphong	1,279
Hanoi*	2,571
Ho Chi Minh City	3,420
W	
Western Samoa	
Apia*	32
Y	
Yemen	
Aden	272
Sanaa*	140
Yugoslavia	
Belgrade*	1,555
Niš	176
Novi Sad	179
Z	
Zaire	
Kananga	291
Kinshasa*	2,654
Lubumbashi	543
Mbuji-Mayi	423
Zambia	
Kitwe	472
Lusaka*	870
Ndola	443
Zimbabwe	
Bulawayo	414
Harare*	656

Dependency

Country / City	Population in thousands
Hong Kong (U.K.)	
Kowloon	2,450
Victoria	1,184
Macau (Port.)	
Macau	342
Puerto Rico (U.S.)	
San Juan	427

Index of the World

This alphabetical list gives countries, cities, regions, political divisions, and physical features for the world. Latitude/longitude coordinates are given for each entry, where possible, followed by the page number for the map on which the entry appears to the best advantage. The entry may be located on other maps as well by the use of the coordinates given. Capitals are designated by asterisks (*).

Index Abbreviations

Afghan.	Afghanistan
Ala.	Alabama
Alg.	Algeria
Alta.	Alberta
Amer.	America
arch.	archipelago
Arg.	Argentina
Ariz.	Arizona
Ark.	Arkansas
Austl.	Australia
Belg.	Belgium
Br. Col.	British Columbia
Calif.	California
Can.	Canada
CAfr.	Central African Republic
chan.	channel
Col.	Colombia
Colo.	Colorado
Conn.	Connecticut
C.R.	Costa Rica
Czech Rep.	Czech Republic
D.C.	District of Columbia
Del.	Delaware
Den.	Denmark
Dom. Rep.	Dominican Republic
E.	East, Eastern
El Sal.	El Salvador
Eng.	England
Eq. Guin.	Equatorial Guinea
Falk. Is.	Falkland Islands
Fla.	Florida
Fr.	France, French
Ga.	Georgia
Ger.	Germany
Guat.	Guatemala
Ill.	Illinois
Ind.	Indiana
Indon.	Indonesia
isl., isls.	island, islands
Kans.	Kansas
Kazak.	Kazakstan
Ky.	Kentucky
La.	Louisiana
Lux.	Luxembourg
Man.	Manitoba
Mart.	Martinique
Mass.	Massachusetts
Md.	Maryland
Mex.	Mexico
Mich.	Michigan
Minn.	Minnesota
Miss.	Mississippi
Mo.	Missouri
Mont.	Montana
Mor.	Morocco
Moz.	Mozambique
mt., mts.	mountain, mountains
N,. No.	North, Northern
Nat'l Pk	National Park
N.B.	New Brunswick
N.C.	North Carolina
N.D.	North Dakota
Neb.	Nebraska
Neth.	Netherlands
Neth. Ant.	Netherlands Antilles
Nev.	Nevada
New Cal.	New Caledonia
Newf.	Newfoundland
N.H.	New Hampshire
Nic.	Nicaragua
N.J.	New Jersey
N. Korea	North Korea
N.M.	New Mexico
No. Ire.	Northern Ireland
No. Terr.	Northern Territory
N.S.	Nova Scotia
N.S.W.	New South Wales
N.W. Terrs.	Northwest Territories (Canada)
N.Y.	New York
N.Z.	New Zealand
Okla.	Oklahoma
Ont.	Ontario
Ore.	Oregon
Pa.	Pennsylvania
Pak.	Pakistan
Para.	Paraguay
P.E.I.	Prince Edward Island
pen.	peninsula
plat.	plateau
P.N.G.	Papua New Guinea
Port.	Portugal, Portuguese
P.R.	Puerto Rico
prom.	promontory
prov.	province, provincial
Qué.	Québec
Queens.	Queensland
Rep.	Republic
res.	reservoir
R.I.	Rhode Island
Rom.	Romania
S., So.	South, Southern
S. Afr.	South Africa
Sask.	Saskatchewan
S.C.	South Carolina
Scot.	Scotland
S. D.	South Dakota
Sol. Is.	Solomon Islands
Sp.	Spain, Spanish
St. Ste.	Saint, Sainte
Switz.	Switzerland
Tanz.	Tanzania
Tas.	Tasmania
Tenn.	Tennessee
Terr.	Territory
Thai.	Thailand
U.K.	United Kingdom
Un.	United
U.S.	United States
Va.	Virginia
Ven.	Venezuela
Vt.	Vermont
W.	West, Western
Wash.	Washington
Wis.	Wisconsin
W. Va.	West Virginia
Wyo.	Wyoming
Yugo.	Yugoslavia
Zim.	Zimbabwe

A

NAME	LATITUDE	LONGITUDE	PAGE
Aberdeen, Scot.	57° 09′ N	02° 06′ W	42
Abidjan, Côte d'Ivoire	05 20 N	04 01 W	68
Abilene, Texas	32 28 N	99 43 W	76
Abu Dhabi,* Un. Arab Emirates	24 28 N	54 22 E	52
Abuja,* Nigeria	67 20 N	09 05 E	68
Acapulco, Mex.	16 51 N	99 55 W	80
Accra,* Ghana	05 33 N	00 12 W	68
Aconcagua (mt.)	32 45 S	70 14 W	88
Adana, Turkey	37 00 N	35 15 E	44
Ad Dahna' (desert)	27 30 N	45 00 E	52
Addis Ababa,* Ethiopia	09 01 N	38 45 E	69
Adelaide, Austl.	34 55 S	138 37 E	59
Aden, Yemen	12 45 N	45 05 E	52
Adirondack (mts.)	44 00 N	74 00 W	78
Adrar de Iforas (plat.)	20 00 N	02 00 E	68
Adriatic (sea)	42 50 N	15 40 E	44
Aegean (sea)	40 23 N	25 00 E	44
Afghanistan	34 00 N	65 00 E	49
Agaña,* Guam	13 29 N	144 47 E	62
Agra, India	27 10 N	78 08 E	53
Aguascalientes, Mex,	21 53 N	102 18 W	80
Agulhas (cape)	34 51 S	19 59 E	70
Ahaggar (mts.)	23 00 N	05 00 E	68
Ahmadabad, India	23 00 N	72 44 E	53
Ahvāz, Iran	31 19 N	48 42 E	52
Aklavik, N.W. Terrs.	68 12 N	135 00 W	79
Akron, Ohio	41 05 N	81 31 W	78
Al Kuwait,* Kuwait	29 20 N	48 02 E	52
Alabama (state), U.S.	33 00 N	87 00 W	78
Åland (isls.)	60 15 N	20 00 E	43
Alaska (gulf)	59 00 N	145 00 W	76
Alaska (pen.)	57 00 N	158 00 W	76
Alaska (range)	63 00 N	151 00 W	76
Alaska (state), U.S.	65 00 N	154 00 W	76
Albania	41 00 N	20 00 E	44
Albany (river)	52 16 N	81 30 W	79
Albany,* N.Y.	42 39 N	73 45 W	78
Albert (lake)	01 45 N	31 00 E	69
Alberta (prov.), Canada	54 00 N	115 00 W	79
Albuquerque, N.M.	35 05 N	106 39 W	76
Aleppo, Syria	36 12 N	37 10 E	52
Aleutian (isls.)	52 00 N	175 00 W	76
Alexandria, Egypt	31 12 N	29 55 E	69
Alexandria, La.	31 18 N	92 27 W	77
Algeria	30 00 N	04 00 E	68
Algiers,* Alg.	36 45 N	03 04 E	68
Alicante, Spain	38 21 N	00 29 W	42
Al Jīsah, Egypt	30 01 N	31 13 E	69
Allahabad, India	25 30 N	81 58 E	69
Allentown, Pa.	40 37 N	75 29 W	77
Almaty, Kazak.	43 15 N	76 57 E	54
Alps (mts.)	46 40 N	10 00 E	42
Alsace (region)	48 30 N	07 35 E	42
Altai (mts.)	47 00 N	92 00 E	54
Altun (mts.)	37 30 N	88 00 E	54
Amarillo, Texas	35 13 N	101 50 W	76
Amazon (river)	00 00	49 00 W	87
American Highland (upland)	72 30 S	78 00 E	71
American Samoa	14 20 S	170 00 W	63
Amherst, N.S.	45 50 N	64 12 W	79
Amman,* Jordan	31 57 N	35 56 E	52
Amritsar, India	31 45 N	74 58 E	53
Amsterdam,* Neth.	52 20 N	04 50 E	42
Amudar'ya (river)	43 40 N	59 01 E	46
Amundsen (sea)	72 00 S	109 00 W	71
Amur (river)	52 56 N	141 10 E	55
Anadyr' (mts.)	67 00 N	176 00 E	47
Anatolia (region)	39 00 N	30 00 E	44
Anchorage, Alaska	61 10 N	149 55 W	76
Andaman (isls.)	12 00 N	92 45 E	53
Andes (mts.)	27 00 S	69 00 W	82
Andorra	42 34 N	01 35 E	42
Angara (river)	56 05 N	101 48 E	47
Angola	12 00 S	17 00 E	70
Ankara,* Turkey	39 55 N	32 52 E	44
Annapolis,* Md.	38 58 N	76 30 W	78
Ann Arbor, Mich.	42 17 N	83 45 W	78
Anshan, China	41 08 N	122 59 E	55
Antananarivo,* Madagascar	18 54 S	47 30 E	70
Antarctic (pen.)	69 30 S	65 00 W	71
Anticosti (isl.)	49 30 N	63 00 W	79
Antigua and Barbuda	17 05 N	61 48 W	81
Antwerp, Belg.	51 20 N	04 25 E	42
Apennines (mts.)	43 00 N	13 00 E	44
Apia,* W. Samoa	13 56 S	171 45 W	63
Appalachian (mts.)	40 00 N	78 00 W	78
Appleton, Wis.	44 16 N	88 25 W	78
Aqaba (gulf)	29 30 N	35 05 E	52
Aqmola,* Kazakstan	51 10 N	71 30 E	62
Aqtōbe, Kazakstan	50 17 N	57 10 E	45
Arafura (sea)	09 00 S	134 00 E	57
Arakan (mts.)	19 00 N	94 00 E	53
Aral (sea)	44 46 N	60 00 E	45
Ararat (mt.)	39 42 N	44 18 E	45
Aras (river)	39 56 N	48 20 E	45
Archangel, Russia	64 34 N	40 32 E	43
Ardennes (region)	50 10 N	05 30 E	42
Arequipa, Peru	16 24 S	71 33 W	86
Argentina	35 00 S	65 00 W	88
Århus, Den.	56 11 N	10 15 E	43
Arizona (state), U.S.	34 00 N	112 00 W	76
Arkansas (river)	33 48 N	91 07 W	77
Arkansas (state), U.S.	34 45 N	92 30 W	77
Armenia	40 15 N	45 00 E	45
Aruba (isl.) Neth.	12 30 N	69 58 W	81
Ascension (isl.)	07 57 S	14 22 W	12
Asheville, N.C.	35 35 N	82 33 W	77
Ashgabat,* Turkmenistan	37 57 N	58 23 E	45
Asir (region)	18 00 N	42 00 E	52
Asmara,* Eritrea	15 20 N	38 57 E	69
Astrakhan', Russia	46 21 N	48 03 E	69
Asunción,* Para.	25 16 S	57 40 W	88
Atacama (desert)	24 00 S	70 00 W	88
Atatürk (res.)	37 30 N	38 30 E	44
Athabasca (lake)	59 20 N	109 00 W	79
Athabasca (river)	58 30 N	111 00 W	79
Athens, Ga.	33 57 N	83 23 W	78
Athens,* Greece	37 59 N	23 44 E	44
Atlanta,* Georgia	33 45 N	84 24 W	78
Atlantic City, N.J.	39 21 N	74 27 W	78
Atlas (mts.)	34 00 N	00 01 W	68
Attu (isl.)	52 55 N	172 55 E	76
Auckland, N.Z.	36 53 S	174 45 E	61
Augsburg, Germany	48 20 N	10 53 E	42
Augusta, Ga.	33 28 N	81 58 W	78
Augusta,* Maine	44 19 N	69 46 W	78
Austin,* Texas	30 16 N	97 45 W	77
Australia	25 00 S	135 00 E	59
Australian Capital Terr.	35 18 S	149 07 E	59
Austria	47 15 N	14 00 E	42
Axel Heiberg (isl.)	79 00 N	90 00 W	79
Azerbaijan	40 30 N	48 00 E	45
Azores (isls.)	38 30 N	28 00 W	12
Azov (sea)	46 00 N	37 00 E	44

B

NAME	LATITUDE	LONGITUDE	PAGE
Baffin (bay)	74° 00′ N	68° 00′ W	79
Baffin (isl.)	68 30 N	70 00 W	79
Baghdad,* Iraq	33 21 N	44 24 E	52
Bahamas	24 00 N	76 00 W	81
Bahrain	26 00 N	50 40 E	52
Baja, California (pen.)	28 00 N	114 00 W	81
Bakersfield, Calif.	35 22 N	119 01 W	76
Bākhtarān, Iran	34 19 N	47 04 E	52
Baku,* Azerbaijan	40 23 N	49 51 E	45
Balaton (lake)	46 50 N	17 50 E	44
Balearic (isls.)	39 30 N	03 00 E	42
Bali (isl.)	08 30 S	115 30 E	56
Balkan (mts.)	43 15 N	23 00 E	44
Balkhash (lake)	46 00 N	74 00 E	54
Baltic (sea)	56 30 N	19 00 E	43
Baltimore, Md.	39 17 N	76 37 W	78
Bamako,* Mali	12 38 N	07 59 W	68
Banaba (isl.)	00 52 S	169 35 E	62
Banda (sea)	06 00 S	128 00 E	57
Bandar Seri Begawan,* Brunei	04 55 N	114 55 E	56
Bandung, Indon.	06 56 S	107 36 E	56
Bangalore, India	12 59 N	77 28 E	53
Bangka (isl.)	02 22 S	106 08 E	56
Bangkok,* Thai.	13 45 N	100 30 E	56
Bangladesh	23 30 N	90 00 E	53
Bangor, Maine	44 48 N	68 46 W	78
Bangui,* CAfr.	04 22 N	18 36 E	69
Bangweulu (lake)	11 00 S	29 45 E	70
Banjul,* Gambia	13 28 N	16 35 W	68
Banks (isl.)	73 00 N	122 00 W	79
Baotou, China	40 40 N	109 59 E	55
Barbados	13 10 N	59 30 W	81
Barcelona, Spain	41 38 N	02 10 E	42
Barents (sea)	70 00 N	45 00 E	46
Bari, Italy	41 07 N	16 52 E	44
Barisan (mts.)	03 00 S	102 15 E	56
Barkly Tableland (plat.)	18 00 S	136 00 E	59
Baroda, India	22 18 N	73 12 E	53
Barquisimeto, Ven.	10 04 N	69 19 W	86
Barranquilla, Col.	10 59 N	74 50 W	86
Basel, Switz.	47 35 N	07 32 E	42
Bass (strait)	40 15 S	146 00 E	61
Bathurst, N.B.	47 36 N	65 39 W	79
Baton Rouge,* La.	30 27 N	91 11 W	78
Battle Creek, Mich.	42 19 N	85 11 W	78
Baykal (lake)	54 00 N	109 00 E	47
Beaufort (sea)	71 00 N	140 00 W	79
Beaumont, Texas	30 05 N	94 06 W	77
Beersheba, Israel	31 14 N	34 47 E	52
Beijing (Peking),* China	39 56 N	116 24 E	55
Beira, Moz.	19 50 S	34 50 E	70
Beirut,* Lebanon	33 55 N	35 30 E	52
Belarus	53 00 N	28 00 E	43
Belém, Brazil	01 28 S	48 27 W	87
Belfast,* No. Ire.	54 35 N	05 55 W	42
Belgium	50 45 N	04 30 E	42
Belgrade,* Yugo.	44 48 N	20 29 E	44
Belitung (isl.)	02 54 S	107 58 E	56
Belize	17 00 N	88 45 W	80
Belle Isle (strait)	51 30 N	56 30 W	79
Bellingshausen (sea)	69 00 S	81 00 E	71
Belmopan,* Belize	17 15 N	88 47 W	80
Belo Horizonte, Brazil	19 56 S	43 57 W	87
Bengal (bay)	18 00 N	90 00 E	53
Benghazi, Libya	32 07 N	20 03 E	69
Benin	09 00 N	02 00 E	68
Benin, Bight of (bay)	05 00 N	04 00 E	68
Ben Nevis (mt.)	56 48 N	04 59 W	42
Bergen, Norway	60 25 N	05 20 E	43
Bering (sea)	55 00 N	180 00	47
Bering (strait)	67 00 N	170 00 W	76
Berkeley, Calif.	37 52 N	122 16 W	76
Berlin,* Germany	52 30 N	13 20 E	42
Bermuda	32 20 N	64 40 W	73
Bern,* Switz.	47 00 N	07 30 E	42
Bhopāl, India	23 16 N	77 24 E	53
Bhutan	27 15 N	90 00 E	53
Bialystok, Poland	53 09 N	23 09 E	44
Bikini (isl.)	11 37 N	165 33 E	62
Bilbao, Spain	43 16 N	03 05 W	42
Biloxi, Miss.	30 24 N	88 53 W	78
Binghamton, N.Y.	42 06 N	75 55 W	78
Birmingham, Ala.	33 31 N	86 49 W	78
Birmingham, Eng.	52 30 N	01 55 W	42
Biscay (bay)	45 00 N	05 00 W	42
Bishkek,* Kyrgyzstan	42 54 N	74 36 E	54
Bismarck (arch.)	04 00 S	150 00 E	62
Bismarck,* N.D.	46 48 N	100 47 W	76
Bissau,* Guinea-Bissau	11 51 N	15 35 W	68

NAME	LATITUDE	LONGITUDE	PAGE
Bitterroot (mts.)	46 30 N	114 25 W	76
Black (sea)	42 30 N	35 00 E	44
Black Hills (mts.)	44 00 N	103 30 W	76
Blanc (mt.)	45 50 N	06 51 E	42
Blantyre, Malawi	15 49 S	35 00 E	70
Bloemfontein, S. Afr.	29 07 S	26 14 E	70
Bloomington, Ill.	40 29 N	88 59 W	78
Bloomington, Ind.	39 10 N	86 32 W	78
Blue Nile (river)	15 37 N	32 31 E	69
Bogotá,* Col.	04 36 N	74 05 W	86
Boise,* Idaho	43 37 N	116 12 W	76
Bolivia	16 00 S	64 00 W	86
Bologna, Italy	44 30 N	11 20 E	42
Bombay, India	19 00 N	72 48 E	53
Bonaire (isl.), Neth. Ant.	12 12 N	68 15 W	81
Bonifacio (strait)	41 18 N	09 15 E	42
Bonn, Germany	50 44 N	07 06 E	42
Boothia (pen.)	70 00 N	95 00 W	79
Bordeaux, France	44 50 N	00 35 W	42
Borneo (isl.)	00 00	113 00 E	56
Bornholm (isl.)	55 10 N	15 00 E	43
Bosnia and Herzegovina	44 00 N	18 00 E	44
Bosporus (strait)	41 15 N	29 10 E	44
Boston,* Mass.	42 21 N	71 03 W	78
Bothnia (gulf)	62 00 N	20 00 E	43
Botou, China	38 05 N	116 30 E	55
Botswana	22 00 S	24 00 E	70
Bougainville (isl.)	06 10 S	155 15 E	62
Bouvet (isl.)	54 26 S	03 24 E	12
Bozeman, Mont.	45 41 N	111 02 W	76
Bradford, Eng.	53 47 N	01 45 W	42
Brahmaputra (river)	29 30 N	95 00 E	53
Brăila, Rom.	45 15 N	27 58 E	44
Brandon, Man.	49 50 N	99 57 W	79
Brasília,* Brazil	15 47 S	47 55 W	87
Braşov, Romania	45 39 N	25 37 E	44
Bratislava,* Slovakia	48 09 N	17 07 E	44
Braunschweig, Germany	52 22 N	10 42 E	42
Brazil	14 00 S	50 00 W	83
Brazos (river)	28 57 N	95 18 W	77
Brazzaville,* Congo	04 17 S	15 14 E	70
Bremen, Germany	53 10 N	08 40 E	42
Brescia, Italy	45 30 N	10 15 E	42
Bridgeport, Conn.	41 11 N	73 12 W	78
Bridgetown,* Barbados	13 06 N	59 37 W	81
Brisbane, Austl.	27 25 S	153 05 E	59
Bristol (bay)	57 45 N	160 00 W	76
Bristol, Eng.	51 28 N	02 35 W	42
Britanny (region)	48 00 N	03 00 W	42
British Columbia (prov.), Canada	55 00 N	125 00 W	79
British Indian Ocean Terr.	06 00 S	72 00 E	13
Brno, Czech Rep.	49 10 N	16 30 E	42
Brooks (mts.)	68 30 N	153 00 W	76
Brownsville, Texas	25 54 N	97 30 W	77
Brunei	04 30 N	115 00 E	56
Brussels,* Belg.	50 50 N	04 22 E	42
Bryan, Texas	30 40 N	96 22 W	77
Bucharest,* Rom.	44 25 N	26 06 E	44
Budapest,* Hungary	47 30 N	19 10 E	44
Buenos Aires,* Arg.	34 36 S	58 26 W	88
Buffalo, N.Y.	42 53 N	78 52 W	78
Bujumbura,* Burundi	03 23 S	29 22 E	70
Bulgaria	42 30 N	25 30 E	44
Burgundy (region)	47 00 N	05 00 E	42
Burkina	12 00 N	01 30 W	68
Burlington, Vt.	44 28 N	73 12 W	78
Burma	20 00 N	96 00 E	49
Bursa, Turkey	40 11 N	29 04 E	44
Burundi	03 30 S	30 00 E	70
Bydgoszcz, Poland	53 50 N	27 35 E	42

C

NAME	LATITUDE	LONGITUDE	PAGE
Caatingas (region)	07° 00′ N	43° 00′ W	87
Cádiz, Spain	36 32 N	06 18 W	42
Cagliari, Italy	39 13 N	09 07 E	42
Cairo,* Egypt	30 03 N	31 15 E	69
Calcutta, India	22 30 N	88 30 E	53
Calgary, Alta.	51 01 N	114 05 W	79
Cali, Col.	03 28 N	76 30 W	86
California (gulf)	28 00 N	112 00 W	81
California (state), U.S.	37 00 N	120 00 W	76
Callao, Peru	12 03 S	77 10 W	86
Camagüey, Cuba	21 53 N	77 55 W	81
Cambodia	12 00 N	105 00 E	56
Cameroon	05 00 N	13 00 E	68
Campbellton, N.B.	48 00 N	66 40 W	79
Campeche (bay)	20 00 N	93 00 W	80
Canada	60 00 N	100 00 W	79
Canadian (river)	35 28 N	95 04 W	76
Canary (isls.)	28 00 N	16 00 W	68
Canaveral (cape)	28 27 N	80 32 W	77
Canberra,* Aust.	35 18 S	149 07 E	61
Cannes, France	43 33 N	07 01 E	42
Cantabrica (mts.)	43 15 N	05 00 W	42
Canton (Guangzhou), China	23 07 N	113 15 E	55
Canton, Ohio	40 48 N	81 23 W	78
Cape Town,* S. Afr.	33 57 S	18 28 E	70
Cape Verde	16 00 N	24 00 W	12
Cape York (pen.)	13 00 S	142 30 E	59
Caprivi Strip (region)	18 00 S	23 00 E	70
Caracas,* Ven.	10 30 N	66 55 W	86
Cardiff,* Wales	51 30 N	03 12 W	42
Caribbean (sea)	15 00 N	75 00 W	81
Caroline (isls.)	08 00 N	150 00 E	62
Carpathian (mts.)	48 00 N	23 00 E	44
Carpentaria (gulf)	15 00 S	139 00 E	59
Carson City,* Nev.	39 10 N	119 45 W	76
Cartegena, Spain	37 36 N	00 59 W	42
Casablanca, Mor.	33 36 N	07 38 W	68
Cascades (mts.)	45 00 N	122 00 W	76
Casper, Wyo.	42 51 N	106 19 W	76
Caspian (sea)	42 00 N	50 00 E	44
Catalonia (region)	41 15 N	02 00 E	42
Caucasus (mts.)	42 30 N	45 00 E	45
Cayenne,* Fr. Guiana	04 56 N	52 20 W	87
Cayman (isls.)	19 30 N	80 40 W	80
Cebu, Philippines	10 18 N	123 54 E	57
Cebu (isl.)	10 18 N	123 54 E	57
Cedar Rapids, Iowa	42 00 N	91 41 W	78
Celebes (isl.)	02 00 S	121 00 E	57
Central African Republic	06 00 N	20 00 E	69
Ceuta, Spain	35 52 N	05 20 W	68
Ceylon (Sri Lanka)	07 00 N	81 00 E	53
Chad	15 00 N	18 00 E	69
Chad (lake)	13 15 N	14 30 E	68
Champaign, Ill.	40 07 N	88 14 W	78
Champlain (lake)	44 30 N	73 20 W	78
Changchun, China	43 53 N	125 18 E	55
Chang (Yangtze) (river)	31 48 N	121 10 E	55
Changsha, China	28 12 N	112 59 E	55
Channel (isls.)	49 30 N	02 30 W	42
Chaozhou, China	23 40 N	116 38 E	55
Charleston, S.C.	32 47 N	79 56 W	78
Charleston,* W. Va.	38 21 N	81 38 W	78
Charlotte, N.C.	35 14 N	80 51 W	78
Charlottesville, Va.	38 02 N	78 30 W	78
Charlottetown,* P.E.I.	46 14 N	63 08 W	79
Chattanooga, Tenn.	35 03 N	85 19 W	78
Chelyabinsk, Russia	55 10 N	61 24 E	45
Chelyuskin (cape)	77 45 N	104 30 E	47
Chemnitz, Germany	50 40 N	12 55 E	42
Chengdu, China	30 40 N	104 04 E	54
Chesapeake (bay)	38 35 N	76 25 W	78
Cheshskaya (bay)	67 30 N	47 00 E	43
Chesterfield Inlet, N.W. Terrs.	63 40 N	91 45 W	79
Cheyenne,* Wyo.	41 08 N	104 49 W	76
Chibougamau, Qué.	49 55 N	74 22 W	79
Chicago, Ill.	41 52 N	87 38 W	78
Chicoutimi, Qué.	48 30 N	71 00 W	79
Chidley (cape)	60 23 N	64 26 W	79
Chihuahua, Mex.	28 38 N	106 05 W	81
Chile	32 00 S	71 00 W	83
Chilliwack, Br. Col.	49 10 N	121 57 W	76
Chiloé (isl.)	42 00 S	74 00 W	88
Chimborazo (mt.)	01 28 S	78 48 W	86
China	35 00 N	105 00 E	54
Chişinău,* Moldova	47 00 N	28 50 E	44
Chittagong, Bangladesh	22 15 N	91 55 E	53
Chongqing, China	29 34 N	106 35 E	54
Chonos (arch.)	45 00 S	74 00 W	88
Christchurch, N. Z.	43 32 S	172 39 E	59
Christmas (isl.)	10 30 S	105 40 E	13
Chuckchi (pen.)	66 00 N	175 00 W	47
Churchill (river)	58 47 N	94 11 W	79
Churchill, Man.	58 46 N	94 10 W	79
Cimarron (river)	36 07 N	96 30 W	76
Cincinnati, Ohio	39 06 N	84 31 W	78
Ciudad Guayana, Ven.	08 22 N	62 40 W	86
Ciudad Juárez, Mex.	31 44 N	106 29 W	81
Cleveland, Ohio	41 30 N	81 42 W	78
Clipperton (isl.)	10 13 N	109 10 W	12
Cluj-Napoca, Romania	46 45 N	23 36 E	44
Coast Ranges (mts.)	42 00 N	123 15 W	76
Cocos (isls.)	05 31 N	87 00 W	13
Cod (cape)	42 04 N	70 10 W	78
Cologne, Germany	51 00 N	07 00 E	42
Colombia	05 00 N	74 00 W	86
Colombo,* Sri Lanka	06 55 N	79 50 E	53
Colorado (river), Arg.	39 51 S	62 08 W	88
Colorado (river), U.S.	28 52 N	96 02 W	76
Colorado (state), U.S.	39 00 N	105 30 W	76
Colorado Springs, Colo.	38 50 N	104 49 W	76
Columbia (river)	46 15 N	123 40 W	76
Columbia, Mo.	38 57 N	92 20 W	78
Columbia,* S.C.	34 00 N	81 02 W	78
Columbus, Ga.	32 28 N	84 59 W	78
Columbus,* Ohio	39 58 N	83 00 W	78
Comorin (cape)	07 37 N	77 28 E	53
Comoros	12 00 S	44 00 E	65
Conakry,* Guinea	09 31 N	13 42 W	68
Concepción, Chile	36 50 S	73 01 W	88
Concord,* N.H.	43 12 N	71 32 W	78
Congo	00 00	15 00 E	65
Congo (basin)	00 00	22 00 E	69
Congo (river)	06 05 S	12 20 E	70
Connecticut (state), U.S.	41 38 N	72 45 W	78
Constantine, Alg.	36 23 N	06 38 E	68
Cook (isls.)	20 00 S	158 00 W	63
Cook (mt.)	43 36 S	170 08 E	59
Cook (strait)	41 15 S	174 30 E	59
Copenhagen,* Denmark	55 40 N	12 35 E	43
Coppermine, N.W. Terrs.	67 50 N	115 05 W	79
Coral (sea)	14 00 S	156 00 E	59
Córdoba, Arg.	31 25 S	64 10 W	88
Córdoba, Spain	37 54 N	04 46 W	42
Corfu (isl.)	39 38 N	19 56 E	44
Corinth (gulf)	38 19 N	22 04 E	44
Cork, Ireland	51 55 N	08 30 W	42
Corner Brook, Newf.	48 57 N	57 56 W	79
Cornwall, Ont.	45 01 N	74 44 W	79
Coromandel Coast	13 00 N	80 15 E	53
Corpus Christi, Texas	27 48 N	97 24 W	77
Corsica (isl.)	42 00 N	09 00 E	42
Corvallis, Ore.	44 34 N	123 16 W	76
Costa del Sol (coast)	36 30 N	04 00 W	42
Costa Rica	10 00 N	84 00 W	80
Côte d'Ivoire	07 00 N	05 00 W	68
Coventry, Eng.	52 25 N	01 33 W	42
Cranbrook, Br. Col.	49 31 N	115 46 W	79
Crete (isl.)	35 15 N	25 00 E	44
Crimea (pen.)	45 00 N	34 00 E	44
Croatia	45 30 N	16 00 E	44
Cuba	22 00 N	80 00 W	81
Curaçao (isl.), Neth. Ant.	12 11 N	69 00 W	81
Curitiba, Brazil	25 25 S	49 15 W	88
Cyclades (isls.)	37 00 N	75 00 E	44
Cyprus	35 00 N	33 00 E	52
Czech Republic	49 00 N	17 00 E	44
Czectochowa, Poland	50 49 N	19 06 E	44

D

NAME	LATITUDE	LONGITUDE	PAGE
Da Hinggang (mts.)	48° 30′ N	120° 00′ E	55
Dacca,* Bangladesh	23 45 N	90 25 E	53
Dakar,* Senegal	14 40 N	17 28 W	68
Dalian, China	38 55 N	121 39 E	55
Dallas, Texas	32 47 N	96 48 W	77
Damascus,* Syria	33 35 N	36 28 E	52
Damavand (mt.)	35 57 N	52 08 E	52
Da Nang, Vietnam	16 04 N	108 13 E	56
Danube (river)	45 20 N	29 40 E	44
Dardanelles (strait)	40 07 N	26 23 E	44
Dar es Salaam,* Tanzania	06 48 S	39 17 E	70
Darling (river)	32 00 S	142 57 E	59
Darwin, Austl.	12 27 S	130 50 E	59
Davao, Philippines	07 18 N	125 25 E	57
Davenport, Iowa	41 31 N	90 34 W	78
Davis (strait)	66 30 N	58 00 W	79
Dawson, Yukon Terr.	64 04 N	139 25 W	79
Dayton, Ohio	39 46 N	84 12 W	78
Daytona Beach, Fla.	29 13 N	81 01 W	78
Dead (sea)	31 30 N	35 30 E	52
Debrecen, Hungary	47 32 N	21 38 E	44
Deccan (plat.)	17 00 N	78 00 E	53
Delaware (state), U.S.	39 00 N	75 30 W	78
Delgado (cape)	10 41 S	40 38 E	70
Delhi, India	28 29 N	77 15 E	53
Denmark	56 00 N	10 30 E	43
Denver,* Colo.	39 45 N	104 59 W	76
Des Moines,* Iowa	41 35 N	93 37 W	78
Detroit, Mich.	42 20 N	83 03 W	78
Devon (isl.)	75 00 N	86 00 W	79
Dezhneva (cape)	66 05 N	169 40 W	47
Diego Garcia (isl.)	07 36 S	72 28 E	13
Dinaric Alps (mts.)	43 30 N	17 00 E	44
District of Columbia, U.S.	38 54 N	77 01 W	78
Diyarbakir, Turkey	37 55 N	40 14 E	44
Djibouti	12 00 N	43 00 E	69
Djibouti,* Djibouti	11 35 N	43 09 E	69
Dnepr (river)	46 30 N	32 36 E	44
Dnestr (river)	46 20 N	30 18 E	44
Dnipropetrovs'k, Ukraine	48 27 N	35 01 E	44
Doğukaradeniz (mts.)	40 30 N	39 00 E	44
Doha,* Qatar	25 17 N	51 32 E	52
Dominica	15 25 N	61 20 W	81
Dominican Republic	19 00 N	70 00 W	81
Don (river)	47 04 N	39 18 E	44
Dondra Head (prom.)	06 00 N	80 30 E	53
Donets (river)	47 36 N	40 54 E	44
Donets'k, Ukraine	48 00 N	37 48 E	44
Dortmund, Germany	51 30 N	07 30 E	42
Douala, Cameroon	04 03 N	09 37 E	68
Douro (river)	41 09 N	08 39 W	42
Dover (strait)	51 00 N	01 30 E	42
Dover,* Del.	39 09 N	75 32 W	78
Drake (passage)	60 00 S	67 00 W	88
Dresden, Germany	51 10 N	13 45 E	42
Dublin,* Ire.	53 20 N	06 10 W	42
Dubrovnik, Croatia	42 38 N	18 07 E	44
Duluth, Minn.	46 47 N	92 06 W	78
Dundee, Scot.	56 30 N	02 58 W	42
Durango, Mex.	24 02 N	104 40 W	81
Durban, S. Afr.	29 51 S	31 00 E	70
Durham, N.C.	35 59 N	78 54 W	78
Dushanbe,* Tajikistan	38 33 N	68 48 E	46
Düsseldorf, Germany	51 20 N	06 40 E	42
Dvina, Northern (river)	64 32 N	40 37 E	46

E

NAME	LATITUDE	LONGITUDE	PAGE
East China (sea)	30° 00′ N	125° 00′ E	55
Easter (isl.)	27 08 S	109 25 W	63
Eastern Ghats (mts.)	17 30 N	83 00 E	53
East London, S. Afr.	33 01 S	27 55 E	70
Eau Claire, Wis.	44 49 N	91 30 W	78
Ebro (river)	40 43 N	00 54 E	42
Ecatepec, Mex.	19 35 N	99 04 W	80
Ecuador	01 00 S	79 00 W	86
Edinburgh,* Scot.	55 55 N	03 10 W	42
Edmonton,* Alta.	53 32 N	113 30 W	79
Edmundston, N.B.	47 22 N	68 20 W	79
Edward (lake)	00 20 S	29 35 E	69
Edwards (plat.)	30 30 N	101 00 W	76
Efate (isl.)	17 40 S	168 23 E	62
Egypt	27 00 N	30 00 E	69
Elbe (river)	53 30 N	09 45 E	42
Elbert (mt.)	39 07 N	106 26 W	76
El'brus (mt.)	43 21 N	42 26 E	45
Elburz (mts.)	36 00 N	52 00 E	52
Ellesmere (isl.)	79 00 N	82 00 W	79
El Paso, Texas	31 45 N	106 29 W	76
El Salvador	13 30 N	89 00 W	80
Enewetak (isl.)	11 11 N	162 21 E	62
England, U.K.	53 00 N	01 00 W	42
English (chan.)	50 00 N	02 30 W	42
Equatorial Guinea	01 30 N	10 00 E	68
Erie (lake)	42 20 N	81 00 W	78
Erie, Pa.	42 07 N	80 05 W	78
Eritrea	15 00 N	40 00 E	69
Erzgebirge ,(mts.)	50 30 N	13 00 E	42
Eşfahān, Iran	32 40 N	51 38 E	52
Espíritu Santo (isl.)	15 15 S	166 55 E	62
Essen, Germany	51 30 N	07 00 E	42
Estonia	59 00 N	26 00 E	43
Ethiopia	10 00 N	40 00 E	69
Eugene, Ore.	44 03 N	123 06 W	76
Euphrates (river)	38 00 N	39 05 E	52
Evansville, Ind.	37 58 N	87 34 W	78
Everest (mt.)	27 58 N	87 05 E	53
Everglades Nat'l Park, U.S.	25 15 N	81 00 W	77
Eyre (lake)	28 30 S	137 15 E	59

F

NAME	LATITUDE	LONGITUDE	PAGE
Fairbanks, Alaska	64° 51′ N	147° 43′ W	76
Faisalabad, Pak.	31 25 N	73 05 E	53
Falkland (isls.)	52 00 S	59 00 W	88
Fall River, Mass.	41 42 N	71 09 W	78
Fargo, N.D.	46 52 N	96 48 W	77
Faroe (isls.)	62 00 N	07 00 W	39
Fayetteville, Ark.	36 04 N	94 09 W	77
Fayetteville, N.C.	35 03 N	78 52 W	78
Ferrara, Italy	44 50 N	11 40 E	42
Fezzan (region)	27 00 N	14 00 E	68
Fiji	17 00 S	179 00 E	62
Finisterre (cape)	42 53 N	09 16 W	42
Finland	64 00 N	26 00 E	43
Finland (gulf)	60 00 N	27 00 E	43
Flin Flon, Man.-Sask.	54 46 N	101 53 W	79
Flint, Mich.	43 01 N	83 42 W	78
Florence, Italy	43 46 N	11 13 E	42
Flores (isl.)	08 30 S	121 00 E	57
Flores (sea)	05 39 S	119 54 E	56
Florida (keys)	24 44 N	81 00 W	78
Florida (state), U.S.	28 00 N	82 00 W	78

NAME	LATITUDE	LONGITUDE	PAGE
Fortaleza, Brazil	03 41 S	38 33 W	87
Fort Collins, Colo.	40 35 N	105 05 W	76
Fort-de-France,* Mart.	14 36 N	61 05 W	81
Fort Frances, Ont.	48 37 N	93 25 W	79
Fort McMurray, Alta.	56 44 N	111 23 W	79
Fort Myers, Fla.	26 38 N	81 52 W	78
Fort Nelson, Br. Col.	58 49 N	122 36 W	79
Fort Smith, Ark.	35 23 N	94 26 W	77
Fort Smith, N.W. Terrs.	60 00 N	112 00 W	79
Fort Wayne, Ind.	41 04 N	85 08 W	78
Fort Worth, Texas	32 45 N	97 20 W	77
Foxe (basin)	68 00 N	78 00 W	79
France	47 00 N	02 00 E	42
Frankfort,* Ky.	38 12 N	84 53 W	78
Frankfurt, Germany	50 10 N	08 30 E	42
Franz Josef Land (isls.)	81 00 N	51 00 E	46
Fraser (river)	49 08 N	123 10 W	79
Fredericton,* N.B.	45 57 N	66 38 W	79
Freetown,* Sierra Leone	08 29 N	13 13 W	68
French Guiana	04 00 N	53 00 W	87
French Polynesia	15 00 S	140 00 W	63
Fresno, Calif.	36 44 N	119 47 W	76
Fukuoka, Japan	33 35 N	130 24 E	55
Funafuti (isl.)	08 31 S	179 08 E	62
Fundy (bay)	45 00 N	66 00 W	79
Fushun, China	41 52 N	123 53 E	55
Fuzhou, China	26 05 N	119 19 E	55

G

NAME	LATITUDE	LONGITUDE	PAGE
Gabon	00° 00′	12° 00′ E	68
Gaborone,* Botswana	24 40 S	25 54 E	70
Gainesville, Fla.	29 39 N	82 20 W	78
Galápagos (isls.)	00 15 S	90 00 W	12
Galaţi, Romania	45 26 N	28 03 E	44
Galveston, Texas	29 18 N	94 48 W	77
Gambia	13 30 N	15 30 W	68
Gäncä, Azerbaijan	40 40 N	46 22 E	45
Ganges (river)	26 00 N	80 15 E	53
Garonne (river)	45 01 N	00 36 W	42
Gary, Ind.	41 35 N	87 20 W	77
Gaspé (pen.)	48 30 N	65 00 W	79
Gaziantep, Turkey	37 05 N	37 22 E	44
Gdańsk, Poland	54 20 N	18 30 E	43
Gdynia, Poland	54 32 N	18 33 E	43
Geneva (lake)	46 25 N	06 25 E	42
Geneva, Switzerland	46 12 N	06 10 E	42
Genoa, Italy	44 25 N	08 55 E	42
Georgetown,* Guyana	06 49 N	58 10 W	68
Georgetown, Malaysia	05 25 N	100 19 E	56
Georgia	42 00 N	43 00 E	45
Georgia (state), U.S.	32 30 N	83 15 W	78
Georgian (bay)	45 15 N	80 45 W	79
Germany	51 00 N	10 00 E	42
Ghana	07 00 N	01 00 W	68
Ghent, Belgium	51 10 N	03 40 E	42
Gibraltar (strait)	35 55 N	05 35 W	42
Gibraltar	36 08 N	05 22 W	42
Gijón, Spain	43 32 N	05 40 W	42
Glacier Nat'l Park, U.S.	48 35 N	114 00 W	76
Glasgow, Scot.	55 50 N	04 10 W	42
Gobi (desert)	43 00 N	110 00 E	54
Godavari (river)	19 00 N	79 00 E	53
Godwin Austen (K2) (mt.)	35 53 N	76 30 E	53
Goiânia, Brazil	16 40 S	49 16 W	87
Good Hope (cape)	34 21 S	18 29 E	70
Göteborg, Sweden	57 43 N	11 58 E	43
Gotland (isl.)	57 45 N	18 45 E	43
Grampians (mts.)	56 45 N	04 30 W	42
Granada, Spain	37 11 N	03 36 W	42
Gran Chaco (region)	24 00 S	62 00 W	88
Grand Canyon Nat'l Park, U.S.	36 03 N	112 08 W	76
Grande Prairie, Alta.	55 10 N	118 48 W	79
Grand Falls, Newf.	48 56 N	55 40 W	79
Grand Forks, N.D.	47 52 N	97 03 W	77
Grand Rapids, Mich.	42 58 N	85 40 W	78
Graz, Austria	47 00 N	15 30 E	42
Great Australian Bight (bay)	33 00 S	130 00 E	59
Great Barrier (reef)	16 00 S	145 50 E	59
Great Bear (lake)	66 00 N	121 00 W	79
Great Britain (isl.)	54 00 N	02 00 W	42
Great Dividing Range (mts.)	35 00 S	149 35 E	59
Great Indian (desert)	28 00 N	73 00 E	53
Great Rift (valley)	09 00 N	41 00 E	69
Great Salt (lake)	41 05 N	112 30 W	76
Great Sandy (desert)	20 00 S	124 00 E	59
Great Slave (lake)	61 00 N	114 00 W	79
Great Victoria (desert)	27 00 S	130 00 E	59
Greater Antilles (isls.)	18 00 N	74 00 W	81
Greece	39 00 N	23 00 E	44
Greeley, Colo.	40 25 N	101 41 W	76
Green Bay, Wis.	44 31 N	88 00 W	78
Greenland (isl.)	70 00 N	40 00 W	73
Greensboro, N.C.	36 04 N	79 47 W	78
Greenland (sea)	75 00 N	15 00 W	71
Greenville, S.C.	34 51 N	82 24 W	78
Grenada	12 05 N	61 40 W	81
Grenoble, France	45 10 N	05 43 E	42
Guadalajara, Mex.	20 40 N	103 20 W	81
Guadalcanal (isl.)	09 40 S	160 15 E	62
Guadalupe (isl.)	29 11 N	118 17 W	73
Guadarrama (mts.)	41 00 N	03 30 W	42
Guadeloupe (isl.)	16 15 N	61 35 W	81
Guajira (pen.)	11 30 N	72 45 W	86
Guam (isl.)	13 30 N	144 47 E	62
Guangzhou, China	23 07 N	113 15 E	55
Guatemala	15 30 N	90 15 W	80
Guatemala,* Guat.	14 37 N	90 31 W	80
Guayaquil, Ecuador	02 12 S	79 53 W	86
Guernsey (isl.)	49 27 N	02 33 W	42
Guiana Highlands (plat.)	05 00 N	60 00 W	86
Guinea	10 00 N	11 00 W	68
Guinea (gulf)	03 00 N	04 00 E	68
Guinea-Bissau	11 50 N	15 00 W	68
Guwāhati, India	26 10 N	91 45 E	53
Guyana	05 00 N	59 00 W	86

H

NAME	LATITUDE	LONGITUDE	PAGE
Hadhramaut (region)	16° 00′ N	51° 00′ E	52
Hague, The,* Netherlands	52 05 N	04 20 E	42
Haifa, Israel	32 50 N	35 00 E	52
Hainan (isl.)	19 00 N	110 00 E	55
Haiphong, Vietnam	20 52 N	106 41 E	55
Haiti	19 00 N	72 30 W	81
Halifax,* N. S.	44 40 N	63 36 W	79
Halle, Germany	51 30 N	12 00 E	42
Halmahera (isl.)	01 30 N	128 00 E	57
Hamburg, Germany	53 30 N	10 00 E	42
Hamilton, Ohio	39 24 N	84 33 W	78
Hamilton, Ont.	43 12 N	79 50 W	79
Hangzhou, China	30 17 N	120 10 E	55
Hannover, Germany	52 20 N	09 30 E	42
Hanoi,* Vietnam	21 02 N	105 50 E	54
Happy Valley-Goose Bay, Newf.	53 18 N	60 23 W	79
Harare,* Zim.	17 50 S	31 03 E	70
Harbin, China	45 42 N	126 36 E	55
Harrisburg,* Pa.	40 16 N	76 53 W	78
Hartford,* Conn.	41 46 N	72 41 W	78
Hatteras (cape)	35 13 N	75 31 W	78
Havana,* Cuba	23 08 N	82 24 W	80
Hawaii (isl.)	19 30 N	155 30 W	76
Hawaii (state), U.S.	21 00 N	00 10 E	76
Hay River, N.W. Terrs.	60 51 N	115 42 W	79
Heard (isl.)	53 07 S	73 20 E	71
Hebrides (isls.)	57 20 N	07 00 W	42
Hecate (strait)	53 20 N	131 00 W	79
Helena,* Mont.	46 36 N	112 02 W	76
Helmand (river)	31 00 N	64 00 E	53
Helsingborg, Sweden	56 07 N	12 45 E	43
Helsinki,* Finland	60 12 N	25 00 E	43
Herāt, Afgh.	34 20 N	62 12 E	52
Hermosillo, Mex.	29 04 N	110 58 W	81
Hijāz (region)	24 30 N	39 00 E	52
Himalaya (mts.)	28 00 N	81 00 E	53
Hindu Kush (mts.)	35 45 N	70 30 E	53
Hiroshima, Japan	34 24 N	132 25 E	55
Hiva Oa (isl.)	09 46 S	139 00 W	63
Hobart, Austl.	42 52 S	147 18 E	59
Ho Chi Minh City, Vietnam	10 47 N	106 41 E	56
Hokkaido (isl.)	43 00 N	143 00 E	55
Homyel', Belarus	52 25 N	31 00 E	43
Honduras	15 00 N	87 00 W	80
Hong Kong	22 15 N	114 10 E	55
Honiara,* Sol. Is.	09 25 S	160 00 E	62
Honolulu,* Hawaii	21 18 N	157 51 W	76
Honshu (isl.)	36 00 N	137 00 E	55
Horn (cape)	55 59 S	67 16 W	88
Houston, Texas	29 45 N	95 22 W	77
Howrah, India	22 35 N	88 20 E	53
Hrodna, Belarus	53 41 N	23 50 E	44
Huang (river)	38 06 N	118 24 E	55
Hudson (bay)	59 00 N	86 00 W	79
Hudson (strait)	61 30 N	72 00 W	79
Hue, Vietnam	16 29 N	107 34 E	56
Hull, Eng.	53 45 N	00 20 W	42
Hull, Qué.	45 26 N	75 44 W	79
Hungary	47 00 N	19 00 E	44
Huntington, W. Va.	38 25 N	82 27 W	78
Huntsville, Ala.	34 44 N	86 35 W	78
Huron (lake)	44 30 N	82 30 W	78
Hyderabad, India	17 15 N	78 30 E	53
Hyderabad, Pak.	25 28 N	68 35 E	53

I

NAME	LATITUDE	LONGITUDE	PAGE
Ibadan, Nigeria	07° 23′ N	03° 54′ E	68
Ibiza (isl.)	39 00 N	01 25 E	42
Iceland	65 00 N	19 00 W	39
Idaho (state), U.S.	44 00 N	114 00 W	76
Iliamna (lake)	59 30 N	155 00 W	76
Illinois (state), U.S.	40 00 N	89 15 W	78
Inch'on, S. Korea	36 51 N	127 26 E	55
India	23 00 N	80 00 E	53
Indiana (state), U.S.	40 00 N	86 00 W	78
Indianapolis,* Ind.	39 46 N	86 10 W	78
Indigirka (river)	70 48 N	149 00 E	47
Indonesia	05 00 S	120 00 E	56
Indore, India	22 40 N	75 58 E	53
Indus (river)	33 00 N	71 30 E	53
Inner Mongolia (region)	42 00 N	110 00 E	55
Inuvik, N.W. Terrs.	68 21 N	133 43 W	79
Ionian (sea)	38 00 N	19 00 E	44
Iowa (state), U.S.	42 00 N	93 30 W	77
Iowa City, Iowa	41 40 N	91 32 W	78
Iqaluit, N.W. Terrs.	63 45 N	68 31 W	79
Iran	33 00 N	55 00 E	52
Iraq	33 00 N	44 00 E	52
Ireland	53 00 N	08 00 W	42
Irish (sea)	53 40 N	04 30 W	42
Irkutsk, Russia	52 16 N	104 20 E	47
Irrawaddy (river)	23 19 N	96 00 E	53
Irtysh (river)	61 02 N	68 47 E	46
Ishevsk, Russia	56 51 N	53 14 E	45
Islamabad,* Pakistan	33 42 N	73 10 E	53
Israel	32 00 N	35 00 E	52
Istanbul, Turkey	41 10 N	29 00 E	44
Itaipu (res.)	25 00 S	54 30 W	88
Italy	42 00 N	13 00 E	39
Ivanovo, Russia	57 00 N	40 59 E	43
Iwo Jima (isl.)	24 47 N	141 20 E	62
Izmir, Turkey	38 25 N	27 10 E	44

J

NAME	LATITUDE	LONGITUDE	PAGE
Jackson,* Miss.	32° 18′ N	90° 11′ W	78
Jacksonville, Fla.	30 20 N	81 40 W	78
Jaipur, India	26 55 N	75 49 E	53
Jakarta,* Indonesia	06 10 S	106 50 E	56
Jamaica	18 15 N	77 30 W	81
James (bay)	53 00 N	80 30 W	79
Jan Mayen (isl.)	71 00 N	08 30 W	39
Japan	38 00 N	138 00 E	55
Japan (sea)	40 00 N	135 00 E	55
Java (isl.)	07 00 S	110 00 E	56
Java (sea)	05 00 S	110 00 E	56
Jayapura, Indon.	02 32 S	140 42 E	57
Jefferson City,* Mo.	38 36 N	92 12 W	78
Jersey (isl.)	49 13 N	02 07 W	42
Jerusalem,* Israel	31 46 N	35 14 E	52
Jidda, Saudi Arabia	21 29 N	39 12 E	52
Jilin, China	43 51 N	126 33 E	55
Jinan, China	36 40 N	117 00 E	55
Johannesburg, S. Afr.	26 12 S	28 03 E	70
Johnston (isl.)	16 44 N	169 31 W	63
Jonquière, Qué.	48 25 N	71 15 W	79
Jordan	31 00 N	37 00 E	52
Juan de Fuca (strait)	49 15 N	123 30 W	79
Juan Fernández (isls.)	33 36 S	78 55 W	12
Juneau,* Alaska	58 18 N	134 25 W	76
Jura (mts.)	47 10 N	07 00 E	42
Jutland (pen.)	56 00 N	09 00 E	43
Juventud (isl.)	21 40 N	82 50 W	80

K

NAME	LATITUDE	LONGITUDE	PAGE
Kabul,* Afgh.	34° 31′ N	69° 00′ E	52
Kahoolawe (isl.)	20 33 N	156 37 W	76
Kaifeng, China	34 48 N	114 21 E	55
Kalaallit Nunaat (Greenland) (isl.)	70 00 N	40 00 W	73
Kalahari (desert)	23 00 S	22 00 E	70
Kalamazoo, Mich.	42 17 N	85 35 W	78
Kalimantan (region)	01 00 S	113 00 E	56
Kalyān, India	19 15 N	73 09 E	53
Kama (river)	55 10 N	49 20 E	45
Kamchatka (pen.)	56 00 N	160 00 E	47
Kamloops, Br. Col.	50 40 N	120 20 W	79
Kampala,* Uganda	00 19 N	32 35 E	69
Kampuchea (Cambodia)	12 00 N	105 00 E	56
Kananga, Zaire	05 54 S	22 25 E	70
Kanazawa, Japan	36 34 N	136 39 E	55
Kanin (pen.)	67 30 N	45 00 E	43
Kano, Nigeria	12 00 N	08 31 E	68
Kanpur, India	26 28 N	80 21 E	53
Kansas (state), U.S.	38 30 N	98 30 W	76
Kansas City, Kans.	39 06 N	94 38 W	77
Kansas City, Mo.	39 05 N	94 35 W	77
Kaohsiung, China	22 38 N	120 17 E	55
Kapuskasing, Ont.	49 25 N	82 26 W	79
Kara (sea)	72 00 N	62 00 E	46
Karachi, Pak.	24 55 N	67 00 E	53
Karaganda, Kazakstan	49 50 N	73 10 E	47
Karakoram (mts.)	36 00 N	77 00 E	53
Karakumy (desert)	41 30 N	58 00 E	45
Karlsruhe, Germany	49 00 N	08 28 E	42
Kasai (river)	03 10 S	16 11 E	70
Kassel, Germany	51 20 N	09 15 E	42
Kathmandu,* Nepal	27 45 N	85 25 E	53
Katowice, Poland	50 16 N	19 00 E	44
Kattegat (strait)	57 00 N	11 30 E	43
Kauai (isl.)	22 05 N	159 30 W	76
Kaunas, Lithuania	54 54 N	23 54 E	43
Kavir, Dasht-e (desert)	35 00 N	55 00 E	52
Kawasaki, Japan	35 30 N	139 47 E	55
Kazakstan	48 00 N	67 00 E	46
Kazan', Russia	55 45 N	49 08 E	45
Kelowna, Br. Col.	49 54 N	119 29 W	79
Kemerovo, Russia	55 20 N	86 05 E	47
Kenora, Ont.	49 46 N	94 28 W	79
Kentucky (lake)	37 00 N	88 16 W	78
Kentucky (state), U.S.	37 30 N	85 00 W	78
Kenya	00 00	38 00 E	69
Kenya (mt.)	00 08 S	37 18 E	69
Kerguélen (isls.)	49 00 S	69 00 E	13
Khabarovsk, Russia	48 30 N	135 06 E	55
Kharkiv, Ukraine	50 00 N	36 15 E	44
Khartoum,* Sudan	15 35 N	32 33 E	69
Khulna, Bangladesh	22 48 N	89 33 E	53
Kiel, Germany	54 20 N	10 10 E	42
Kiev,* Ukraine	50 27 N	30 32 E	44
Kigali,* Rwanda	01 57 S	30 04 E	70
Kilimanjaro (mt.)	03 04 S	37 21 E	70
Kimberley, S. Afr.	28 43 S	24 46 E	70
Kimberley (plat.)	16 00 S	127 00 E	59
Kingston,* Jamaica	18 00 N	76 48 W	81
Kingston, Ont.	44 10 N	76 44 W	79
Kinshasa,* Zaire	04 19 S	15 23 E	70
Kirgiz Steppe (grassland)	49 30 N	57 00 E	45
Kiribati	00 00	175 00 E	62
Kitakyushu, Japan	33 53 N	130 50 E	55
Kjölen (mts.)	65 00 N	15 00 E	43
Knoxville, Tenn.	35 58 N	83 55 W	78
Kobe, Japan	34 41 N	135 10 E	55
Kodiak (isl.)	57 30 N	153 30 W	76
Kola (pen.)	67 20 N	37 00 E	43
Kolguyev (isl.)	68 30 N	49 00 E	43
Kolyma (mts.)	63 00 N	160 00 E	47
Kolyma (river)	69 30 N	161 12 E	47
Komandorskiye (isls.)	55 00 N	167 00 E	47
Konya, Turkey	37 52 N	32 31 E	44
Korea, North	40 00 N	127 00 E	55
Korea, South	37 30 N	128 00 E	55
Koror,* Palau	07 20 N	134 28 E	62
Kosciusko (mt.)	36 28 S	148 16 E	59
Kota Kinabalu, Malaysia	05 59 N	116 04 E	56
Kowloon, Hong Kong	22 20 N	114 11 E	55
Kraków, Poland	50 05 N	19 55 E	44
Krasnodar, Russia	45 02 N	39 00 E	44
Krasnoyarsk, Russia	56 02 N	92 48 E	46
Krishna (river)	15 57 N	80 59 E	53
Krung Thep (Bangkok),* Thailand	13 45 N	100 30 E	56
Kryvyy Rih, Ukraine	47 55 N	33 21 E	44
Kuala Lumpur,* Malaysia	03 09 N	101 42 E	56
Kuching, Malaysia	01 34 N	111 22 E	56
Kumamoto, Japan	32 48 N	130 43 E	55
Kumasi, Ghana	06 41 N	01 37 W	68
Kunming, China	25 04 N	102 41 E	54
Kunlun (mts.)	36 00 N	90 00 E	54
Kura (river)	39 24 N	49 19 E	45
Kuril (isls.)	45 00 N	150 00 E	47
Kutch (Kachchh), Rann of (salt lake)	24 00 N	70 00 E	53
Kuwait	29 30 N	47 45 E	52
Kwajalein (isl.)	08 43 N	167 44 E	62
Kyoto, Japan	34 58 N	135 45 E	55
Kyrgyzstan	41 00 N	75 00 E	46
Kyushu (isl.)	33 00 N	131 00 E	55

L

NAME	LATITUDE	LONGITUDE	PAGE
Labrador (region)	54° 00′ N	60° 00′ W	79
Laccadive, (sea)	11 00 N	73 00 E	53

NAME	LATITUDE	LONGITUDE	PAGE
Ladoga (lake)	61 00 N	31 00 E	43
Lafayette, Ind.	40 25 N	86 53 W	78
Lagos, Nigeria	06 27 N	03 25 E	68
Lahore, Pak.	31 37 N	74 18 E	53
Lake of the Woods (lake)	49 30 N	94 30 W	79
Lancaster (sound)	74 15 N	84 00 W	79
Lancaster, Pa.	40 02 N	76 18 W	78
Land's End (prom.)	50 05 N	05 30 W	42
Languedoc (region)	43 00 N	03 00 E	42
Lansing,* Mich.	42 44 N	84 33 W	78
Lanzhou, China	36 03 N	103 41 E	54
Laos	19 00 N	103 00 E	49
La Paz,* Bolivia	16 29 S	68 09 W	86
La Pérouse (strait)	45 45 N	142 00 E	55
La Plata (river)	36 00 S	55 00 W	88
Lapland, (region)	68 00 N	23 00 E	43
Laptev (sea)	76 00 N	126 00 E	47
Laramie, Wyo.	41 19 N	105 35 W	76
Las Cruces, N.M.	32 18 N	106 46 W	76
Las Palmas, Canary Is., Spain	28 06 N	15 24 W	65
Las Vegas, Nev.	36 10 N	115 09 W	76
Latvia	57 00 N	24 00 E	43
Lausanne, Switz.	46 31 N	06 37 E	42
Laval, Qué.	45 36 N	73 45 W	77
Lebanon	33 45 N	35 45 E	52
Leeds, Eng.	53 50 N	01 25 W	42
Leeward, (isls.)	18 00 N	61 00 W	81
Le Havre, France	49 25 N	00 10 E	42
Leipzig, Germany	51 20 N	12 20 E	42
Lena (river)	72 00 N	127 00 E	47
León, Mex.	21 07 N	101 40 W	80
Lesotho	29 15 S	28 15 E	70
Lesser Antilles, (isls.)	12 00 N	67 00 W	81
Lésvos (Lesbos) (isl.)	39 20 N	26 15 E	44
Lethbridge, Alta.	49 42 N	112 50 W	79
Lexington, Ky.	38 03 N	84 30 W	78
Leyte (isl.)	10 50 N	125 00 E	57
Liard (river)	61 50 N	121 19 W	79
Liberia	06 00 N	09 00 W	68
Libreville,* Gabon	00 24 N	09 27 E	68
Libya	27 00 N	17 30 E	69
Libyan (desert)	28 00 N	25 00 E	69
Liechtenstein	47 10 N	09 32 E	42
Liège, Belgium	50 40 N	05 35 E	42
Ligurian, (sea)	43 00 N	09 00 E	42
Lille, France	50 40 N	03 00 E	42
Lilongwe,* Malawi	13 59 S	33 47 E	70
Lima, Ohio	40 44 N	84 06 W	78
Lima,* Peru	12 03 S	77 03 W	86
Limpopo (river)	25 12 S	33 31 E	70
Lincoln,* Neb.	40 49 N	96 42 W	77
Line, (isls.)	04 00 S	155 00 W	63
Linz, Austria	48 18 N	14 15 E	42
Lion (gulf)	43 00 N	03 45 E	42
Lisbon,* Port.	38 43 N	09 10 W	42
Lithuania	55 00 N	24 00 E	43
Little Rock,* Ark.	34 45 N	92 17 W	78
Liverpool, Eng.	53 28 N	02 55 W	42
Livorno, Italy	43 33 N	10 19 E	42
Ljubljana,* Slovenia	46 03 N	14 31 E	44
Llanos (plain)	14 00 N	70 00 W	86
Lloydminster, Alta.-Sask.	53 17 N	110 00 W	79
Lódź, Poland	51 46 N	19 25 E	44
Logan (mt.)	60 34 N	140 24 W	79
Logan, Utah	41 44 N	111 50 W	76
Loire (river)	47 20 N	02 00 E	42
Lomas de Zamora, Arg.	34 46 S	58 24 W	88
Lombok (isl.)	08 48 S	115 52 E	56
Lomé,* Togo	06 07 N	01 14 E	68
London,* Eng.	51 30 N	00 07 W	42
London, Ont.	43 02 N	81 30 W	79
Long (isl.)	40 45 N	73 00 W	78
Long Beach, Calif.	33 47 N	118 11 W	76
Longview, Tex.	32 29 N	94 44 W	77
Lopatka (cape)	50 52 N	156 40 E	47
Lorraine (region)	49 00 N	06 00 E	42
Los Angeles, Calif.	34 03 N	118 14 W	76
Louisiana (state), U.S.	31 00 N	92 30 W	77
Louisville, Ky.	38 15 N	85 46 W	78
Lowell, Mass.	42 38 N	71 19 W	78
Loyalty (isls.)	21 00 S	168 00 E	62
Luanda,* Angola	08 49 S	13 14 E	70
Lubbock, Texas	33 35 N	101 50 W	76
Lübeck, Germany	53 50 N	10 40 E	42
Lubumbashi, Zaire	11 40 S	27 28 E	70
Lucknow, India	26 46 N	80 59 E	53
Ludhiāna, India	30 54 N	75 51 E	53
Lusaka,* Zambia	15 25 S	28 18 E	70
Luxembourg	49 45 N	06 10 E	42
Luxembourg,* Lux.	49 35 N	06 12 E	42
Luzon (isl.)	15 00 N	121 00 E	57
L'viv, Ukraine	49 51 N	24 02 E	44
Lynchburg, Va.	37 25 N	79 08 W	78
Lyon, France	45 40 N	04 40 E	42

M

NAME	LATITUDE	LONGITUDE	PAGE
Maanselkä (mts.)	66° 30′ N	29° 00′ E	43
Macau,* Macau	22 12 N	113 33 E	55
Macedonia	42 00 N	21 26 E	44
Maceió, Brazil	09 40 S	35 44 W	87
Mackenzie (river)	68 00 N	134 00 W	79
Macon, Ga.	32 50 N	83 38 W	77
Madagascar	18 00 S	47 00 E	70
Madeira (isl.)	32 45 N	17 00 W	68
Madeira (river)	03 23 S	58 45 W	86
Madeleine (isls.)	47 26 N	61 44 W	79
Madison,* Wis.	43 04 N	89 23 W	78
Madras, India	13 05 N	80 15 E	53
Madrid,* Spain	40 25 N	03 42 W	42
Madura (isl.)	07 00 S	113 00 E	54
Madurai, India	09 55 N	78 15 E	53
Magdalena (river)	11 06 N	75 00 W	86
Magdeburg, Germany	52 10 N	11 00 E	42
Magellan (strait)	54 00 S	71 00 W	88
Magnitogorsk, Russia	53 28 N	59 00 E	46
Maine (state), U.S.	45 30 N	69 00 W	78
Majorca (isl.)	39 35 N	03 00 E	42
Majuro,* Marshall Is.	07 04 N	171 12 E	62
Makassar (strait)	03 57 S	119 32 E	56
Malabar Coast	12 50 N	75 00 E	53
Malabo,* Eq. Guin.	03 45 N	08 46 E	68
Malacca (strait)	03 10 N	100 45 E	56
Málaga, Spain	36 43 N	04 25 W	42
Malang, Indonesia	07 59 S	112 37 E	56
Malatya, Turkey	38 21 N	38 19 E	44
Malawi	13 30 S	34 30 E	70
Malay (pen.)	05 00 N	102 00 E	56
Malaysia	04 00 N	102 00 E	56
Maldives	04 00 N	73 00 E	49
Mali	17 30 N	04 00 W	68
Malmö, Sweden	55 35 N	13 00 E	43
Malta	35 55 N	14 23 E	44
Man (isl.)	54 15 N	04 30 W	42
Managua,* Nic.	12 08 N	86 18 W	80
Manaus, Brazil	03 08 S	60 01 W	86
Manchester, Eng.	53 30 N	02 13 W	42
Manchester, N.H.	42 60 N	71 28 W	78
Mandab, Bab al (strait)	12 39 N	43 26 E	52
Mandalay, Burma	21 59 N	96 05 E	53
Manicouagan (res.)	51 24 N	68 44 W	79
Manila,* Philippines	14 36 N	120 59 E	57
Manitoba (lake)	50 30 N	98 20 W	79
Manitoba (prov.), Canada	55 00 N	97 00 W	79
Manitoulin (isl.)	45 50 N	82 25 W	79
Mannar (gulf)	08 00 N	79 00 E	53
Mannheim, Germany	49 30 N	08 28 E	42
Maputo,* Moz.	25 58 S	32 35 E	70
Maracaibo (lake)	09 20 N	71 30 W	86
Maracaibo, Venez.	10 38 N	71 38 W	86
Marajó (isl.)	01 00 S	50 00 W	87
Marañón (river)	04 30 S	73 26 W	86
Margarita (isl.)	11 00 N	64 00 W	86
Marie Byrd Land (region)	80 00 S	120 00 W	71
Mariupol', Ukraine	47 05 N	37 36 E	44
Marmara (sea)	40 42 N	28 12 E	44
Marquesas (isls.)	09 00 S	139 30 W	63
Marrakech, Morocco	31 38 N	08 00 W	68
Marsala, Italy	37 48 N	12 26 E	42
Marseille, France	43 18 N	05 23 E	42
Marshall Islands	09 00 N	168 00 E	62
Martinique (isl.)	14 40 N	61 00 W	81
Maryland (state), U.S.	39 00 N	76 30 W	78
Mashhad, Iran	36 18 N	59 36 E	52
Massachusetts (state), U.S.	42 20 N	72 00 W	78
Massif Central (plat.)	45 00 N	08 00 E	42
Mato Grosso (plat.)	14 30 S	54 00 W	87
Maui (isl.)	20 48 N	156 20 W	76
Mauna Loa (mt.)	19 29 N	155 36 W	76
Mauritania	20 00 N	11 00 W	68
Mauritius	20 15 S	57 30 E	13
Mayotte (isl.)	13 00 S	45 00 E	65
Mazār-e Sharif, Afgh.	36 42 N	67 06 E	52
McAllen, Tex.	26 12 N	98 14 W	77
M'Clintock (chan.)	71 30 N	103 00 W	79
McKinley (mt.)	63 04 N	151 00 W	76
Mecca, Saudi Arabia	21 29 N	39 45 E	52
Medan, Indon.	03 35 N	98 40 E	56
Medellín, Col.	06 15 N	75 34 W	86
Medicine Hat, Alta.	50 02 N	110 41 W	79
Mediterranean (sea)	40 00 N	10 00 E	42
Mekong (river)	16 00 N	105 00 E	56
Melanesia (isls.)	10 00 S	160 00 E	62
Melbourne, Fla.	28 05 N	80 36 W	78
Melbourne, Austl.	37 50 S	145 00 E	59
Melville (isl.)	75 30 N	112 00 W	79
Memphis, Tenn.	35 09 N	90 03 W	78
Mendocino (cape)	40 27 N	124 26 W	76
Mendoza, Arg.	32 53 S	68 49 W	88
Mérida, Mex.	20 58 N	89 37 W	80
Mesopotamia (region)	34 00 N	44 00 E	52
Meuse (river)	51 49 N	05 01 E	42
Mexico	22 00 N	102 00 W	80
Mexico (gulf)	25 00 N	90 00 W	80
Mexico City,* Mex.	19 26 N	99 01 W	80
Miami, Fla.	25 47 N	80 12 W	78
Michigan (lake)	44 00 N	87 00 W	78
Michigan (state), U.S.	44 00 N	85 00 W	78
Micronesia	12 00 N	154 00 E	62
Micronesia, Fed. States of	08 00 N	150 00 E	62
Midway (isls.)	28 15 N	177 20 W	62
Milan, Italy	45 30 N	09 10 E	42
Milwaukee, Wis.	43 02 N	87 54 W	78
Minami-Tori-Shima (isl.)	24 20 N	154 00 E	62
Mindanao (isl.)	08 00 N	125 00 E	57
Mindoro (isl.)	12 50 N	121 10 E	57
Minneapolis, Minn.	44 59 N	93 16 W	78
Minnesota (state), U.S.	46 30 N	94 30 W	77
Minorca (isl.)	40 00 N	04 00 E	42
Minsk,* Belarus	53 50 N	27 35 E	44
Miskolc, Hungary	48 10 N	20 50 E	44
Mississippi (river)	29 10 N	89 16 W	78
Mississippi (state), U.S.	33 00 N	89 45 W	78
Missoula, Mont.	46 52 N	114 00 W	76
Missouri (river)	38 50 N	90 10 W	77
Missouri (state), U.S.	38 30 N	92 30 W	77
Mitchell (mt.)	35 46 N	82 16 W	78
Mobile, Ala.	30 42 N	88 03 W	78
Modesto, Calif.	37 38 N	121 00 W	76
Mogadishu,* Somalia	02 03 N	45 20 E	69
Mojave (desert)	35 00 N	117 00 W	76
Moldova	47 00 N	29 00 E	44
Molokai (isl.)	21 08 N	157 00 W	76
Moluccas (isls.)	02 30 S	129 00 E	57
Mona (passage)	18 15 N	68 00 W	81
Monaco	43 44 N	07 25 E	42
Moncton, N.B.	46 05 N	64 46 W	79
Mongolia	47 00 N	102 00 E	54
Monrovia,* Liberia	06 19 N	10 48 W	68
Montana (state), U.S.	47 00 N	110 00 W	76
Montenegro (rep.), Yugo.	42 30 N	19 15 E	44
Monterrey, Mex.	25 45 N	100 20 W	80
Montevideo,* Uruguay	34 53 S	56 10 W	88
Montgomery,* Ala.	32 23 N	86 19 W	78
Montpelier,* Vt.	44 16 N	72 35 W	78
Montréal, Qué.	45 35 N	73 40 W	79
Montserrat	16 44 N	62 10 W	81
Moose Jaw, Sask.	50 24 N	105 33 W	79
Morelia, Mex.	19 42 N	101 07 W	80
Morena (mts.)	38 30 N	05 00 W	42
Morocco	33 00 N	07 00 W	68
Morón, Arg.	34 39 S	58 37 W	88
Moscow (Moskva),* Russia	55 45 N	37 35 E	43
Moscow (upland)	55 00 N	33 00 E	43
Mosquitos (coast)	13 00 N	88 00 W	80
Mozambique	18 00 S	35 00 E	70
Mozambique (channel)	22 00 S	38 00 E	70
Multān, Pakistan	30 11 N	71 29 E	53
Muncie, Ind.	40 11 N	85 23 W	78
Munich (München), Germany	48 10 N	11 30 E	42
Murcia, Spain	37 43 N	01 08 W	42
Murmansk, Russia	68 58 N	33 05 E	43
Murray (river)	35 33 S	144 00 E	59
Muscat,* Oman	23 37 N	58 35 E	52
Muskegon, Mich.	43 14 N	86 15 W	78
Myanmar (Burma)	20 00 N	96 00 E	49
Mykolayiv, Ukraine	46 58 N	32 00 E	44

N

NAME	LATITUDE	LONGITUDE	PAGE
Naberezhnye Chelny, Russia	55° 42′ N	52° 19′ E	45
Nafūd (desert)	28 00 N	41 00 E	52
Nagoya, Japan	35 10 N	137 55 E	55
Nagpur, India	21 15 N	79 12 E	53
Nairobi,* Kenya	01 17 S	36 49 E	69
Najd (region)	25 00 N	43 00 E	52
Namib (desert)	23 00 S	14 00 E	70
Namibia	23 00 S	17 00 E	70
Nanchang, China	28 40 N	115 53 E	55
Nancy, France	48 40 N	06 10 E	42
Nanjing, China	32 03 N	118 48 E	55
Nantes, France	47 15 N	01 30 W	42
Nantucket (isl.)	41 16 N	70 05 W	78
Naples, Italy	40 51 N	14 15 E	42
Nashville,* Tenn.	36 10 N	86 47 W	78
Nassau,* Bahamas	25 05 N	77 21 W	81
Nasser (lake)	24 00 N	32 50 E	69
Naucalpan, Mex.	19 28 N	99 14 W	80
Nauru	00 32 S	166 56 E	62
N'Djamena,* Chad	12 07 N	15 04 E	68
Nebraska (state), U.S.	41 30 N	100 00 W	76
Negrais (cape)	16 02 N	94 12 E	56
Negro (river), Arg.	41 02 S	62 47 W	88
Negro (river), Brazil	03 10 S	59 55 W	68
Negros (isl.)	10 00 N	123 00 E	57
Nelson (river)	57 00 N	92 38 W	79
Nepal	28 00 N	84 00 E	53
Netherlands	52 00 N	05 30 E	42
Netherlands Antilles	12 10 N	69 00 W	81
Nevada (state), U.S.	39 00 N	117 00 W	76
Nevis (isl.)	17 10 N	62 38 W	81
Newark, N.J.	40 44 N	74 10 W	78
New Bedford, Mass.	41 38 N	70 55 W	78
New Britain (isl.)	05 55 S	150 20 E	62
New Brunswick (prov.), Canada	46 30 N	66 45 W	79
New Caledonia (isl.)	21 30 S	165 30 E	62
Newcastle, N.S.W.	32 55 S	151 45 E	59
Newcastle upon Tyne, Eng.	55 00 N	01 35 W	42
New Delhi,* India	28 19 N	77 15 E	53
Newfoundland (isl.)	49 30 N	57 30 W	79
Newfoundland (prov.), Canada	51 30 N	55 45 W	79
New Guinea (isl.)	05 00 S	141 00 E	57
New Hampshire (state), U.S.	43 30 N	71 45 W	78
New Haven, Conn.	41 18 N	72 55 W	78
New Ireland (isl.)	04 00 S	152 00 E	62
New Jersey (state), U.S.	40 00 N	74 30 W	78
New Mexico (state), U.S.	34 30 N	106 00 W	76
New Orleans, La.	29 57 N	90 04 W	77
Newport News, Va.	36 58 N	76 25 W	78
New Siberian (isls.)	75 00 N	142 00 E	47
New South Wales, Austl.	32 00 S	147 00 E	59
New York, N.Y.	40 45 N	74 00 W	78
New York (state), U.S.	43 00 N	76 00 W	78
New Zealand	41 00 S	173 00 E	59
Niagara Falls, Ont.	43 06 N	79 03 W	79
Niamey,* Niger	13 31 N	02 07 E	68
Nicaragua	13 00 N	85 00 W	80
Nicaragua (lake)	11 30 N	85 30 W	80
Nice, France	43 42 N	07 16 E	42
Nicobar (isls.)	07 45 N	93 30 E	53
Nicosia,* Cyprus	35 12 N	33 22 E	52
Niger	17 00 N	08 00 E	68
Niger (river)	04 17 N	06 04 E	68
Nigeria	09 00 N	08 00 E	68
Niihau (isl.)	21 53 N	160 10 W	76
Nile (river)	31 50 N	32 00 E	69
Ningbo, China	29 54 N	121 32 E	55
Niue (isl.)	19 02 S	169 52 W	63
Nizhniy Novgorod, Russia	56 20 N	44 00 E	45
Norfolk (isl.)	29 02 S	167 57 W	62
Norfolk, Va.	36 51 N	76 17 W	78
Norman Wells, N.W. Terrs.	65 17 N	126 51 W	79
Normandy (region)	49 00 N	00 00	42
Norrköping, Sweden	58 30 N	16 10 E	43
Norrland (region)	66 00 N	20 00 E	43
North (cape)	71 11 N	25 40 E	39
North (isl.), N.Z.	39 00 S	176 00 E	59
North (sea)	55 20 N	03 00 E	42
North Battleford, Sask.	52 46 N	108 17 W	79
North Bay, Ont.	46 16 N	79 30 W	79
North Carolina (state), U.S.	35 30 N	79 00 W	78
North Dakota (state), U.S.	47 30 N	100 30 W	76
Northern Ireland, U.K.	54 30 N	06 30 W	42
Northern Marianas	18 00 N	145 45 E	62
Northern Territory, Austl.	20 00 S	134 00 E	59
North Magnetic Pole	75 00 N	100 00 W	71
Northwest Territories, Canada	66 00 N	102 00 W	77
Norton (sound)	64 00 N	164 00 W	42
Norway	65 00 N	11 00 E	43
Norwegian (sea)	70 00 N	00 00	39
Nottingham, Eng.	52 58 N	01 10 W	42
Nouakchott,* Mauritania	18 06 N	15 57 W	68
Nouméa,* New Cal.	22 17 S	166 26 E	62
Nova Scotia (prov.), Canada	45 00 N	63 00 W	79
Novaya Zemlya (isls.)	74 00 N	57 00 E	46
Novosibirsk, Russia	55 02 N	82 53 E	46
Nubian (desert)	21 00 N	33 00 E	69
Nürnberg, Germany	49 20 N	11 05 E	42
Nuuk (Godthab),* Greenland	64 11 N	51 45 W	73
Nyasa (lake)	12 00 S	34 30 E	70

O

NAME	LATITUDE	LONGITUDE	PAGE
Oahu (isl.)	21° 30′ N	158° 00′ W	76
Oakland, Calif.	37 48 N	122 16 W	76
Ob' (river)	66 45 N	69 07 E	46

NAME	LATITUDE	LONGITUDE	PAGE
Odense, Denmark	55 24 N	10 23 E	43
Oder (river)	53 30 N	14 30 E	42
Odesa, Ukraine	46 29 N	30 44 E	44
Ogbomosho, Nigeria	08 08 N	04 16 E	68
Ogden, Utah	41 13 N	111 58 W	76
Ohio (river)	36 59 N	89 08 W	78
Ohio (state), U.S.	40 00 N	82 45 W	78
Oka (river)	56 00 N	43 57 E	43
Okeechobee (lake)	27 00 N	80 50 W	78
Okhotsk (sea)	55 00 N	150 00 E	47
Okinawa (isls.)	26 30 N	128 00 E	55
Oklahoma (state), U.S.	35 30 N	97 30 W	77
Oklahoma City,* Okla.	35 28 N	97 31 W	77
Olenek (river)	73 00 N	119 55 E	47
Olympia,* Wash.	47 02 N	122 53 W	76
Olympic Nat'l Park, U.S.	47 45 N	123 40 W	76
Omaha, Neb.	41 16 N	95 56 W	77
Oman	21 00 N	57 00 E	52
Oman (gulf)	24 30 N	58 45 E	52
Omdurman, Sudan	15 37 N	32 30 E	69
Omsk, Russia	55 00 N	73 24 E	46
Onega (bay)	64 15 N	37 00 E	43
Onega (lake)	61 30 N	35 00 E	43
Ontario (lake)	43 40 N	78 00 W	78
Ontario (prov.), Canada	50 00 N	87 00 W	79
Oradea, Rom.	47 03 N	21 54 E	44
Oran, Algeria	35 43 N	00 38 W	68
Orange (river)	28 39 S	16 29 E	70
Oregon (state), U.S.	44 00 N	120 30 W	76
Orenburg, Russia	51 45 N	55 06 E	45
Orinoco (river)	09 00 N	60 45 W	86
Orkney (isls.)	59 00 N	03 00 W	42
Orlando, Fla.	28 33 N	81 23 W	78
Osaka, Japan	34 40 N	135 30 E	55
Oslo,* Norway	59 55 N	10 40 E	43
Ostrava, Czech Rep.	49 45 N	18 20 E	44
Otranto (strait)	40 30 N	19 00 E	44
Ottawa (river)	45 26 N	74 00 W	77
Ottawa,* Canada	45 30 N	75 44 W	77
Ouagadougou,* Burkina	12 22 N	01 30 W	68
Oulu, Finland	65 00 N	25 28 E	43
Owen Sound, Ont.	44 34 N	80 51 W	79
Oxford, Eng.	51 45 N	01 15 W	42

P

NAME	LATITUDE	LONGITUDE	PAGE
Pago Pago,* Amer. Samoa	14° 17′ S	170° 40′ W	63
Pakistan	30 00 N	69 00 E	49
Palau	07 30 N	134 30 E	62
Palembang, Indonesia	02 55 S	104 55 E	56
Palawan (isl.)	10 30 N	118 30 E	56
Palermo, Italy	38 07 N	13 20 E	44
Palma, Spain	39 34 N	02 39 E	42
Pamir (plat.)	38 00 N	73 50 E	54
Pampas (plains)	35 00 S	63 00 W	88
Panama	08 30 N	80 00 W	80
Panamá,* Panama	08 57 N	79 32 W	81
Panay (isl.)	10 42 N	122 33 E	57
Pangnirtung, N.W. Terrs.	66 08 N	65 44 W	79
Papeete,* Fr. Polynesia	17 32 S	149 34 W	63
Papua (gulf)	08 30 S	145 00 E	57
Papua New Guinea	06 00 S	148 00 E	62
Paraguay	24 00 S	58 00 W	83
Paraguay (river)	27 18 S	58 36 W	88
Paramaribo,* Suriname	05 50 N	55 09 W	87
Paraná (river)	31 44 S	60 32 W	83
Paris,* France	48 45 N	02 20 E	42
Parry (chan.)	74 30 N	100 00 W	79
Parry Sound, Ont.	45 20 N	80 02 W	79
Patagonia (region)	44 00 S	68 00 W	88
Paterson, N.J.	40 55 N	74 10 W	78
Patos (lagoon)	31 00 S	51 20 W	88
Peace (river)	58 59 N	111 25 W	79
Peace River, Alta.	56 14 N	117 17 W	79
Pechora (river)	67 40 N	52 30 E	43
Pecos (river)	29 40 N	101 40 W	76
Peel (river)	67 41 N	134 32 W	79
Peipus (lake)	58 45 N	27 30 E	43
Pemba (isl.)	05 15 S	39 45 E	70
Pennsylvania (state), U.S.	41 00 N	77 30 W	78
Pensacola, Fla.	30 25 N	87 13 W	78
Penza, Russia	53 12 N	45 03 E	45
Peoria, Ill.	40 42 N	89 36 W	77
Perm', Russia	58 00 N	56 15 E	45
Persian (gulf)	26 30 N	52 45 E	52
Perth, Austl.	31 55 S	115 50 E	59
Peru	10 00 S	75 00 W	86
Peshāwar, Pakistan	34 01 N	71 33 E	53
Petare, Ven.	10 29 N	66 49 W	86
Peterborough, Ont.	44 18 N	78 20 W	79
Petropavlovsk-Kamchatskiy, Russia	53 01 N	158 39 E	47
Philadelphia, Pa.	39 57 N	75 09 W	78
Philippine (sea)	19 00 N	135 00 E	57
Philippines	12 00 N	122 00 E	57
Phnom Penh,* Cambodia	11 33 N	104 55 E	56
Phoenix (isls.)	03 43 S	171 00 W	63
Phoenix,* Ariz.	33 27 N	112 04 W	76
Pierre,* S.D.	44 22 N	100 21 W	76
Pietermaritzburg, S. Afr.	29 37 S	30 16 E	70
Pilcomayo (river)	25 16 S	57 43 W	88
Pisa, Italy	43 45 N	10 21 E	42
Pitcairn (isls.)	25 05 S	130 05 W	63
Pittsburgh, Pa.	40 26 N	80 00 W	78
Platte (river)	41 05 N	95 55 W	77
Ploiești, Rom.	44 57 N	26 02 E	44
Plovdiv, Bulgaria	42 09 N	24 45 E	44
Plymouth, Eng.	50 24 N	04 07 W	42
Plzeň, Czech Rep.	49 45 N	13 22 E	44
Po (river)	45 00 N	12 25 E	42
Pocatello, Idaho	42 52 N	112 27 W	76
Pohnpei (isl.)	06 54 N	158 14 E	62
Poland	52 00 N	19 00 E	39
Polynesia	10 00 S	160 00 W	63
Pomerania (region)	53 00 N	16 30 E	43
Poona, India	18 30 N	73 45 E	53
Poopó (lake)	19 10 S	67 00 W	86
Portage la Prairie, Man.	49 58 N	98 18 W	79
Port-au-Prince,* Haiti	18 33 N	72 21 W	81
Port Elizabeth, S. Afr.	33 58 S	25 37 E	70
Portland, Maine	43 40 N	70 15 W	78
Portland, Ore.	45 31 N	122 41 W	76
Port Moresby,* P.N.G.	09 29 S	147 09 E	57
Porto, Portugal	41 10 N	08 36 W	42
Porto Alegre, Brazil	30 02 S	51 14 W	88
Port of Spain,* Trinidad and Tobago	10 39 N	61 31 W	81
Porto-Novo,* Benin	06 28 N	02 38 E	68
Port Said, Egypt	31 16 N	32 18 E	69
Portsmouth, Eng.	50 47 N	01 05 W	42
Portugal	39 00 N	08 00 W	42
Poznań, Poland	52 25 N	16 58 E	44
Prague,* Czech Rep.	50 05 N	14 20 E	44
Pretoria,* S. Afr.	25 45 S	28 11 E	70
Prince Albert, Sask.	53 12 N	105 45 W	79
Prince Edward Island (prov.), Canada	46 20 N	63 30 W	79
Prince George, Br. Col.	53 55 N	122 46 W	79
Prince of Wales (isl.)	72 30 N	98 30 W	79
Prince Rupert, Br. Col.	54 19 N	130 20 W	79
Provence (region)	43 30 N	06 00 E	42
Providence,* R.I.	41 50 N	71 25 W	78
Provo, Utah	40 14 N	111 39 W	76
Prut (river)	45 29 N	28 13 E	44
Puebla, Mex.	19 03 N	98 10 W	80
Puerto Rico	18 15 N	66 30 W	81
Puget (sound)	47 30 N	122 29 W	79
Purus (river)	03 43 S	61 28 W	86
Pusan, S. Korea	35 06 N	129 03 E	55
P'yongyang,* N. Korea	39 01 N	125 45 E	55
Pyrenees (mts.)	42 45 N	00 05 E	42

Q

NAME	LATITUDE	LONGITUDE	PAGE
Qandahār, Afgh.	31° 32′ N	65° 30′ E	52
Qatar	25 30 N	51 15 E	52
Qingdao, China	36 04 N	120 19 E	55
Qiqihar, China	47 19 N	123 55 E	55
Qom, Iran	34 39 N	50 54 E	52
Québec (prov.), Canada	52 00 N	72 00 W	79
Québec,* Qué.	46 50 N	71 12 W	79
Queen Charlotte (isls.)	53 00 N	132 00 W	79
Queen Elizabeth (isls.)	77 00 N	100 00 W	79
Queen Maud Land (region)	72 30 S	12 00 E	71
Queensland, Austl.	23 00 S	145 00 E	59
Quesnel, Br. Col.	52 59 N	122 29 W	79
Quezon City, Philippines	14 38 N	121 03 E	57
Quito,* Ecuador	00 13 S	78 30 W	86

R

NAME	LATITUDE	LONGITUDE	PAGE
Rabat,* Mor.	34° 00′ N	06° 51′ W	68
Rabaul, P.N.G.	04 12 S	152 12 E	62
Race (cape)	46 30 N	53 15 W	79
Racine, Wis.	42 43 N	87 48 W	77
Raleigh,* N.C.	35 47 N	78 38 W	78
Rangoon,* Burma	16 48 N	96 09 E	56
Rankin Inlet, N.W. Terrs.	62 49 N	92 05 W	79
Rann of Kutch (salt lake)	24 00 N	70 00 E	53
Rarotonga (isl.)	21 14 S	159 46 W	63
Rāwalpindi, Pakistan	33 36 N	73 04 E	53
Reading, Pa.	40 20 N	75 56 W	78
Recife, Brazil	08 04 S	34 53 W	87
Red (river)	30 58 N	91 40 W	78
Red (sea)	20 00 N	39 00 E	52
Red Deer, Alta.	52 16 N	113 48 W	79
Red River of the North (riv.)	49 00 N	97 14 W	77
Reggio di Calabria, Italy	38 06 N	15 39 E	44
Regina,* Sask.	50 27 N	104 37 W	79
Reims, France	49 15 N	04 00 E	42
Reindeer (lake)	57 15 N	102 15 W	79
Rennes, France	48 05 N	01 40 W	42
Reno, Nev.	39 31 N	119 48 W	76
Réunion (isl.)	21 00 S	55 30 E	13
Revelstoke, Br. Col.	51 00 N	118 11 W	79
Revillagigedo (isls.)	19 00 N	111 30 W	73
Reykjavík,* Iceland	64 10 N	21 58 W	39
Rhine (river)	52 00 N	04 00 E	42
Rhode Island (state), U.S.	41 49 N	71 30 W	78
Rhodes (isl.)	36 15 N	28 00 E	44
Rhodope (mts.)	41 50 N	24 00 E	44
Rhône (river)	45 00 N	05 00 E	42
Richmond,* Va.	37 32 N	77 26 W	78
Riga,* Latvia	56 55 N	24 15 E	43
Rijeka, Croatia	45 21 N	14 24 E	44
Rio de Janeiro, Brazil	22 54 S	43 15 W	87
Rio Grande (river)	25 58 N	97 09 W	76
Riverside, Calif.	33 59 N	117 22 W	76
Rivière-du-Loup, Qué.	47 50 N	69 32 W	79
Riyadh,* Saudi Arabia	24 45 N	46 45 E	52
Roanoke, Va.	37 16 N	79 56 W	78
Roberval, Qué.	48 31 N	72 13 W	79
Robson (mt.)	53 07 N	119 08 W	79
Rochester, N.Y.	43 10 N	77 36 W	78
Rockford, Ill.	42 16 N	89 06 W	78
Rocky (mts.)	50 00 N	117 00 W	76
Rodrigues (isl.)	19 45 S	63 25 E	13
Romania	46 00 N	25 00 E	44
Rome,* Italy	41 54 N	12 30 E	42
Rosario, Arg.	32 57 S	60 40 W	88
Ross Ice Shelf	81 30 S	175 00 W	71
Ross (sea)	75 00 S	180 00	71
Rostov, Russia	47 15 N	39 53 E	45
Rotterdam, Neth.	51 55 N	04 25 E	42
Rotuma (isl.)	12 30 S	177 05 E	62
Rouyn-Noranda, Qué.	48 15 N	79 02 W	79
Rub' al Khali (desert)	20 00 N	52 00 E	52
Russia	60 00 N	90 00 E	46
Rwanda	02 00 S	30 00 E	70
Ryazan', Russia	54 38 N	39 44 E	43

S

NAME	LATITUDE	LONGITUDE	PAGE
Sabah (state), Malaysia	05° 00′ N	117° 00′ E	56
Sable (cape)	43 24 N	65 37 W	79
Sable (isl.)	43 55 N	60 00 W	79
Sacramento (mts.)	33 15 N	105 40 W	76
Sacramento,* Calif.	38 35 N	121 30 W	76
Saginaw, Mich.	43 26 N	83 56 W	78
Sahara (desert)	23 00 N	10 00 E	68
Saigon (Ho Chi Minh City), Vietnam	10 47 N	106 41 E	56
Saint Cloud, Minn.	45 34 N	94 10 W	78
Saint-Étienne, France	45 25 N	04 25 E	42
Saint Helena (isl.)	15 58 S	05 21 W	65
Saint John, N.B.	45 16 N	66 04 W	79
Saint John's,* Newf.	47 40 N	52 45 W	79
Saint Kitts and Nevis	17 17 N	62 40 W	81
Saint Lawrence (isl.)	63 00 N	170 00 W	76
Saint Lawrence (river)	49 30 N	66 00 W	79
Saint Louis, Mo.	38 38 N	90 12 W	78
Saint Lucia	14 00 N	61 00 W	81
Saint Paul,* Minn.	44 57 N	93 05 W	78
Saint Petersburg, Fla.	27 46 N	82 38 W	78
St. Petersburg (Leningrad), Russia	59 55 N	30 15 E	43
Saint Pierre & Miquelon (isls.)	46 47 N	56 21 W	79
Saint Vincent and the Grenadines	13 15 N	61 15 W	81
Saipan (isl.)	15 12 N	145 45 E	62
Sakhalin (isl.)	50 00 N	143 00 E	47
Sala y Gómez (isl.)	26 27 S	105 28 W	12
Salado (river)	32 30 S	60 47 W	88
Salem,* Ore.	44 56 N	123 02 W	76
Salinas, Calif.	36 40 N	121 39 W	76
Salt Lake City,* Utah	40 45 N	111 53 W	76
Salton Sea (lake)	33 15 N	115 48 W	76
Salvador, Brazil	13 00 S	38 30 W	87
Salween (river)	25 00 N	98 45 E	54
Samar (isl.)	12 00 N	125 00 E	57
Samara, Russia	53 12 N	50 09 E	45
Samsun, Turkey	41 17 N	36 20 E	44
Sanaa,* Yemen	15 21 N	44 12 E	52
San Antonio, Texas	29 26 N	98 29 W	77
San Bernardino, Calif.	34 07 N	117 17 W	76
San Diego, Calif.	32 43 N	117 09 W	76
San Francisco, Calif.	37 47 N	122 25 W	76
San Jose, Calif.	37 20 N	121 53 W	76
San José,* C.R.	09 56 N	84 05 W	80
San Juan,* P.R.	18 28 N	66 07 W	81
San Luis Potosí, Mex.	22 09 N	100 59 W	80
San Marino	43 56 N	12 28 E	42
San Miguel de Tucumán, Arg.	26 50 S	65 12 W	88
San Pedro Sula, Honduras	15 27 N	88 02 W	80
San Salvador (Watling) (isl.)	24 02 N	74 28 W	81
San Salvador,* El Sal.	13 41 N	89 12 W	80
Santa Barbara, Calif.	34 25 N	119 42 W	76
Santa Cruz, Bolivia	17 48 S	63 10 W	86
Santa Fe, Arg.	31 38 S	60 43 W	88
Santa Fe,* N.M.	35 41 N	105 56 W	76
Santa Rosa, Calif.	38 26 N	122 43 W	76
Santiago,* Chile	33 26 S	70 42 W	88
Santiago, Dom. Rep.	19 27 N	70 42 W	81
Santiago de Cuba, Cuba	20 01 N	75 49 W	81
Santo André, Brazil	23 40 S	46 31 W	87
Santo Domingo,* Dom. Rep.	18 28 N	69 53 W	81
Santos, Brazil	23 57 S	46 19 W	87
São Francisco (river)	10 30 S	36 23 W	87
São Paulo, Brazil	23 33 S	46 37 W	87
São Roque (cape)	05 26 S	35 15 W	87
São Tomé and Príncipe	01 00 N	07 00 E	68
Sapporo, Japan	43 04 N	141 22 E	55
Saragossa (Zaragoza), Spain	41 39 N	00 51 W	42
Sarajevo,* Bosnia and Herzegovina	43 52 N	18 25 E	44
Saratov, Russia	51 34 N	46 02 E	45
Sarawak (state), Malaysia	02 30 N	113 00 E	56
Sardinia (isl.)	40 00 N	09 00 E	42
Saskatchewan (prov.), Canada	54 00 N	106 00 W	79
Saskatchewan (river)	53 11 N	99 17 W	79
Saskatoon, Sask.	52 09 N	106 45 W	79
Satpura Range (mts.)	21 25 N	76 10 E	53
Saudi Arabia	24 00 N	45 00 E	52
Sault Sainte Marie, Ont.	46 38 N	84 20 W	79
Sava (river)	44 51 N	20 27 E	44
Savai'i (isl.)	13 35 S	172 25 W	63
Savannah (river)	32 03 N	80 55 W	78
Savannah, Ga.	32 05 N	81 06 W	78
Sayan (mts.)	53 00 N	95 00 E	46
Schefferville, Qué.	54 48 N	66 50 W	79
Scotia (sea)	57 00 S	40 00 W	71
Scotland, U.K.	57 00 N	04 00 W	42
Scranton, Pa.	41 25 N	75 40 W	77
Seattle, Wash.	47 37 N	122 20 W	76
Seine (river)	49 20 N	00 20 E	42
Selvas (region)	06 00 S	64 00 W	86
Semarang, Indon.	06 58 S	110 25 E	56
Sendai, Japan	38 15 N	140 53 E	55
Senegal	15 00 N	15 00 W	68
Senegal (river)	15 51 N	17 29 W	68
Seoul,* S. Korea	37 34 N	127 00 E	55
Sept-Îles, Qué.	50 13 N	66 24 W	79
Severnaya Zemlya (isls.)	79 30 N	98 00 E	46
Seville, Spain	37 24 N	06 00 W	42
Seychelles	04 30 S	55 30 E	13
's Gravenhage (The Hague),* Neth.	52 05 N	04 20 E	42
Shanghai, China	31 14 N	121 30 E	55
Shannon (river)	52 39 N	09 00 W	42
Shaoxing, China	30 00 N	120 35 E	55
Shasta (mt.)	41 24 N	122 12 W	76
Shatt-al-'Arab (river)	30 00 N	48 30 E	52
Sheffield, Eng.	53 22 N	01 30 W	42
Shelekhov (gulf)	60 00 N	158 00 E	47
Shenyang, China	41 48 N	123 26 E	55
Sherbrooke, Qué.	45 25 N	71 54 W	79
Shetland (isls.)	60 30 N	01 00 W	42
Shikoku (isl.)	34 00 N	140 00 E	55
Shiraz, Iran	29 37 N	52 33 E	52
Shreveport, La.	32 31 N	93 45 W	77
Sicily (isl.)	37 00 N	14 00 E	44
Sicily (str.)	37 30 N	12 00 E	42
Sidra (gulf)	32 00 N	18 00 E	68
Sierra Leone	08 00 N	12 00 W	68
Sierra Madre Occidental (mts.)	26 00 N	106 20 W	81
Sierra Madre Oriental (mts.)	23 30 N	100 00 W	80
Sierra Nevada (mts.)	38 00 N	119 30 W	76
Sikhote-Alin' (mts.)	48 00 N	138 00 E	55
Silesia (region)	51 30 N	17 00 E	44
Simbirsk, Russia	54 20 N	48 24 E	43
Sinai (pen.)	29 00 N	34 00 E	52
Singapore	01 17 N	103 51 E	56
Singapore,* Singapore	01 17 N	103 51 E	56
Skagerrak (strait)	58 00 N	09 30 E	43
Skeena (mts.)	56 30 N	129 00 W	79
Skopje,* Macedonia	42 00 N	21 26 E	44
Slovakia	48 30 N	19 00 E	44

NAME	LATITUDE	LONGITUDE	PAGE
Slovenia	46 00 N	15 00 E	44
Snake (river)	46 12 N	119 02 W	76
Society (isls.)	17 00 S	152 00 W	63
Socotra (isl.)	12 30 N	54 00 E	52
Sofia,* Bulgaria	42 42 N	23 20 E	44
Solomon (sea)	08 00 S	152 00 E	62
Solomon Islands	09 00 S	160 00 E	62
Somalia	05 00 N	47 00 E	69
Somerset (isl.)	73 30 N	93 30 W	79
South (isl.), N.Z.	44 00 S	171 00 E	59
South Africa	30 00 S	25 00 E	70
Southampton (isl.)	64 45 N	84 30 W	79
Southampton, Eng.	50 55 N	01 28 W	42
South Australia, Austl.	31 00 S	136 00 E	59
South Bend, Ind.	41 40 N	86 15 W	78
South Carolina (state), U.S.	34 00 N	81 00 W	78
South China (sea)	15 00 N	115 00 E	56
South Dakota (state), U.S.	44 30 N	100 30 W	76
South Georgia (isl.)	54 20 S	36 40 W	88
South Orkney (isls.)	60 38 S	45 35 W	71
South Sandwich (isls.)	56 00 S	26 30 W	12
South Shetland (isls.)	62 00 S	58 00 W	71
Spain	40 00 N	04 00 W	42
Spokane, Wash.	47 40 N	117 26 W	76
Spratly (isls.)	08 00 N	113 00 E	56
Springfield,* Ill.	39 48 N	89 39 W	78
Springfield, Mass.	42 06 N	72 35 W	78
Springfield, Mo.	37 13 N	93 18 W	78
Springfield, Ohio	39 55 N	83 48 W	78
Sri Lanka	07 00 N	81 00 E	53
Srinagar, India	34 07 N	74 45 E	53
Stanley,* Falk. Is.	51 42 S	57 51 W	88
Stanovoy (mts.)	55 40 N	126 00 E	47
Stavanger, Norway	58 58 N	05 45 E	43
Stikine (river)	56 37 N	132 21 W	79
Stockholm,* Sweden	59 16 N	18 00 E	43
Stockton, Calif.	37 57 N	121 17 W	76
Strasbourg, France	48 35 N	07 45 E	42
Stuttgart, Germany	48 40 N	09 10 E	42
Subotica, Yugo.	46 06 N	19 40 E	44
Sucre,* Bolivia	19 03 S	65 18 W	86
Sudan	13 00 N	30 00 E	69
Sudan (region)	12 00 N	10 00 E	68
Sudbury, Ont.	46 32 N	81 15 W	79
Sudd (swamp)	08 00 N	30 00 E	69
Sudeten (mts.)	51 00 N	17 00 E	44
Suez (canal)	30 45 N	32 20 E	69
Sulu (arch.)	09 00 N	120 30 E	57
Sulu (sea)	09 08 N	120 00 E	57
Sumatra (isl.)	00 00	102 00 E	56
Sumba (isl.)	10 00 S	120 00 E	57
Sumbawa (isl.)	08 30 S	117 26 E	56
Sunda (isls.)	09 00 S	105 00 E	57
Sunda (strait)	06 28 S	105 24 E	56
Sundsvall, Sweden	62 23 N	17 19 E	43
Superior (lake)	87 00 N	48 00 W	77
Surabaya, Indon.	07 16 S	112 44 E	56
Surat, India	21 10 N	72 50 E	53
Suriname	04 00 N	56 00 W	87
Sutlej (river)	30 00 N	73 00 E	53
Suva,* Fiji	18 08 S	178 24 E	62
Svalbard (arch.)	79 00 N	19 00 E	71
Swansea, Wales	51 58 N	03 55 W	42
Swaziland	26 30 S	31 30 E	70
Sweden	62 00 N	16 00 E	43
Swift Current, Sask.	50 17 N	107 46 W	79
Switzerland	46 48 N	08 00 E	42
Sydney, Austl.	33 52 S	151 10 E	59
Sydney, N.S.	46 09 N	60 10 W	79
Syracuse, N.Y.	43 03 N	76 09 W	78
Syrdar'ya (river)	46 03 N	61 06 E	45
Syria	35 00 N	38 00 E	52
Szczecin, Poland	53 50 N	14 30 E	44

T

NAME	LATITUDE	LONGITUDE	PAGE
Tacoma, Wash.	47° 15′ N	122° 26′ W	76
Tagus (river)	38 45 N	09 00 W	42
Tahiti (isl.)	17 38 S	149 25 W	63
Tai'an, China	36 12 N	117 07 E	55
Taipei,* Taiwan, China	25 02 N	121 31 E	55
Taiwan	24 00 N	121 00 E	55
Taiyuan, China	37 52 N	112 35 E	55
Tajikistan	39 00 N	71 00 E	46
Takla Makan (desert)	39 20 N	83 00 E	54
Tallahassee,* Fla.	30 27 N	84 17 W	78
Tallinn,* Estonia	59 25 N	24 45 E	43
Tampa, Fla.	27 57 N	82 27 W	78
Tampere, Finland	61 30 N	23 45 E	43
Tampico, Mex.	22 13 N	97 51 W	80
Tana (lake)	12 00 N	37 20 E	69
Tanganyika (lake)	06 00 S	29 30 E	70
Tangier, Morocco	35 48 N	05 45 W	68
Tangshan, China	39 38 N	118 11 E	55
Tanzania	07 00 S	35 00 E	70
Tapajós (river)	02 24 S	54 47 W	87
Taranto (gulf)	40 15 N	17 15 E	44
Tarawa (isl.)	01 27 N	172 58 E	62
Tashkent,* Uzbekistan	41 20 N	69 18 E	46
Tasman (sea)	35 00 S	160 00 E	62
Tasmania, Austl.	42 00 S	147 00 E	59
Tatar (strait)	50 25 N	140 30 E	47
Taurus (mts.)	36 45 N	32 00 E	44
Taymyr (pen.)	76 00 N	104 00 E	46
Tbilisi,* Georgia	41 42 N	44 46 E	45
Tegucigalpa,* Honduras	14 06 N	87 13 W	80
Tehran,* Iran	35 41 N	51 26 E	52
Tehuantepec (isth.)	17 00 N	95 00 W	80
Tel Aviv-Jaffa, Israel	32 02 N	34 49 E	52
Tenerife (isl.)	28 15 N	16 35 W	68
Tennessee (river)	37 04 N	88 33 W	78
Tennessee (state), U.S.	36 00 N	86 00 W	78
Terre Haute, Ind.	39 28 N	87 24 W	78
Texas (state), U.S.	31 00 N	99 00 W	76
Thailand	14 00 N	101 00 E	56
Thailand (gulf)	10 00 N	102 30 E	56
The Hague,* Netherlands	52 05 N	04 20 E	42
The Pas, Man.	53 49 N	101 14 W	79
Thessaloniki, Greece	40 39 N	22 56 E	44
Thimphu,* Bhutan	27 29 N	89 37 E	53
Thompson, Man.	55 45 N	97 52 W	79
Thunder Bay, Ont.	48 24 N	89 19 W	79
Tianjin, China	38 59 N	117 24 E	55
Tian Shan (mts.)	42 12 N	78 13 E	54
Tiber (river)	41 44 N	12 14 E	42
Tibesti (mts.)	20 30 N	18 00 E	68
Tibet, China	30 00 N	90 00 E	54
Tierra del Fuego (isl.)	54 00 S	68 00 W	88
Tigris (river)	32 30 N	45 45 E	52
Tijuana, Mex.	32 32 N	117 01 W	81
Timişoara, Rom.	45 45 N	21 20 E	44
Timmins, Ont.	48 28 N	81 19 W	79
Timor (isl.)	09 30 S	125 00 E	57
Timor (sea)	11 00 S	125 00 E	59
Tinian (isl.)	15 01 N	145 38 E	62
Tiranë,* Albania	41 20 N	19 48 E	44
Tisza (river)	45 15 N	20 17 E	44
Titicaca (lake)	16 00 S	69 00 W	86
Tlalnepantla, Mex.	19 33 N	99 12 W	80
Tobago (isl.)	11 15 N	60 40 W	81
Tocantins (river)	01 50 S	49 10 W	87
Togo	08 00 N	01 00 E	68
Tokelau (isls.)	09 00 S	172 00 W	63
Tokyo,* Japan	35 42 N	139 46 E	55
Toledo, Ohio	41 39 N	83 33 W	78
Tol'yatti, Russia	53 31 N	49 26 E	45
Tomsk, Russia	56 30 N	84 58 E	46
Tonga	21 00 S	175 15 W	63
Tonkin (gulf)	19 40 N	107 30 E	56
Topeka,* Kans.	39 03 N	95 40 W	77
Toronto,* Ont.	43 38 N	79 27 W	79
Torrens (lake)	31 00 S	137 45 E	59
Torreón, Mex.	25 33 N	103 26 W	81
Torres (strait)	10 25 S	142 12 E	59
Toulon, France	43 08 N	05 56 E	42
Toulouse, France	43 36 N	01 27 E	42
Trail, Br. Col.	49 06 N	117 43 W	76
Transantarctic (mts.)	85 00 S	175 00 W	71
Transylvania (region)	47 00 N	23 30 E	44
Trenton,* N.J.	40 14 N	74 44 W	78
Trinidad and Tobago	10 30 N	61 15 W	81
Tripoli,* Libya	32 54 N	13 11 E	68
Tristan da Cunha (isl.)	37 00 S	12 30 W	12
Trivandrum, India	08 29 N	76 55 E	53
Trois-Rivières, Qué.	46 27 N	72 30 W	79
Tromsø, Norway	69 40 N	18 58 E	43
Trondheim, Norway	63 25 N	10 26 E	43
Troy, N.Y.	42 44 N	73 41 W	78
Truk (isls.)	07 25 N	151 45 E	62
Tuamotu (arch.)	17 00 S	142 00 W	63
Tucson, Ariz.	32 13 N	110 58 W	76
Tuktoyaktuk, N.W. Terrs.	69 27 N	133 03 W	79
Tula, Russia	54 12 N	37 36 E	43
Tulsa, Okla.	36 09 N	96 00 W	77
Tunis,* Tunisia	36 48 N	10 10 E	68
Tunisia	35 00 N	10 00 E	68
Turin, Italy	45 04 N	07 40 E	42
Turkana (lake)	03 30 N	36 00 E	69
Turkey	39 00 N	35 00 E	44
Turkmenistan	39 00 N	60 00 E	46
Turks and Caicos (isls.)	22 00 N	71 30 W	81
Tuscaloosa, Ala.	33 12 N	87 34 W	78
Tutuila (isl.)	14 17 S	170 40 W	63
Tuvalu	08 00 S	178 00 E	62
Tuz (lake)	38 00 N	33 30 E	44
Tuzla, Bosnia	44 32 N	18 41 E	44
T'ver, Russia	56 50 N	35 55 E	43
Tyrrhenian (sea)	39 00 N	13 00 E	42

U

NAME	LATITUDE	LONGITUDE	PAGE
Ucayali (river)	04° 30′ S	73° 26′ W	86
Ufa, Russia	54 43 N	55 55 E	45
Uganda	01 00 N	32 00 E	69
Ukraine	49 00 N	32 00 E	44
Ulaanbaatar,* Mongolia	45 55 N	106 53 E	54
United Arab Emirates	24 00 N	55 00 E	52
United Kingdom	55 00 N	02 00 W	42
United States	44 58 N	103 46 W	76-77
Ural (mts.)	56 00 N	60 00 E	46
Ural (river)	47 00 N	51 48 E	45
Urfa, Turkey	37 10 N	38 50 E	44
Urmia (lake)	37 35 N	45 05 E	52
Uruguay	33 00 S	56 00 W	88
Uruguay (river)	34 05 S	58 20 W	88
Ustyurt (plat.)	43 00 N	56 00 E	45
Utah (state), U.S.	39 30 N	111 30 W	76
Utica, N.Y.	43 06 N	75 13 W	78
Utrecht, Neth.	52 05 N	05 08 E	42
Uzbekistan	41 00 N	62 00 E	46

V

NAME	LATITUDE	LONGITUDE	PAGE
Vaal (river)	29° 04′ S	23° 38′ E	70
Val-d'Or, Qué.	48 07 N	77 46 W	79
Valencia, Spain	39 29 N	00 23 W	42
Valencia, Ven.	10 11 N	68 00 W	86
Valladolid, Spain	41 39 N	04 43 W	42
Valletta,* Malta	35 53 N	14 30 E	44
Valparaíso, Chile	33 01 S	71 38 W	88
Van (lake)	38 36 N	42 49 E	45
Vancouver (isl.)	49 40 N	125 50 W	79
Vancouver, Br. Col.	49 15 N	123 08 W	79
Vänern (lake)	59 00 N	13 30 E	43
Vanua Levu (isl.)	16 30 S	179 15 E	62
Vanuatu	17 00 S	168 30 E	62
Vārānāsi, India	25 17 N	83 08 E	53
Varna, Bulgaria	43 13 N	27 55 E	44
Vatican City	41 54 N	12 30 E	42
Vättern (lake)	58 20 N	14 30 E	43
Venezuela	08 00 N	66 00 W	86
Venice, Italy	45 26 N	12 20 E	42
Veracruz, Mex.	32 25 N	115 05 W	80
Verde (cape)	14 43 N	17 30 W	68
Verkhoyansk (mts.)	65 00 N	130 00 E	47
Vermont (state), U.S.	44 00 N	72 45 W	78
Vernon, Br. Col.	50 16 N	119 16 W	76
Verona, Italy	45 29 N	11 00 E	42
Victoria (falls)	17 57 S	25 52 E	70
Victoria (isl.)	71 00 N	110 00 W	79
Victoria (lake)	01 00 S	33 00 E	69
Victoria, Austl.	37 00 S	145 00 E	59
Victoria,* Br. Col.	48 27 N	123 25 W	79
Victoria,* Hong Kong	22 17 N	114 09 E	55
Vienna,* Austria	48 20 N	16 30 E	44
Vientiane,* Laos	17 58 N	102 37 E	56
Vietnam	16 00 N	108 00 E	49
Vila,* Vanuatu	17 44 S	168 19 E	62
Vilnius,* Lithuania	54 41 N	25 19 E	43
Virgin (isls.)	18 20 N	64 40 W	81
Virginia (state), U.S.	37 30 N	76 30 W	78
Visalia, Calif.	36 20 N	119 18 W	76
Vistula (river)	54 20 N	18 50 E	44
Viti Levu (isl.)	17 50 S	178 00 E	62
Vladivostok, Russia	43 06 N	131 50 E	55
Volcano (isls.)	24 43 N	141 20 E	62
Volga (river)	46 15 N	48 24 E	45
Volgograd, Russia	48 42 N	44 30 E	45
Volta (lake)	07 00 N	00 00	68
Volta (river)	05 45 N	00 41 E	68
Voronezh, Russia	51 40 N	39 00 E	45
Vyatka, Russia	58 33 N	49 42 E	45

W

NAME	LATITUDE	LONGITUDE	PAGE
Wabash (river)	37° 48′ N	88° 01′ W	78
Waco, Tex.	31 33 N	97 08 W	77
Wake (isl.)	19 18 N	166 38 E	62
Wales, U.K.	52 30 N	04 00 W	42
Wallis and Futuna (isls.)	13 18 S	176 10 W	62
Walvis Bay, S. Afr.	22 57 S	14 30 E	70
Warsaw,* Poland	52 10 N	21 00 E	44
Wasatch Range (mts.)	41 00 N	111 35 W	76
Washington, D.C.,* U.S.	38 54 N	77 01 W	78
Washington (state), U.S.	47 15 N	121 00 W	76
Waterloo, Iowa	42 30 N	92 20 W	78
Weddell (sea)	70 00 S	40 00 W	71
Wellington,* N.Z.	41 19 S	174 47 E	59
Weser (river)	53 30 N	08 34 E	42
Western Australia, Austl.	25 00 S	122 00 E	59
Western Ghats (mts.)	15 00 N	74 30 E	53
Western Sahara	25 00 N	14 00 W	68
Western Samoa	14 00 S	172 00 W	63
West Palm Beach, Fla.	26 43 N	80 03 W	78
West Virginia (state), U.S.	38 30 N	81 00 W	78
Wheeling, W. Va.	40 04 N	80 43 W	78
White (sea)	65 30 N	38 00 E	43
Whitehorse,* Yukon Terr.	60 45 N	135 04 W	79
White Nile (river)	15 37 N	32 31 E	69
Whitney (mt.)	36 35 N	118 18 W	76
Wichita, Kans.	37 42 N	97 20 W	77
Wiesbaden, Germany	50 05 N	08 15 E	42
Wilkes-Barre, Pa.	41 15 N	75 53 W	78
Willemstad,* Neth. Ant.	12 07 N	68 57 W	81
Wilmington, Del.	39 45 N	75 33 W	78
Windhoek,* Namibia	22 34 S	17 06 E	70
Windsor, Ont.	42 19 N	83 02 W	79
Windward (isls.)	13 00 N	62 00 W	81
Windward (passage)	20 00 N	73 50 W	81
Winnipegosis (lake)	52 30 N	100 00 W	79
Winnipeg (lake)	49 50 N	97 10 W	79
Winnipeg,* Man.	49 53 N	97 10 W	79
Wisconsin (state), U.S.	44 30 N	90 00 W	78
Woods, Lake of the (lake)	49 30 N	94 30 W	79
Worcester, Mass.	42 16 N	71 48 W	78
Wrangel (isl.)	71 00 N	180 00	47
Wroclaw, Poland	51 10 N	17 02 E	44
Wuhan, China	30 35 N	114 16 E	55
Würzburg, Germany	49 48 N	09 58 E	42
Wyoming (state), U.S.	43 00 N	107 30 W	76

X

NAME	LATITUDE	LONGITUDE	PAGE
Xi'an, China	34° 16′ N	108° 54′ E	54
Xiantao, China	30 25 N	113 25 E	55
Xingu (river)	01 44 S	51 56 W	87

Y

NAME	LATITUDE	LONGITUDE	PAGE
Yablonovyy (mts.)	52° 30′ N	113° 00′ E	47
Yakima, Wash.	46 36 N	120 31 W	76
Yamoussoukro,* Côte d'Ivoire	06 49 N	05 17 W	68
Yamal (pen.)	70 00 N	70 00 E	46
Yaoundé,* Cameroon	03 53 N	11 32 E	68
Yap (isl.)	09 30 N	138 10 E	62
Yarmouth, N.S.	43 50 N	66 07 W	79
Yaroslavl', Russia	57 35 N	39 50 E	45
Yekaterinburg, Russia	56 50 N	60 38 E	45
Yellow (sea)	37 00 N	123 00 E	55
Yellowknife,* N.W. Terrs.	62 27 N	114 21 W	79
Yellowstone (river)	48 00 N	104 00 W	76
Yellowstone Nat'l Park, U.S.	44 30 N	110 30 W	76
Yemen	15 00 N	44 00 E	52
Yenisey (river)	69 35 N	84 25 E	46
Yerevan,* Armenia	40 11 N	44 30 E	45
Yogyakarta, Indon.	07 48 S	110 22 E	56
Yokohama, Japan	35 25 N	139 31 E	55
York, Pa.	39 57 N	76 44 W	78
Yorkton, Sask.	51 13 N	102 28 W	79
Youngstown, Ohio	41 06 N	80 39 W	78
Yucatán (pen.)	20 00 N	89 00 W	80
Yugoslavia	44 00 N	21 00 E	44
Yukon (river)	62 36 N	164 46 W	79
Yukon Territory, Canada	65 00 N	137 00 W	79
Yuzhno-Sakhalinsk, Russia	46 58 N	142 42 E	47

Z

NAME	LATITUDE	LONGITUDE	PAGE
Zagreb,* Croatia	45° 48′ N	16° 00′ E	44
Zagros (mts.)	34 00 N	47 30 E	52
Zaire	02 00 S	24 00 E	65
Zaire (Congo) (river)	06 05 S	12 20 E	70
Zambezi (river)	18 50 S	36 15 E	70
Zambia	14 00 S	27 00 E	70
Zanzibar (isl.)	06 00 S	39 30 E	70
Zaozhuang, China	34 53 N	117 34 E	55
Zaporizhzhya, Ukraine	47 50 N	35 10 E	44
Zaragoza (Saragossa), Spain	41 39 N	00 51 W	42
Zhengzhou, China	34 48 N	113 39 E	55
Zhytomyr, Ukraine	50 16 N	28 40 E	44
Zibo, China	36 47 N	118 01 E	55
Zimbabwe	19 00 S	30 00 E	70
Zürich, Switz.	47 22 N	08 22 E	42

World Statistics

The Continents

	Area in: Sq. Miles	Sq. Kms.	Percent of World's Land
Asia	17,128,500	44,362,815	29.5
Africa	11,707,000	30,321,130	20.2
North America	9,363,000	24,250,170	16.2
South America	6,875,000	17,806,250	11.8
Antarctica	5,500,000	14,245,000	9.5
Europe	4,057,000	10,507,630	7.0
Australia	2,966,136	7,682,300	5.1

Dimensions of the Earth

	Area in: Sq. Miles	Sq. Kilometers
Superficial area	196,939,000	510,073,000
Land surface	57,506,000	148,941,000
Water surface	139,433,000	361,132,000
	Distance in: Miles	**Kilometers**
Equatorial circumference	24,902	40,075
Polar circumference	24,860	40,007
Equatorial diameter	7,926.4	12,756.4
Polar diameter	7,899.8	12,713.6
Equatorial radius	3,963.2	6,378.2
Polar radius	3,949.9	6,356.8
Volume of the Earth	2.6×10^{11} cubic miles	10.84×10^{11} cubic kilometers
Mass or weight	6.6×10^{21} short tons	6.0×10^{21} metric tons
Maximum distance from Sun	94,600,000 miles	152,000,000 kilometers
Minimum distance from Sun	91,300,000 miles	147,000,000 kilometers

Oceans and Major Seas

	Area in: Sq. Miles	Sq. Kms.	Greatest Depth in: Feet	Meters
Pacific Ocean	64,186,000	166,241,700	36,198	11,033
Atlantic Ocean	31,862,000	82,522,600	28,374	8,648
Indian Ocean	28,350,000	73,426,500	25,344	7,725
Arctic Ocean	5,427,000	14,056,000	17,880	5,450
Caribbean Sea	970,000	2,512,300	24,720	7,535
Mediterranean Sea	969,000	2,509,700	16,896	5,150
South China Sea	895,000	2,318,000	15,000	4,600
Bering Sea	875,000	2,266,250	15,800	4,800
Gulf of Mexico	600,000	1,554,000	12,300	3,750
Sea of Okhotsk	590,000	1,528,100	11,070	3,370
East China Sea	482,000	1,248,400	9,500	2,900
Yellow Sea	480,000	1,243,200	350	107
Sea of Japan	389,000	1,007,500	12,280	3,740
Hudson Bay	317,500	822,300	846	258
North Sea	222,000	575,000	2,200	670
Black Sea	185,000	479,150	7,365	2,245
Red Sea	169,000	437,700	7,200	2,195
Baltic Sea	163,000	422,170	1,506	459

Largest Islands

	Area in: Sq. Miles	Sq. Kms.
Greenland	840,000	2,175,600
New Guinea	305,000	789,950
Borneo	290,000	751,100
Madagascar	226,400	586,376
Baffin, Canada	195,928	507,454
Sumatra, Indonesia	164,000	424,760
Honshu, Japan	88,000	227,920
Great Britain	84,400	218,896
Victoria, Canada	83,896	217,290
Ellesmere, Canada	75,767	196,236
Celebes, Indonesia	72,986	189,034
South I., New Zealand	58,393	151,238
Java, Indonesia	48,842	126,501
North I., New Zealand	44,187	114,444
Newfoundland, Canada	42,031	108,860
Cuba	40,533	104,981
Luzon, Philippines	40,420	104,688
Iceland	39,768	103,000
Mindanao, Philippines	36,537	94,631
Ireland	31,743	82,214
Sakhalin, Russia	29,500	76,405

Principal Mountains

	Height in: Feet	Meters
Everest, Nepal-China	29,023	8,846
K2 (Godwin Austen), Pakistan-China	28,250	8,611
Dhaulagiri, Nepal	26,810	8,172
Annapurna, Nepal	26,504	8,078
Rakaposhi, Pakistan	25,550	7,788
Tirich Mir, Pakistan	25,230	7,690
Communism Peak, Tajikistan	24,590	7,495
Pobedy Peak, Kyrgyzstan	24,406	7,439
Muztag, China	23,891	7,282
Cerro Aconcagua, Argentina	22,831	6,959
Ojos del Salado, Chile-Argentina	22,572	6,880
Tupungato, Chile-Argentina	22,310	6,800
Huascarán, Peru	22,205	6,768
Nevada Ancohuma, Bolivia	21,489	6,550
Chimborazo, Ecuador	20,561	6,267
McKinley, Alaska	20,320	6,194
Logan, Yukon, Canada	19,524	5,951
Kilimanjaro, Tanzania	19,340	5,895
Pico Cristóbal Colón, Colombia	18,947	5,775
Citlaltépetl (Orizaba), Mexico	18,701	5,700
Damavand, Iran	18,606	5,671
El'brus, Russia	18,510	5,642
Batian (Kenya), Kenya	17,058	5,199
Ararat, Turkey	16,946	5,165
Margherita (Ruwenzori), Africa	16,795	5,119
Puncak Jaya, Indonesia	16,503	5,030
Blanc, France	15,771	4,807
Dufourspitze (Mte. Rosa), Italy-Switzerland	15,203	4,634
Matterhorn, Switzerland	14,691	4,478
Whitney, California, U.S.A.	14,494	4,418

Longest Rivers

	Length in: Miles	Kms.
Nile, Africa	4,145	6,671
Amazon, S. America	3,915	6,300
Chang Jiang (Yangtze), China	3,900	6,276
Mississippi-Missouri-Red Rock, U.S.A.	3,741	6,019
Ob'-Irtysh-Black Irtysh, Russia-Kazakstan	3,362	5,411
Yenisey-Angara, Russia	3,100	4,989
Huang He (Yellow), China	2,877	4,630
Amur-Shilka-Onon, Asia	2,744	4,416
Lena, Russia	2,734	4,400
Congo (Zaire), Africa	2,718	4,374
Mackenzie-Peace-Finlay,Canada	2,635	4,241
Mekong, Asia	2,610	4,200
Missouri-Red Rock, U.S.A.	2,564	4,125
Niger, Africa	2,548	4,101
Paraná-La Plata, S. America	2,450	3,943
Mississippi, U.S.A.	2,348	3,778
Murray-Darling, Australia	2,310	3,718
Volga, Russia	2,194	3,531
Madeira, S. America	2,013	3,240
Purus, S. America	1,995	3,211
Yukon, Alaska-Canada	1,979	3,185
St. Lawrence, Canada-U.S.A.	1,900	3,058
Rio Grande, Mexico-U.S.A.	1,885	3,034
Syrdar'ya-Naryn, Asia	1,859	2,992
São Francisco, Brazil	1,811	2,914
Indus, Asia	1,800	2,897
Danube, Europe	1,775	2,857
Salween, Asia	1,770	2,849
Brahmaputra, Asia	1,700	2,736
Euphrates, Asia	1,700	2,736

Principal Natural Lakes

	Area in: Sq. Miles	Sq. Kms.	Max. Depth in: Feet	Meters
Caspian Sea, Asia	143,243	370,999	3,264	995
Lake Superior, U.S.A.-Canada	31,820	82,414	1,329	405
Lake Victoria, Africa	26,724	69,215	270	82
Lake Huron, U.S.A.-Canada	23,010	59,596	748	228
Lake Michigan, U.S.A.	22,400	58,016	923	281
Aral Sea, Kazakstan-Uzbekistan	15,830	41,000	213	65
Lake Tanganyika, Africa	12,650	32,764	4,700	1,433
Lake Baykal, Russia	12,162	31,500	5,316	1,620
Great Bear Lake, Canada	12,096	31,328	1,356	413
Lake Nyasa (Malawi), Africa	11,555	29,928	2,320	707
Great Slave Lake, Canada	11,031	28,570	2,015	614
Lake Erie, U.S.A.-Canada	9,940	25,745	210	64
Lake Winnipeg, Canada	9,417	24,390	60	18
Lake Ontario, U.S.A.-Canada	7,540	19,529	775	244
Lake Ladoga, Russia	7,104	18,399	738	225
Lake Balkhash, Kazakstan	7,027	18,200	87	27
Lake Maracaibo, Venezuela	5,120	13,261	100	31
Lake Chad, Africa	4,000 – 10,000	10,360 – 25,900	25	8
Lake Onega, Russia	3,710	9,609	377	115